PARRY BEFORE *JERUSALEM*

To Michael Kennedy, Bruce Roberts
and the R.V.W. Trust

Parry before *Jerusalem*

Studies of his Life and Music
with Excerpts from his Published Writings

Bernard Benoliel

Ashgate

Aldershot • Brookfield USA • Singapore • Sydney

Published by
Ashgate Publishing Limited
Gower House
Croft Road
Aldershot
Hants GU11 3HR
England

Ashgate Publishing Company
Old Post Road
Brookfield
Vermont 05036-9704
USA

British Library Cataloguing-in-Publication data.

Benoliel, Bernard
  Parry before *Jerusalem* : studies of his life and music with
  excerpts from his published writings
  1.Parry, Hubert   2.Composers – Great Britain – Biography
  3.Historians – Great Britain – Biography
  I.Title
  780.9'2

Library of Congress Cataloging-in-Publication data

Benoliel, Bernard.
  Parry before *Jerusalem* : studies of his life and music with
  excerpts from his published writings / by Bernard Benoliel.
    Includes bibliographical references and index.
    ISBN 0–85967–927–6 (cloth)
    1. Parry, C. Hubert H. (Charles Hubert Hastings), 1848–1918.
  2. Composers—England—Biography.   3. Music—History and criticism.
  I. Parry, C. Hubert H. (Charles Hubert Hastings), 1848–1918.
  II. Title.
  ML410.P173B46 1997
  780'.92—dc20
  [B]   96–32134
            CIP
            MN

ISBN 0 85967 927 6

Typeset in Sabon by Manton Typesetters, 5–7 Eastfield Road, Louth, Lincolnshire and printed in Great Britain by Biddles Limited, Guildford.

Contents

List of plates

Preface and acknowledgements

For the greater part of this century, Hubert Parry's artistic legacy suffered from inaccessibility: his music remained almost unplayed and his books went out of print. For the general public his name lingered on essentially through one work, *Jerusalem*, composed at the end of his life, and even this piece was rarely, if ever, performed in his own orchestration. The exception to this bleak picture was the Church of England musicians who consistently played the small body of his music written for their services. Intermittently over the decades musicologists and Parry's surviving pupils would resume the debate over his merits as a composer. But the debate usually concentrated on the same pieces, especially two of the oratorios, and each time the advocates, including Vaughan Williams, never succeeded in convincing the sceptics. It was a case of always returning to the same old battleground where George Bernard Shaw had won the decisive victory in 1893.

By a curious twist of fate it was Shaw himself who immortalized Parry; by the 1950s Parry was known best through Shaw's fierce but highly amusing attack on the oratorios *Job* and *Judith*. Shaw's injunction that Parry should erect a funeral pyre and burn all the copies is a classic piece of destructive criticism. But was Shaw right about Parry's entire *œuvre*? This was the question I wanted to answer nearly twenty-five years ago. I was sceptical that Parry, before *Jerusalem*, had produced no other music worth playing, because *Jerusalem* is one of the world's great tunes. In fact Shaw himself had given praise to a few of Parry's cantatas.

It was Adrian Boult's performance of *Blest Pair of Sirens*, then the only recording of a Parry work for chorus and orchestra, that convinced me a major revaluation was long overdue.[1] As I gradually examined and played through Parry's scores two basic criteria became relevant: was the contrapuntal harmonic texture comparably elaborate to that of Brahms and Wagner, and was there an athletic thrust to the way the music moved? No thin static foursquare Parry was great Parry.

My primary concern, once this assessment had been completed, was to cut through the inaccessibility by promoting performances and recordings of the finest music. I was particularly struck that many works I regarded as his masterpieces, such as the *Ode on the Nativity*, *The Soul's Ransom*, the *Elegy for Brahms* and Symphony No. 4 had achieved no critical reputation whatever. For the next two decades Bruce Roberts and I actively promoted performances of Parry's music, supported by our own programme notes; this endeavour culminated in 1991 when the Ralph Vaughan Williams Trust went into partnership with Chandos Records to produce six CDs. His music could finally speak, or more appropriately sing, for itself. The consistently positive critical reaction to the Chandos series has more than vindicated the enterprise. (Since the Second World War active devotees of Parry's music have been rare, but I would like to draw attention to Sir George Thalban-Ball, Michael Pope, Malcolm MacDonald, Alasdair Mitchell and Lewis Foreman).

Over these years I had evolved a critique of Parry fundamentally at odds with C.L. Graves' biography, published in the 1920s.[2] When Dr Jeremy Dibble's Oxford biography appeared in 1992[3] I found myself in equal disagreement. At this point I felt it was important to set out my alternative perspectives on Parry's music, Parry the man and Lady Maude Parry. This book incorporates much new material, which itself is only a small portion of the still unpublished sources; the most important is the collection of family papers, letters and diaries deposited at Shulbrede Priory, the home of Parry's elder daughter Dorothea, Lady Ponsonby and her descendants.[4] Of equal importance, it became essential to reorganize the known material to effect a satisfactory reinterpretation of Parry's development as a creative artist. A series of 'Studies' provided the opportunity for the more kinetic treatment that I felt the subject demanded.

Parry's life is remarkable for the diversity of his involvements and accomplishments. It soon became evident, on the basis of his published articles and books, that he was the most significant music historian Britain had produced since Dr Burney. It is not possible to reach a balanced assessment of Parry before *Jerusalem* without encountering his engaging enthusiasm and thought-provoking insight as a writer on music. Moreover it was Parry the writer – not Parry the composer – who provided the key to his distinguished thirty-five year academic career at the Royal College of Music. Therefore the second part of this book is devoted to a selection of his writings.

I would like to acknowledge the constant assistance of Mr Bruce Roberts of the Ralph Vaughan Williams Trust Committee for historical research and the task of deciphering the handwriting of Parry and Lady Maude. I wish to thank the R.V.W. Trust for its encouragement, Miss Dee Platt for typing the manuscript and Mr Nigel Farrow for asking me to write this book. I am grateful to the Hon. Laura Ponsonby and the Hon. Kate Russell for making the material at Shulbrede Priory so freely available.

I Parry before *Jerusalem*

1 Formation of a Creative Personality

There is no other source of beauty than the wound – unique, different for each person, hidden or visible, that every man keeps within, that he preserves and whither he withdraws when he wants to leave the world behind for a temporary but deep solitude.

(Jean Genet)[1]

Parry's life is unusual for a composer in that so many of the material facts of his biography were not determined by his musical career. Despite his obsession with the art of music, his domestic life, friendships, economic situation and class status were defined by non-musical influences; his later career as a composer, teacher and historian, to a large extent, can be seen as a belated overlay. Any evaluation of the man must be conditioned by this element of dualism in both his character and his subsequent mode of existence. His social status was determined by his father's position as a Gloucestershire landowner – Highnam Court covered 2,400 acres (almost 1,000 hectares) with eight tenant farmsteads. His friendship with the Pembrokes, Lytteltons, Arthur Balfour and Robert Bridges dated back to his days at Eton and Oxford. His life-long connection with the late nineteenth-century artists, Lord Leighton, Burne-Jones, William Blake Richmond, William de Morgan and William Morris evolved naturally from his father's position as a major art collector and a talented painter in his own right.

Indeed, Parry's close association with the Three Choirs Festival, especially with Gloucester, was essentially a family legacy; his father Thomas Gambier Parry (1816–88) was a Steward and financial guarantor of the Festival who fought for its survival in the 1860s. Through his father he established friendly relations with the leading British composers: Sterndale Bennett, Samuel Sebastian Wesley and Henry Hugo Pierson. Parry's own house parties at Highnam during the Festival merely continued a tradition in which he had participated from childhood. When in 1896 he took over the running of Highnam Court on the death of his step-mother, Ethelinda, the inheritance of his father's mantle was complete. He even became a local magistrate, though not Sheriff of Gloucestershire or Deputy Lieutenant of the shire, as Gambier Parry had in the 1850s.

It is important to bear in mind that at the time of his marriage to Lady Maude Herbert (1851–1933), there was no question of Parry pursuing a career in music. In 1872 Parry was an educated English country gentleman with a city career and a strong interest in music. It was a far cry from the over-stretched Director of the

Royal College of Music and composer of an annual Cantata to whom Maude found herself married thirty years later.

Parry's overt commitment to music in the late 1870s came when he was already 30 and father of two children. It was inevitable that he would bring to bear on his artistic career a system of values and a mode of conduct conditioned by the social structures in which he grew up and a personality that was strongly extrovert. His later criticisms of the aristocracy, his liberal politics and avid agnosticism (clearly distinguished from atheism), should not blind one to his deep-seated conservatism, his Victorian faith in institutions, and his unswerving belief in the spiritual and moral foundations of man's nature.

These values, fortified by his devotion to Bach, led him to a conception of the composer as public servant and moral instructor. It was not a wholly positive role-model for later English composers, but at least it was a working role model and one which had enormous influence. However, in its identification of the composer with the role of the academic and supplier of annual novelties to regional festivals – 'the commission composer' – it helped to shape the yoke under which British composers still labour in the mid-1990s – arguably to their detriment as creative artists. Arguably it confirms Parry's own view that 'man is doomed by the fatality of his birth to be part and parcel of the age in which he is born'.

Although Parry died almost eighty years ago, in terms of artistic time we are still close to his legacy. Herbert Howells, his last major pupil, died in 1983. Howells' magnificent *Stabat Mater*, written in 1963, is possibly the last tribute to a composer who breathed new life into English music so long before and helped to change every aspect of the art form in England.

Parry's birth on 27 February, in that year of revolutions 1848, was hardly propitious: twelve days later his mother Anna Maria Isabella Fynes Clinton died of consumption in Bournemouth at the age of 32.[2] Thomas Gambier Parry buried her in the seaside resort where he had brought her in the vain hope of securing remission in the disease. Sixty years later Hubert took time away from Bournemouth Symphony performances of his music to maintain the grave of a mother he never knew. Three elder brothers had died in infancy and no doubt there was a tacit assumption that Hubert would soon follow them; his hyperactivity, nervousness, heart irregularities and premature ageing all suggest lasting repercussions from the circumstances of his birth.

His early life was spent at Highnam Court, in the care of a wet nurse, nannies and, later, governesses. Gambier Parry was frequently absent, in London or abroad, and throughout Hubert's youth his elder brother Charles Clinton (1840–83) and sister Lucy Anne (1841–61) carried precedence for his father's attentions.

By the time he was three, his father Gambier Parry at 35 had remarried: Ethelinda Lear (1826–96) was a younger cousin of Isabella and in time produced six children, all of whom lived. Essentially it was the failure of his stepmother Ethelinda to take the place of Isabella that worked its detrimental effect on Clinton's and, more subtly, Hubert's personality. His elder daughter Dorothea (1876–1963) writes that Ethelinda 'was the antithesis of his first [wife]. Being extremely calm and phlegmatic and absolutely conventional. She too was absorbed by church matters and the bearing of children. With her love of young ones she had not time for Hubert.'[2] Her mother Mrs Lear, the narrow-minded wife of the Dean of Salisbury, disliked Isabella and considered Gambier Parry with his £10,000 a year income too good for her impecunious niece.

Once Isabella died Mrs Lear took advantage of Gambier Parry's bereavement to promote the cause of her daughter, and evidently Ethelinda was all too ready. Dorothea considered her stern religious propriety had a stifling effect on Gambier Parry's thinking and one suspects he had grown up with a natural tendency to be dominated by the women around him. (His father and grandfather had died shortly after his birth in 1816). C.L. Graves points out that Parry's undisciplined table manners arose as a natural rebellion against the very formal eating rituals Ethelinda insisted on at Highnam and her stiff letter of congratulation when Parry received his Cambridge doctorate in 1882 speaks volumes on the non-relationship with her stepson: 'I hope people won't think it necessary to call you *Dr. Parry!*'

Dorothea states that her father 'looked back with amazement at the blind complacency of his parents, who appeared to him to have been shirking all responsibility to himself and his brother' and 'He felt his brother could have been saved.' Clinton's wild behaviour, a combination of drinking, womanizing and opium, ruined his Oxford career and prepared the twenty-year decline to his death. Ethelinda's religious feelings did not extend to Clinton. He had been 'neglected' and 'was regarded by the family as past praying for', as Parry explained to Dorothea.

Neglect arose partly from Gambier Parry's wanderlust, especially his travels to Italy. Clinton and Hubert were separated from their father and stepmother – and each other – for long stretches. In January 1856 Parry was sent to Malvern, and later Twyford and Eton; the boarding school regime had begun. The fact that it was welcomed by the boy is indicative of the absence of a close interdependent family life.

C.L. Graves make much of the fact that Parry's interests are discernible in, and therefore inherited from, his forebears; there is a more interesting thesis, namely that Parry deliberately emulated them. The process became a positive means of forging a connection with the dead mother's and absent father's wider families. These were rich in achievement and diversity. There had been East India administrators, diplomats, admirals, scholars and clergymen within the preceding hundred years, including one diplomat, Richard Oakes, who became a favourite of Catherine the Great. Hence the evolution of Hubert Parry the Renaissance man. Gambier Parry was left a workable fortune by his grandfather Thomas Parry, which paid for Highnam in 1837 and enabled him to accumulate an unique collection of Renaissance art ranging from Giotto, Albertinelli and Giorgione to Albrecht Dürer, whose carved panels became part of the library mantelpiece in Highnam.

Isabella, like Gambier Parry, was descended from Huguenot stock and her son's name, Charles Hubert, betrays his French origins: he shared his name with the neglected French composer, Charles-Hubert Gervais (1671–1744). Isabella's father, Henry Fynes Clinton, was a scholar whose work in chronology, and his Greek and Latin verse compilations *Fasti Hellenici* and *Fasti Romani*, secured his reputation for research. His obsession with hard work and periodic fits of melancholy

were matched by an equal capacity for rigorous exercise; contradictory characteristics more than apparent in his grandson. Fynes Clinton's reaction to Highnam
Church built, by Gambier Parry, in memory of his daughter Isabella is indicative
'April 29, 1851 – At Highnam, Construction of Church, Tower 97 ft., spire 85 ft.,
vane 15 ft., total 197 ft.'[3] More significant is the fact that Hubert visited the old
scholar at Welwyn the following year shortly before his death and always recalled
the visit with affection.

Parry knew Isabella only from her portraits from which she regards the world
with an expression at once guarded and considerate. But Henry Fynes Clinton
provided his large family with an excellent education. Isabella was a proficient
scholar in French, Latin and Italian. She used an Italian Bible and studied philosophy, especially Carlyle. The constant travel throughout the nine-year marriage
undermined her delicate health, but her stamp of character remained and Hubert
would have learned much about her from Clinton and Lucy. The marriage was
dedicated to the pursuit of art; their collection adorned Highnam and throughout
Parry's life continued to draw artists, collectors and historians there.

Gambier Parry was a proficient musician and composer, a talent inherited by
Clinton who performed his own compositions before the Prince of Wales at Oxford. It was therefore logical for Parry to emulate his father and elder brother. This
conclusion has to be qualified by Parry's reported complaint to Dorothea that: 'He
himself was never encouraged to play the piano; in fact he was discouraged.'
Gambier Parry's and Ethelinda's refusal to nurture Hubert's musical talent probably ensured he would never become a professional pianist despite years of practice in the 1860s and 1870s. It is an important point that he took piano lessons at
Oxford and went to Dannreuther in 1873 not because the latter was a composer
but because he was a renowned pianist and piano teacher.

But Parry never became a successful soloist. Had he done so the compositional
and academic career might have taken a quite different course. Nonetheless the
power of Parry's playing should not be underestimated, as Mary Gladstone, daughter
of the Prime Minister, has testified:

> Anything that is appealing in my pianoforte playing, anything that is tender, or wistful,
> or passionate, is entirely owing to Hubert; it was he who first revealed to me how to
> express in music the emotions of the human heart. Two things he played that first time I
> met him as a beautiful boy at Wilton, in all the glory of a first and last love. The
> Schumann *Reverie* in F sharp major and the Chopin Prelude in D . . . It is more than fifty
> years ago, yet never in this life can I forget the effect on me of his rendering of these two
> pieces.[4]

There is evidence that Parry consciously felt neglected by his father in his youth,
and this response remained with him throughout his life. Dorothea recounts that,
'A short time before he died he talked to me of his childhood bringing-up somewhat bitterly',[5] and several pieces of information testify to the continuation of that
emotional void. Parry confessed to her that he relied on a 'little imaginary friend'
with whom he talked, for the lack of a companion. There is other corroborative
evidence: in 1854 Ethelinda wrote in her diary that Hubert had been sufficiently
troublesome with his governess Mlle Foertsch that she took over his lessons
herself. Later she told her eldest son Ernest Gambier Parry that of all the children

she taught to read, Hubert was the most difficult: 'So difficult indeed as to approach the impossible.' In December 1864 Parry writes a telling scene in his first diary.

> On our way home, we came through the churchyard; as we neared *oxcp* [darling] Lucy's grave I stayed behind and when Clin passed on, stood beside the grave and there I thought of 'the days that are no more' and those 'tears, idle tears' rose in my heart and gathered in my eyes as that dear dear face once more rose in my mind's eye and I thought of that face that I should see no more, Clin came back when he found that I had stayed behind; and there we stood beside the grave, the only sad remnants of our dear mother; as we turned away Clin said, 'I wonder who will be the next to lie there'.

The description confirms the two brothers' sense of discontinuity and separateness from the second family. Lucy's death in 1861 continued to haunt Hubert: In 1868 he wrote to the 17-year-old Lady Maude of Lucy 'my only sister – the only person in the world whose loss I still regret'. Yet during Lucy's final months the young schoolboy had paid little attention to her, a fact that Parry surely remembered, probably with remorse. There are three surviving letters from Lucy to Hubert, all written in the last year of her life. Only the first, sent in May 1861 from Genoa, refers to her health and only in reference to alternative travel arrangements, either 'the steamer . . . which will be horrid or whether we shall cross the Alps which would be *much* pleasanter and altogether nicer only Dr. Bennet would not allow it for me when we were at Mentone.' Her last letters, dated 23 September and 8 October, to 'my own darling Hubert' were written when Parry was in his first term at Eton. They still display the same animation, but despite her request that 'when you write to me you will tell me all about it' (that is, Eton) by 8 October she had received only 'a little note' which failed to confirm receipt of her earlier letter.

No doubt the distraction of Eton pushed Highnam and Lucy into the background and Parry would have underestimated her illness. She speaks of 'driving Jack [her horse], generally in the afternoons', hopes Clinton 'may have learned a little wisdom in his past experience' and laughs about a local singer pronouncing *pro nobis* from a Bach aria as 'nobees or perhaps nobus with the *s* sharp of course'. Parry might have remembered this anecdote when he came to set the same words so memorably in the *Ode on the Nativity* (1912). It is Lucy's last extant letter; within a month she had died of consumption.

Twenty years later, Clinton died in Australia, a forlorn victim of his own dissipation. When the family wrangles opened up with Ernest in 1896 over the Highnam inheritance, Parry would splutter 'it's as if the first family didn't exist'.[6] Surviving paintings and photographs testify that Isabella and 'the first family' were attractive; Ethelinda and the second family, much less so. None of the latter was exceptionally gifted or achieved a distinguished career. Yet Hubert was a great favourite and always remained close to Sidney and his four sisters. In 1873 it was Beatrice and Linda who took his compositions to their piano teacher Edward Dannreuther, and throughout the First World War Parry looked after Hilda and her family while her husband was fighting at the Front. But these relationships were formed too late to impact on Parry's formative years. Sidney was only born in 1859 and Hilda, his youngest sister, not until 1866, five years after Lucy's death. By that time Parry was already writing his Oxford Cantata.

Yet everyone concludes that Gambier Parry was a warm-hearted father who cared for his sons: Hubert related strongly to a father figure. Gambier Parry's years of dangerous creative work completing the frescos on the nave roof of Ely Cathedral, initiated by his friend Henry Le Strange, set a powerful example of concentrated artistic endeavour to his son. Gambier Parry carried out his work at his own expense after Le Strange died unexpectedly in 1862.

Fortunately Gambier Parry ensured that Hubert was provided with several people *in loco parentis* who gave him the opportunity to develop as a musician. At Twyford School (1858–61) the Revd Kitchen fostered a liberal regime. As Parry wrote in the *Musical Times* (1898), Kitchen, later Dean of Winchester and Durham, 'was sympathetic to music' and 'allowed strumming at certain rare hours on the cottage pianoforte in his drawing room'. Kitchen remained a friend until his death in 1912. At Eton (1861–6) Parry followed his father's and brother's footsteps by entering Evans' house. The reclusive Evans had taught his father drawing and Parry recalled 'I remember "Beeves" was especially kind to me on account of his having known my father for many years.' Eton College in the 1860s was eminently civilized if academically lax. Boys had their own rooms and Parry was one of the first to have his own piano. These facts have to be weighed with Parry's complaint that he was actively discouraged from playing the piano by his father.

This habit of attracting and attaching himself to father figures persisted into adult life when it culminated in his 25-year association with Sir George Grove, a man 28 years his senior. These men provided the environment in which Parry's musical endeavours could flourish. Their encouragement was essential because all musical training in the 1860s was an extra-curricular activity; at Twyford, Eton or Oxford. All Parry's early training was limited to local organists of varying ability who were bound by high Anglican conventions. Despite the fact that Parry's earliest compositions date from childhood, composition would always remain only one element of his musical interests, clearly to its detriment.

It is a reasonable supposition that Parry's earliest musical stimulus came from Clinton and Lucy. Music would have been both the vehicle for relating to the elder brother and sister and a powerful medium for emulation. Parry asserted to Dorothea that Clinton's 'touch on the piano was the most brilliant he ever heard' and as Parry grew up Clinton replaced the imaginary companion as 'a real living companion'.

At Twyford Hubert took lessons from a local organist who made the boy learn the accompaniments to his own direful anthems: 'Did you ever see such stuff?', Parry wrote later. But a rewarding by-product of Highnam Church was Gambier Parry's appointment of Edward Brind as organist in 1860. For the next three years Brind gave Parry piano lessons and taught him harmony and counterpoint. In the Church built to the memory of his mother Parry heard his earliest compositions, chants and hymn tunes, performed by the chapel choir.

This essential experience of hearing his music performed carried over on a grander scale under Sir George Elvey. Elvey was organist of St George's Chapel, Windsor and from 1863 to 1866 he was responsible for Parry's musical training; a vigorous study of fugue and the production of anthems, cantatas and part-songs. Elvey is now a forgotten figure but he raised performing standards at Windsor and composed the funeral music for Prince Albert in December 1861. He remains the formative influence on Parry's compositional techniques. His kindness and championship is beyond reproach though Parry chafed at his restrictive aesthetic. He performed Parry's compositions with the chapel choir – sometimes to an audience of the royal family – and secured the publication of two anthems *Blessed is He* and *Prevent Us O Lord* by Novello in 1865.

The culmination of these years was the composition of the Cantata *Oh Lord Thou Hast Cast Us Out*. Its creation enabled Parry to become the youngest candidate ever to be awarded a B.Mus. degree from Oxford University in December 1866. Football injuries to his ankle meant Parry literally hobbled into the examination room. It is a testament to his ability that a quarter of the way through the final paper 'they told me I need not do more and let me go'. The examiners Sir Frederick Arthur Gore Ouseley, Dr Charles William Corfe, organist of Christchurch, and the young John Stainer wasted no time making up their minds. 'Sir Frederick was very kind and they came out about a quarter of an hour afterwards and I heard that I had got my *testamur* – Glorious'.[7] Sir George Elvey himself led the first violins in the Eton College performance of the Cantata on 8 December with Parry conducting.

Parry became friends with all three examiners, in particular John Stainer (1844–1900): as an undergraduate he worked as Stainer's *répétiteur* with the Exeter College Musical Society. He received no formal musical training at Oxford but did take piano lessons from James Taylor, Stainer's successor as conductor of the Oxford Philharmonic Society. With hindsight the training he did receive was narrow, provincial and old fashioned, inured in an Anglican cocoon, isolated from the momentous developments in European composition. Fortunately his social position and extrovert personality brought him into contact with more stimulating influences, strong enough to challenge the conservatism of his training.

At Twyford he met Samuel Sebastian Wesley (1810–76), organist of Winchester and a composer, capable of embracing some modern tendencies. Parry would sit in Winchester organ loft while 'old Wesley with his eyebrows raised and chin sticking out ruminated on the organ.' Wesley was friendly with Gambier Parry and visited Highnam. In 1865 he succeeded as organist of Gloucester Cathedral where he gave Parry freedom of the organ loft; and he included a part-song by Parry in a cathedral concert and sang in the performance. In the concert William Sterndale Bennett conducted his cantata *The May Queen*; Parry commented 'I think he is one of the most kind and delightful men I ever met'. Despite their later relegation to the sidelines of music history these two men were the leading English composers of their day and their positive impression on Parry cannot be overestimated. In later life Parry talked with admiration of Wesley's *The Wilderness* and pointed out the essential Englishness of his music. The nineteenth-century English tradition was desperately weak in musical originality but these men showed Parry that a tradition did exist.

Proximity to the Three Choirs Festival confronted him with the powerful experience of massed choirs and orchestra performing Handel, Bach, Mendelssohn, Spohr and Beethoven, whose Mass in C in 1865 impressed him by the severe strain it placed on the sopranos. According to his diary, his delight at *Walpurgisnacht* was enhanced by sitting next to Miss Nettie Ward all through the evening. Nettie Ward came from a local family and, as Parry's diary indicates, was a favourite companion during this period.

Practical music-making soon became a means of defining relationships at both school and university where he was active as performer and composer; his rooms were a focal point for his peers and lifelong friendships were forged from a shared love of music. Parry was haunted by the need for ceaseless activity, be that music, reading, religious study, convivial socializing, dancing and an insatiable appetite for sport. His academic performance was only moderate; he failed to get an exhibition to Oxford and struggled through with second class honours. The chronicle of this hyperactivity throughout his early diaries makes exhausting reading. The inner man is oblique behind a welter of action and distraction that was often self-destructive. The result was salutary. He excelled best at the extreme points of his range, music and sports. This combination is not without precedent: to the ancient Greeks they became essential expressions of a civilization.

In 1861 that conjunction had been reaffirmed close to hand when the leading athletes of the day founded the Eton Musical Society, one of the founders being Stephen Fremantle, Captain of Evans, who later took an active interest in Parry's own compositions before his untimely death in 1875. He was one of the subscribers to the publication of Parry's *Oh Lord Thou Hast Cast Us Out* in 1866. In time Parry became the society's president. With his cousin Edward Hamilton and Spenser Lyttelton he 'worked away at part songs and madrigals and Handel choruses and Mendelssohn's psalms and gave concerts'.[8] On the playing field he was no less distinguished becoming Keeper of the Field (in football) and deputy Keeper of the Wall (in the Eton form of rugby). Robert Lyttelton remembered that 'His nature delighted in the concentrated essence of excitement found at the highest in Eton football as played in the field, and I can see him now rushing all over the ground, rash and therefore always injuring himself, shouting to his side and bubbling over with joy at the rush and tumble.'[9] Parry's 'smashes' – as he put it – were frequent and extreme; on one occasion he was carried off unconscious on a sheep hurdle.

Such behaviour by one blessed with charm and good looks endeared him to his peers, but his Eton chronicle obscures the darkening situation at home. In early 1861 Clinton had been sent down from Christ Church, Oxford, his intentions to obtain a B.Mus. and a first class degree in modern history ruined by a destructive mode of life that suggests a mind deeply disturbed. His return in 1862 saw a repetition of the same collapse of intentions and in 1863 he was sent down for good. Gambier Parry, despite his love, was unable to understand the root of his son's problems. Clinton's rejection of Christianity only increased his distress, and in 1864 he sent his son to Paris in a face-saving exercise. In the same year Clinton became involved with Florence Hinde, whose dubious family Gambier Parry viewed with undisguised horror. That November an alcoholic Clinton visited Eton to tell Hubert that he was marrying Florence and leaving Highnam; Gambier Parry forbade any member of the family to attend the wedding. Parry commendably always remained loyal to his flawed elder brother and continued to correspond with Florence long after Clinton's death.

Parry's reaction to Clinton's collapse was not restricted to an emotional response. Emulation of his aspirations intensified and the determination to excel at music, sport and philosophy was fuelled by a desire to compensate for a brother he believed to be more talented than himself. He drew closer to his father, an outcome of their inability to solve Clinton's problems and Gambier Parry's desire that Hubert should take his elder brother's place. These demands on a schoolboy, who used activity to fill the void of a lost mother and sister, took its toll. He began to experience 'heart trouble' which manifested itself as palpitations, irregularity of the heart beat and dizziness. These unpleasant symptoms which were to plague him throughout his life, were alarming and increased his feelings of vulnerability. It was not until the mid-1880s that doctors finally assured him the heart itself was not diseased.

In compensation for Clinton's decline, Parry selected his elder cousin Lewis Majendie as a mentor and for the first time spoke of following a musical career. C.L. Graves points out that he was influenced by the romantic novel *Charles Auchester* by Miss E.S. Sheppard, published in 1853 'a sort of hidden life of Mendelssohn', at that time still Parry's musical God. Majendie wisely encouraged his musical aspirations but warned against slavish imitation of an idol, literary or otherwise, 'and so losing one's own individuality'.[10]

Social distraction posed a more serious threat to Parry's individuality than imitation of any idol. In mitigation it has to be stressed that when he was young his physical presence cast a spell on all who came into its orbit. 'Hubert Parry was extraordinarily handsome, I might say he was beautiful', Mrs Frank Pownall recalled later; and Frederick Leighton after his first meeting with the young man referred to him as 'a Greek God'.[11]

At Oxford Stainer continued to encourage the younger composer who dedicated his *Morning Service in D* to him. Parry soon became on friendly terms with the Donkin family (W.P. Donkin was Savilian Professor of Astronomy); all talented players, they gave regular performances of chamber music in their home. In Gloucester S.S. Wesley continued to take an interest and on his advice Gambier Parry sent his son to Stuttgart to spend the summer vacation of 1867 with Henry Hugo Pierson (1815–73). Pierson was the only English composer of his generation to embrace the Romantic spirit and break loose from the Anglican stranglehold, literally by going into voluntary exile to Germany. If his compositions lack that essential expression of a strong personality, his incidental music to Goethe's *Faust Part 2* and the tone-poem *Macbeth* are conceived on a scale beyond the comprehension of his English contemporaries. The full scores of his operas and choral works including *Faust Part 2* are missing, perhaps still resting on a library shelf in Germany.

Parry was sent to Stuttgart to improve his German but Pierson gave him the only training in orchestration he would ever receive. They met at the Gare du Nord in Paris, Parry noting that Pierson was 'German in appearance with long dark hair, greyish eyes, tallish and slightly Beethovenish altogether – not quite what I expected, I must say'.

After a day's sight-seeing in Paris, they travelled via Strasbourg and Kehl to Stuttgart. Pierson's villa was on high ground surrounded by vineyards. Parry was taken up with enthusiasm by Pierson and his German-speaking sons who introduced him to every palace and gallery in the area, interspersed with 'rambling, bathing, and the consumption of a good deal of Bavarian beer ...'. 'I couldn't help thinking of the rum position: the German student and the English Varsity man; Oxford and Würzburg, fraternising on sofas with beer and smoke'. The Jägerhaus with its views of the Swabian Alps was their favourite beer hall.

Music lessons 'if lessons they were' followed an eccentric but demanding course: 'We sit with reeds in our mouths', Parry wrote, 'while Dr. Pierson descants on the peculiarities of different instruments for nearly two hours before luncheon. After luncheon we smoke and have coffee. Then I practise and after that we go for a walk'. Pierson was concerned to disabuse him of Bach and Mendelssohn, and exercises included 'instrumentating', from piano scores, the overture to *Der Freischütz*, excerpts from *William Tell*, the Entr'acte from *Egmont* and the March from Pierson's *Faust*.

During his two month stay he studied viola with a local musician, Huhn, who introduced him to the viola d'amour; he played various church organs and heard Auber's *Masaniello* at the Opera 'with unexpected pleasure'. The most stimulating experience was a concert by a Hungarian band: 'only eleven of them – violins and two clarinets and an instrument I'd never seen before [probably the czimbalon or Hungarian dulcimer]. They played like madmen or wild beasts'.[12]

Pierson was erudite and encouraged Parry to read Goethe's *Faust* and Shakespeare's plays. He talked to him about Wagner – Parry already knew the *Tannhäuser* overture: 'I couldn't understand the reason of a great deal of it. Some of it was very fine; somewhat giving the sensation of Chaos, with Creation and Form beginning to be perceptible'.

At the end of August Parry attended the funeral of the oldest General in Württemberg. The burial, with full military honours, regiments of horse and foot, each with their own band, and 'a tremendous salvo of guns' as the body was lowered into the grave, made a deep impression. His stay ended on 11th September, but his return journey took in Heidelberg, its castle and the route along the Rhine to Cologne. There he heard vespers in a side chapel of the Cathedral: 'The voices of the choristers chanting, with an occasional booming chord from the organ rolling out into the dim stillness and the scent of incense all combined to make the scene solemn and memorable'.[13]

His German visit stimulated a burst of compositional activity which included two string quartets, several other chamber works, the *Morning Service in D* and three pieces he orchestrated with Pierson: the song *Autumn*, the *Intermezzo Religioso* which S.S. Wesley was able to have performed at Gloucester in 1868 and the *Allegretto Scherzando*, composed at Stuttgart and intended to form part of a symphony, never to be completed. Parry and Pierson nurtured hopes of his returning to Stuttgart in the following summer, 1868, but Pierson's letter to 'My best Uberto' from 'your affectionate Padre della musica'[14] indicates that Gambier Parry was 'not complimentary to the musical profession' and the plan was rejected. Gambier Parry's decision to thwart his son's musical ambitions at this crucial stage had far reaching repercussions.

Parry's inability to return to Pierson halted his technical development as a composer for five, possibly ten years.[15] From 1868 to 1873 he completed a mere handful of pieces, all small scale. In contrast, the score of the 1866 Oxford Cantata still testifies that the First Symphony (1881) could have been written much earlier had he continued to study with Pierson. The decision also halted his maturity as a man. Musical composition was the one activity which required Parry to develop the introspective side of his personality. Composition demands solitude, reflection, and the ability to concentrate on one constellation of processes for long stretches of time every day. Gambier Parry's decision flung his son back on an already over-extrovert personality; by severing his son's relationship with Pierson he led him directly into his obsessive quest for a relationship with the 17-year-old Lady Maude Herbert.

For the next four years Parry would pursue Lady Maude with a single-minded intensity that previously had been channelled diversely into sport, music and socializing. With a logic that was surely unconscious, Parry applied the same techniques he learned in the playing fields of Eton to win her, and employed a mix of finesse, sleight of hand and unfaltering determination. The price of marriage into the aristocratic class would be high; others would be allowed to set the rules. Domestic obligations and a partial downturn in Gambier Parry's finances would force Parry to expend a further five years of fruitless energy (1871–6) on one activity he did not like, a city career as an underwriter at Lloyds Register of Shipping. This forced extroversion, combined with Parry's strong moral sense, laid the foundations for the future teacher and public servant, but the harm to the future composer was no doubt considerable.

Throughout the rest of Parry's life there is consistent evidence from his diaries that he suffered from a psychological breach between extreme extroversion, constant hyper-activity, an obsession with sport, administration and distraction by social engagements, and a blocked process of introversion, an inability to sit alone and contemplate. In later life he constantly complained in letters and diary entries that there was insufficient time to compose. Yet paradoxically he fought against the solitary conditions that are a necessary pre-requisite for the compositional process. Parry constantly equated 'solitary' with 'lonely', a negative rather than a positive experience. For example, when Lady Maude was away, resting at Roehampton during her second pregnancy, Parry wrote in his diary: 'Tried to work but was very depressed and didn't succeed much, it is horrid this loneliness, not a soul to speak to, or to look into their eyes and catch a gleam of sympathy.' (24 September 1877). Thirteen years later he is still using the word 'lonely' in the same way. In a letter to Maude, referring to a visit from Frank Pownall he says that 'at times I do feel that lonely and disheartened I am almost desperate. But when Frank comes I feel there's someone worth playing to. I think it's the total lack of sympathy that's made me give up my playing.' (26 October 1890). For a man then at the height of his fame, this highly charged need for company and sympathy could only spring from a strong psychological root, never properly understood at the time and now problematic to isolate.

It is possible that the lack of a mother caused a rift between the masculine and feminine aspects of Parry's personality. By the nineteenth century it was generally known that deprivation of a maternal relationship had a detrimental effect on any child, but before the dawn of modern psychology there were no theories, based on empirical evidence, to suggest what the more profound aspects could be.[16]

Parry felt the loss keenly, but the ways in which it affected his personality remained unconscious. It is significant that two of his most enduring friendships were with Alfred Lyttelton and Edward Burne-Jones, both of whom lost their mothers at birth. Parry and Burne-Jones were consistently drawn, sometimes obsessively, to an elusive feminine ideal, originally projected onto their wives and later onto their daughters; throughout their lives they were drawn to other young women who conformed to their idealized image including Laura Tennant who married Alfred Lyttelton (see Chapter 8). In both men this quest was caught up with an acute sense of loneliness never properly assuaged.

Another artist who suffered the same deprivation of the mother and close family was Jean Genet (1910–89); Genet, writing in a more self-analytical age, defines the source of beauty, and therefore creative inspiration, as 'the wound'. The artist unconsciously 'preserves' the wound because the healing of the wound would remove the wellsprings of his creativity. So the wound becomes the source of the creativity, which is in itself the only activity which offers a temporary alleviation of the wound's negative attributes. It is a circular process – a conundrum.

In Parry's case the unconscious longing for his mother may have been the nucleus of his wound, a longing intensified by a stepmother to whom he did not relate emotionally, and a sister who died prematurely. The wound was deepened by the tragic decline of his elder, and in his opinion more talented, brother Clinton and a father who was intent on Parry becoming a conventional member of the establishment. In the process Gambier Parry deprived his son of further contact with Pierson, who was to be one of his principal role models both musically and domestically, since it could be argued that at Rustington Parry created an environment comparable to Pierson's in Stuttgart. So the privilege and affluence of Parry's childhood environment concealed the fact that Parry lacked love – the greatest of all wounds. Because he remained unconscious of this until the last years of his life, Parry became the prisoner and the gaoler of his own personality.

2 Lady Maude

I think special pleading is out of place in a biography.

(Lady Maude, Diaries)

It is certainly rather a trial to take aristocrats to concerts.

(Lady Maude, Diaries)

Maudie is keener about Wagner's music than I ever saw her about anything except the rights of women.

(Parry, Diary, 18 May 1877)

The earldom of Pembroke had been in the Herbert family for hundreds of years and Wilton, their country seat was rich in history; in particular, it was famous for its literary associations with Sir Philip Sidney and his sister the Countess of Pembroke. Lady Maude Herbert grew up surrounded by a loving family, luxury and a succession of the illustrious to grace each house party. Her father Baron Herbert of Lea (1810–61) played a notable part as Secretary of War in supporting Florence Nightingale's nursing mission during the Crimean War. Shortly after Parry entered Eton, Maude's elder brother George (1850–95) inherited the earldom. Parry's cousin Edward Hamilton (1848–1907), a fellow boarder in Evans house, was a family friend of the Herberts and Parry soon became acquainted with the young earl.

In the summer of 1863 Pembroke invited Hamilton and Parry to Wilton. The 15-year-old schoolboy was attracted to its environment, evocative of Tudor times with its architecture, landscaped grounds and heirlooms such as the Wilton Diptych of Richard II, all of which hearkened back to the age of Sidney, Spenser, Tallis and Byrd. In particular he was attracted to the 12-year-old Lady Maude Herbert. An extended visit a year later was filled with 'picnics, music, fencing, fishing, bathing, riding, and moonlight walks', with his 'lady love'. Parry's private thoughts about Maude were committed to his diary in code; an action that drew her into the world of Lucy and Clinton. Wilton's calm contrasted with the tension of Highnam where Clinton was now embroiled with Florence Hinde.

A mixture of ancestries endowed Lady Maude with memorable features: dark intense eyes and dark swept-back hair contrasted with an ivory complexion more Russian than English in effect. High cheek bones, a delicate prominence to the nose and a determined line to the jaw marked a countenance that must have been ever changing in expression. She retained her willowy figure and even in her careless old age people described her as 'wondrously beautiful'.[1] In youth her clothes were an impressive testament to her natural instinct for the dramatic. There was a resemblance to Parry's own mother Isabella and his sister Lucy. Striking looks were bestowed on the whole Pembroke family: Mary Gladstone and Margot Tennant testify to the handsome demeanour of the six-foot-five George Pembroke with 'the most beautiful eyes I have ever seen', and Lady Maude's sister Constance Gladys was one of the great beauties of her day.

For the next four years there is less mention of Parry's 'lady love' though he remained good friends with her brother and in 1866 left Eton, travelling with Pembroke. Throughout these years the rich social life of Highnam, Eton and Oxford provided outlets for the pleasure loving aspect of Parry's personality. His diary displays an appreciation of other feminine distractions: Nettie Ward, the Miss Liddells, and Miss Beach who 'dances gloriously and is one of the most delightful creatures', but they were a series of transient attractions illuminating his early diaries without any evidence of deeper involvements.

A result of Gambier Parry's refusal to fund a second visit to Pierson was an opportunity to spend a week at Wilton. It is not surprising that Parry arrived in a susceptible mood, wanting emotional compensation after the frustration to his creative ambitions. The elegant Lady Maude was an ideal object for his affections. Hubert, the handsome undergraduate, sporting a moustache, and with a Gloucester Festival performance to his name the following month, appeared at his most desirable. Maude clearly enjoyed being the centre of his attention. The gushing mentions she elicits in Parry's 1868 diary suggest that part of the charm of Lady Maude was the context of Wilton: 'Maude and I were like brother and sister always together', 'Both she and Mary are the most wonderfully well read ... ', 'Dear Lady Herbert is as fascinating and impulsive as ever' and 'Sidney and Reggie are a perfect pair of little boys'. It is clear that the Pembrokes had become a substitute family, a compensation for his lost 'first family' at Highnam, his uninterested stepmother, and the denied musical family of Pierson.

Maude at 17 was a perfect replacement for the lost sister Lucy. The romance was soon aided and abetted by Maude's elder sister Mary and cousin 'Sandy'. Several letters survive from Lady Mary Herbert secretly encouraging Parry's suit. An exchange of letters following the Gloucester Festival has Parry replying to his 'dear little Fairie Queene' by return of post. Maude appears cautious, under pressure from her widowed mother and the imminence of her coming out.[2] In fairness Lady Herbert (1822–1911) would be planning a prestigious marriage for her second daughter. Mary would wed Baron von Heugel and Constance Gladys would become the wife respectively of the Earl of Lonsdale and the second Marquess of Ripon. Parry, a younger son without title, income or career, was not an acceptable suitor, but in the event Lady Herbert's opposition proved too half-hearted.

The letters were followed by clandestine meetings in London chaperoned by Lady Mary Herbert who drew Mary Gladstone into the courtship conspiracy. The Gladstones' home at Hawarden and Pembroke's yacht *Jem* provided additional lustre to the undergraduate's quest for romance and a surrogate family. At Highnam, Clinton's decline was confirmed by an awkward family reunion in 1869.

It is clear that social constraints imposed on the young couple precluded intimacy, as Parry was the first to acknowledge, and these same constraints allowed

Maude to remain his 'Fairie Queene', a perfect unruffled object for her lover's romantic projections. After 18 months' courtship she agreed to become unofficially engaged but in the spring of 1870, under pressure from her brother, she informed her mother. Maude wrote to 'My dear Hubert', telling him: 'Don't be downhearted whatever happens as really opposition can make no earthly difference to me'. Within a month, as Parry graphically described, 'the crash came' in a lengthy letter from Lady Herbert. All too late, she introduced an element of common sense into the proceedings. It is a fair letter and not to be condemned; Lady Herbert's mistake was timing. If she wanted to act she should have acted earlier and more decisively.

The letter accuses Parry of 'entangling Maude into an engagement' and taking advantage of George's inexperience and her own widowhood. At the conclusion it shows an ominous perspicacity:

> Dear Hubert, if I have written severely it is not that I do not care for you but that for both your sakes I feel and see the utter madness of such a marriage to an extent of which you can have no idea. After all, Maude and you would never get on even if you had the means of living. She hates music except for your sake and you have a passion for it, and she is thoroughly unbusiness like and would make the worst poor man's wife in the world![3]

From this point events are unclear and one can only hazard interpretations in the face of the partial evidence. Gambier Parry was busy establishing his son's career at Lloyds before Lady Herbert's letter arrived: so the decision was not the outcome of demands from the Pembrokes. Why Gambier Parry was content to tie Hubert to the unedifying position of an underwriter, a career in which Parry had no interest, needs investigation. Parry referred to it as 'the hateful occupation of money making'.

But the city career suited the Pembrokes and the impact of Lady Herbert's letter was limited. Within a 'short while' communication was resumed and by Christmas 1870 Parry was visiting Wilton again. There he and Maude had 'a gorgeous ride in the Woronzoff sledge with bells and all'. 'I drove and both ponies were very fresh, much excited by the jangling of the bells and went like the wind'. The sledge was a legacy of Maude's Russian ancestry (her grandmother was the Countess Woronzoff) and provided one more glamorous image for Parry's delectation. By June 1871 Lady Herbert had given permission for the engagement and on 27 June 1872 they were married at St Paul's, Knightsbridge; Parry called it 'the supreme event of my life'.

However Parry's comment was set down almost two years later. It is revealing that he felt no desire to record the early day-to-day experiences of his engagement and marriage, but the diary was rarely an outlet for intense, personal experiences. Some of the missing details are furnished by surviving letters from Parry and Lady Maude. There is a marked contrast between Parry's outpourings to his 'Darlingest of Pets' and Maude's poised to 'My dear Hubert.' To the modern eye his letters are curiously exhausting. The endless protestations of love appear self-centred, demanding and sometimes border on the hysterical. On Christmas Day 1871 he wrote

> All day long I am thinking of you and praying for your happiness and all night I think of you and dream of you. Even at the celebration this morning I discovered that I was utterly unable to listen to the prayers, or pray for myself for my whole soul was so consumed with thoughts of you that there was no room for any thoughts of myself except in so far as I might be worthy of you.

Maude was the object of his desire, not the subject of his understanding. In fairness, this example was prompted by a minor but illuminating point of tension in their engagement.

In contrast to Lady Herbert's warm Christmas greeting 'God bless you dear boy', Parry is shocked by Maude's short, casual letter. The couple are in daily correspondence at this time[4] but Maude departs from her normal 'My dear Hubert' and 'Your very loving Maudie' nomenclature for the altogether colder 'Dear Hubert' and 'Yr affect. Md. H.'.

> Dear Hubert
> I wish you a happy Xmas. Its a pity you can't be in two places at a time. I enjoyed myself tremendously at Torquay. Found all the Froudes more or less congenial and Devonshire House lovely to look upon. I find a truly match making spirit pervades this family with the exception of Maude. It is a phase and may pass. Mr. Manners [?] preached a beautiful sermon last Sunday on how many high and noble earthly aspirations would be realised to the full in heaven. – I saw a view just like a Turner from out of the train. A ship with brown sails reflected into still water, the background of trees and houses half hidden in a mist and the whole enveloped in a most delicious pink light. It was wonderful. Do you know Miss Byron nearly dined with us one night in Torquay. The man who sings.
> Ys affect.
Md. H.

The letter is memorable for its disjunct syntax and images of isolation: the sermon on earthly aspirations linked to the solitary boat in the mist. Maude is clearly proclaiming her independence from Parry's effusions, but other factors are also at play.

Parry does not notice its more curious contents; the match-making spirit that will pass, the dinner with Miss Byron that never happened and the man who sings. Instead he reacts rather pompously to the letter's distant overall tone: 'Though you are the biggest darling in the world my precious Maudie, I declare you are very funny. Your letters are so matter of fact that they very often act as a positive damper to the intensity of my affection. I daresay it is very good for me'.

By the time Maude receives Parry's letter she has already pre-empted any crisis by writing a second affectionate letter in her usual manner. This prompts an immediate retraction from her fiancé: 'Darlingest of pets, I am so glad another letter came this morning. I am sure I should have been quite grumpy if it hadn't. Instead whereof I am in a state of reaction from the state of lowness which I was in yesterday and the day before for want of you'. In the stress of this emotional square dance Parry is not lacking in spirit and signs the letter initially with 'Your very loving C. Hubert H. Parry. Hello! What did I sign myself like that for' before ending in his usual more intimate style.

The letter gives Maude a convenient escape and she writes on 27 December 1871: 'My Dear Hubert, I was delighted at getting your second letter, because now

I needn't answer the first need I? So glad you are happy again'. She ends the letter by writing all round the edges with a statement that is perhaps a credo:

> I daresay you are thinking this letter terribly matter of fact but it is always an effort for me to speak out my affection. There is a lot of reserve in my nature which forbids me doing so. My letters may be seemingly cold but they don't mean to be so. But I think you understand the reason without my explaining it. I shouldn't at all like you to be matter of fact. Evelyn has sent a Happy Xmas to the 'love birds' as she calls us. Only 3 days now before I shall see you again. It seems as if you had been away a month at least. M.H. I hope we shall spend next Xmas together. Your very very very very loving Maudie. I send you a pretended and a real one.

Parry, in reply, protests: 'Why didn't you want to answer the letter you speak of? I shall demand an explanation when I come' but one suspects he never received one. Unfortunately, on the evidence of the letters, one has to conclude that Parry as suitor was never mysterious or intriguing, and anything but hard-to-get. Maude's capriciousness allowed the fresh air of drama to cut through the repetitiousness of Parry's sentiments.

Maude was not a figure of Romance, nor the Snow White of his dreams,[5] but an attractive aristocrat caught up in the only significant decision permitted by the strictures of her class and Lady Herbert may have felt her daughter had been allowed more than her own say in the marital decision making. Later Maude gradually loosened ties with her mother, forbidding her presence at the birth of her daughters and refusing to see her on her deathbed in 1911. Parry would go upstairs alone. Perhaps she felt Lady Herbert had let her down profoundly. Whether this related to her marriage we may never know.

Parry's letters throughout the courtship may be ardent but they are often superficial, showing little understanding of the complexity of Maude's character. It is likely that she had private doubts about the marriage – perhaps any marriage. There is insufficient evidence to deduce her private attitude to Lady Herbert's letter or how actively she encouraged her mother to back down so easily with regard to renewed correspondence and social meetings. Nonetheless, since the marriage proved to be difficult from almost the beginning, perhaps Maude began to have her serious doubts at the same time as Lady Herbert had been finally won over. If Lady Herbert had believed in her own letter she would have stuck by it. One suspects that the redoubtable 48-year-old widow of Lord Herbert ('our marriage was one big crescendo!' she once wrote to Parry with un-English enthusiasm) and 'friend of Liszt', was not insensible to Parry's famous charms. Her own behaviour is also difficult to disentangle from the surviving evidence.

Maude's letters may have been designed to elicit certain responses from her fiancé; to test his reactions when she withdrew or became moody. It allowed her to discover in advance how he reacted when she was not responsive. Later he would not be able to claim ignorance. This is not to imply she did not take a conscious decision that marriage to Parry was her best choice. But in her own mind perhaps, she laid down her terms. His consistent importuning would reasonably have convinced her of his devotion and his determination to make her the centre of his life. This was to prove not to be the case.

After her death Arthur Ponsonby wrote at length about Maude's inadequacies, of her being a poor wife. In contrast, nothing has been written about Parry's inadequacies as a husband. This is not surprising; Maude with nonchalant disdain published no testimonies, no self defences, no charming reminiscences and no special pleadings to salvage her image from the narrow scrutiny of sons-in-laws. The major surprise was to discover her diary for seven consecutive years from 1887 to 1893 from which no extracts have been published.[6] There are also numerous letters to Parry throughout her marriage usually addressed to 'my dearest darling'. Maude comes over as neither helpless and hapless nor neurotic but witty, sophisticated and fired with an eccentric sense of humour which delighted in human foibles.[7] By the late 1880s she lived an elaborate self-sufficient social life, with younger men, Philip Burne-Jones (1861–1925) in particular,[8] dancing attendance and the willing butt for her whims and fancies. Hubert floated in and out of Maude's social panoply which she used adeptly to keep his role within defined limits.

It is unfair of Ponsonby to claim that Maude had no interest in her husband's music. The diary shows she attended many performances and took pride in his success. But sensibly she avoided the cliché role of the admiring composer's wife, as her story of *The Lotos-Eaters* shows:

> To Cambridge. Travelled with a woman in the train who ate till she was sick so I tried to frighten her by pretending to shoot her with my umbrella and she did try to change carriages when we stopped but couldn't find another.
> Great squash at the concert. The rude Vice Chancellor's wife refused to let me sit down declaring that all the seats belonged to herself and 'friends' till Stanford called out from the orchestra 'let me introduce you to Lady Maude Parry' and that put everything right. *The Lotos-Eaters* was lovely but Mrs. Hutchinson did not do it justice. June 13th. [1892 Sh.P.]
> June 14th Tuesday. Horrid critic on *Lotos-Eaters* by Graves which I saw at the dentists.

Lady Maude did not care for C.L. Graves and refused to co-operate on his biography. Neither Graves or Ponsonby would credit her for responding positively to Parry's most forward-looking score to date.

The romantic impetus of Maude's marriage to Hubert continued through the first 18 months. A house at Bengeo close to Hertford was rented from Gambier's relatives and Parry's city duties were interspersed with elaborate house parties and extended visits to relations and acquaintances; Parry fitted in uncomplainingly with a social round predetermined by Lady Maude's station and his dependency on the generosity of aristocratic in-laws. His finances remained precarious and, against the background of Clinton's disastrous emigration to South Africa, his father was in no position to help. Parry resorted to a £400 gift from the Earl of Pembroke in addition to Maude's allowance of £600 *per annum*. In fairness to Parry, Clinton by November 1872 had gone through his £500 annual allowance and two-thirds of the £5,000 provided by Gambier Parry 'to establish his family for their future existence'.[9]

In July 1873 Parry and Lady Maude moved to 7 Cranley Place, lavishly furnished by Lady Herbert to Parry's aesthetic horror. But the move allowed Parry to begin his thirty-year association with Edward Dannreuther; on 11 November 1873 he took up his bi-weekly Sunday afternoon piano lessons. In the same month,

August Manns played through Parry's overture *Vivien;*[10] thus after five years the impetus to resume serious composition presented itself.

Maude could be forgiven for believing she alone would be the centre of her husband's attentions. Yet Edward Dannreuther (1844–1905) was to emerge as an unexpectedly powerful influence over her husband. Four years younger than Clinton, the German émigré soon stepped into the position left vacant by Clinton's disintegration – he became the replacement for the elder brother and compensation for Parry's inability to return to Pierson. Gifted, sensitive, married into the powerful Ionides family[11], and a friend of George Eliot, his early biography reveals interesting parallels with Klesmer in Eliot's novel, *Daniel Deronda*. One wonders if he provided a conscious model. (Parry and Lady Maude named their two daughters after the heroines of *Middlemarch* and *Daniel Deronda*. It should be noted that Daniel, in George Eliot's novel, grew up never knowing his mother, a subject of some importance to his character and the novel's development.)

Four years later (after Parry had completed his *Concertstück* and the Wind *Nonet*) the intensity of their relationship is evident from Parry's diary: 'He said he had been so lonely for so long and I might be a brother to him and help him in life and he would not let me consider myself as having lessons from him any longer and so on. I can't write all the sweet things he said.[12]

With a curious synchronicity, as Dannreuther replaced Clinton, Maude began to echo the role of Parry's lost sister Lucy. With the move to London she fell ill: 'Poor little Maudie is very low ... always so tired ... and sad.'[13] Lady Herbert and Pembroke considered Parry's poor finances were aggravating Maude's condition. Between Parry's required presence in the city and his increased involvement with music, Maude seemed without a *raison d'être*. Her illnesses, psychosomatic and real, begin to exert a strong hold on her husband's attention. This is reminiscent of Freud's comment to Mahler during their 1910 meeting in Holland: 'You loved your mother, and you look for her in every woman. She was careworn and ailing and unconsciously you wish your wife to be the same.'[14]

Fear of losing Maude, with the reminder of Lucy's understated decline, exercised a profound effect on Parry. Maude could maintain an emotional hold on her husband by a supreme display of inactivity. Parry noted in 1876: 'Maudie takes up a good deal of time, exercising her and doing various things she cannot do herself'. The illnesses had other advantages; they commanded the sympathy of family, friends and servants. Maude could continue to be the static centre of her social domestic world just as she had been during the courtship.

Maude's health encouraged Parry to find a home outside London. An appeal to Gambier Parry for finance to build a house in 1875 was met with a polite refusal: 'I have not £5,000 available anyhow for you – and indeed if I had, I should need to be very far better informed of the scheme'.[15] Parry found an initial solution by renting a house in Ottershaw, within commuting distance of London. It was the first step to the building of Knights Croft, Rustington in 1880–81 which would become Maude's main abode for the rest of their married life but for Parry only a holiday and weekend home.

In January 1876 Maude returned to London for the birth of Dorothea, named 'after our favourite character in *Middlemarch*.' Although Parry could write on the day of the birth to Lady Herbert about Maudie's 'being safe', she remained bedbound and 'wavered between a little better and a little worse for weeks and weeks'. He hints delicately that one problem was that control of the urinary tract failed to return for some time. To Parry's fury the first recovery was wrecked by Lady Herbert reducing Maude to hysterics with a fallacious story that Mary von Heugel was not returning from Germany to stay with her – 'Lady Herbert loves to produce strong emotions in the minds of her hearers,' he wrote acidly – but it is clear that Maude's decision to keep her mother away from the confinement only aggravated relations.

If the experience of childbirth was a trauma little helped by the gynaecological inadequacies of the 1870s, Maude now faced further emotional upheaval in the form of a new competitor for Parry's affections: 'I also had a very sweet little Idyll which cheered my somewhat dreary and sorrowful life a great deal and this was the friendship which grew up between Tora Gordon and me.'[16] The friendship even survived her engagement, for which Parry wrote the Piano Sonata in A major. 'I began to idealise the object of it and to make a Romance out of it and love grew till in my heart she was second only to Maudie.[17] Even today, in our brave new world of sexual freedom and unstable liaisons, this would be considered emotional disloyalty, especially by a young father. In the face of this development Maude soon rallied and resumed her social rounds including Wilton where fate decided to give a twist of black humour: she succumbed to diphtheria and scarlatina which banished both her and Hubert to total isolation. Although she soon recovered, later a persistent lung infection required her to winter abroad – several months in a cramped hotel in Cannes where Dorothea managed to fall sick with croup. 'I spent part of each day and all the evening swearing at my exile', Parry wrote of the outward journey.

The realities of childbirth and illness must have forced Maude into serious thinking. Her husband's impatience with the trappings of the aristocratic life and his desire to make a career in music demonstrated clearly that Parry was incapable of arranging his life around a private world centred on Maude. 'She wants to go to Highnam straight after the sea and straight away to Hugh Montgomery's from Highnam. It doesn't give a chap much chance. It's that diseased aristocratic education which emasculates both moral and physical. ... ',[18] he complained to Eddie Hamilton during their diphtheria isolation. But even in Cannes Parry discovered a musical distraction: he fell in with a young Italian violinist Guerini and his wife, and by January 1877 he was busy as performer and composer in Guerini's chamber music concerts.

Hyperactivity attracted another accomplice, a Mr Hawkins. On one expedition to Mont du Cheivon they 'walked forty miles, climbed 4,000 ft., passed the night at Grässe and returned next morning by a 5.45 train to Cannes.' Maude's afternoon walk entailed Parry pushing her along the promenade in a bath chair. Nonetheless her health improved and they journeyed back in April 1877 via Paris, where they attended Meyerbeer's *Robert le Diable*. Of the Opera House Parry noted: 'I never saw the nude female form made so much use of in my life before.'

After her return there was a change in Maude's *modus operandi*. The excuse of pregnancy in the spring of 1877 encouraged her regime of distancing herself from her husband by extended visits to her sister Mary (at Hampstead), Mrs Morrison (at Roehampton) the Majendies (at Hedingham Castle) and finally Rustington. The effect of this tactic was to make Parry 'wretchedly lonely' whenever they were parted and no doubt more attentive and less nervous when he was allowed to be reunited with Maude.

Maude now evolved a positive policy towards Parry's emerging roles as composer, musicologist and academic. She attended performances even to the extent of sitting through the rehearsal of the E Minor Piano Trio only six days before the birth of Gwendolen in February 1878. She was present at the first performance of all the first four symphonies and as late as 1915 attended the second performance of *From Death to Life*. Her response to the Cambridge performance of *Prometheus* in 1881 confounds Ponsonby's assertion that she 'never cared for his music.' Parry recounted to his cousin Eddie Hamilton that 'Maude was so wild with delight over your telegram that she told me that bad as she was, she got up and jumped about the room.'[19]

There is evidence that she encouraged Parry's academic career and placed considerable importance on Sir George Grove, with whom she enjoyed a flirtatious relationship. 'I can't help liking Mr. Grove though he is a wicked old humbug!'[20] In her diaries and letters Maude emerges as a born humorist and actress who probably crossed the fine line between acting and acting-up all too frequently. Her delight in theatre and especially modern drama, including Ibsen and Wilde, remained undiminished. Parry mentions attending *The Importance of Being Earnest* in 1909: 'Very lively dialogue, but very thin and trivial. Maude enjoyed it very much.'

It is surprising, considering her reputed lack of interest in music, that the composer to whom Maude responded most strongly was the ultra-progressive Wagner. The Parry's met Richard and Cosima Wagner at Orme Square when Dannreuther and the Wagner Society organized the 1877 London concerts.[21] 'Wagner talks so fast that I could catch but very little of what he said', Parry recounted, but 'I enjoyed them [the concerts] fully and so did Maudie who is keener about Wagner's music than I ever saw her about anything except the rights of women. We sat with George Eliot and Madame Wagner'. Maude's interest would continue unabated, and in 1913 she attended the English première of *Parsifal*.

Involvement in Women's Rights was stimulated by Agnes and Rhoda Garrett. They were interior designers who worked with Morris and de Morgan. Agnes's sister Mrs Fawcett, married to the blind Postmaster-General Henry Fawcett, was a leader of the women's suffrage movement and soon Maude and Parry were attending meetings. In later life Maude's concern went further and embraced the more revolutionary suffragettes. She became friendly with the Pankhursts, and Kensington Square was a frequent venue for committee meetings and gatherings. Maude made speeches, apparently with some success, and on at least one occasion she marched with suffragettes in Littlehampton. The surviving photographs capture her in front staring out with her habitual quizzical gaze and dressed for the part. It was fortunate for Parry's equilibrium that she never chained herself to the Downing Street railings. The support of women from Maude's social class lent prestige to the movement and gives the lie to Ponsonby's criticism of her smallness of vision. It testifies to her belief that there was a richer role for women than the narrow alternatives of social adornment or domestic drudgery, accorded by the accidents of birth and class.

The movement provided Maude with ammunition to defend her role in her circumscribed relationship with Parry. Her attitude did not stop with herself but carried over to Dorothea, later Lady Ponsonby, who produced the ultimate justification of the non-supportive wife in a diary entry about the wife of one of her husband's friends, Mrs E.D. Morel:

> She is a wonderful woman almost too good – and puts one to shame. Slaving for other people and doing the housework all day – and she's very intelligent too and much more sympathetic than he – she is very bad for him giving him unstinted and unlimited admiration and praise, consequently encouraging his self absorbed nature. How bad good women are for men. This is the only comfort I can take in my own selfishness and my requiring consideration and attention – it is so good for A [Arthur] and especially the children.[22]

Dorothea's dismay at Mrs Morel's 'slaving' suggests she learned first-hand from her mother that domestic inactivity could work far more effectively for marital survival. But inactivity made Maude a splendid observer and raconteur with a relish for gossip. Her diaries record a series of memorable vignettes either heard or experienced: 'Lady Brooke lives separate from her husband. Miss Wakefield gives him dinner in her bedroom together with Marion Ivry and Maude White. They drink oceans of champagne and take baths under the table.' (The beautiful Daisy, Lady Brooke – nicknamed 'Babbling Brooke' – was Edward VII's mistress at the time).

Maude's delight in practical jokes persisted into old age, as Parry's own diaries record. Philip Burne-Jones in particular was rarely spared her humour, often at the receiving end of practical jokes and the sharpness of her pen: 'Phil gobbles all day and the noise he makes when he eats is simply sickening. He is literally bursting out of his clothes'. On one bizarre occasion Maude put sticking plasters on her own and all the servants' faces to dupe Phil into believing they had broken out in a pox-like allergy acquired from the chickens. To Maude's delight Phil fell for it. But when he returned two days later to visit all concerned, he was outraged to find Maude with no plasters and no *scars*. 'I hadn't thought of that', she adds regretfully. In contrast, at other times they discussed more profound issues: 'To the New Gallery with Phil. We talked seriously in the evening about our beliefs & how it was really quite impossible that we shouldn't all meet again.'[23] Essentially her humour is most apparent in social situations, at house parties, dinner parties and concerts. For example, although Maude made use of her illnesses all her life, occasionally the situation was reversed and she wasn't above seeing the funny side of it: 'All too ill to go to the Wyndhams. Sidney has a clot. Hubert a throat. Getey a heart. George a liver and Margaret indigestion!'

Her sister-in-law, the auburn-haired Lady Getey Talbot was ten years older than Lord Pembroke; their marriage in 1874 shocked the Herberts. The eccentric Getey was more than a match for Maude: in middle age she employed a red headed footman at Wilton expressly to provide locks of hair for her coiffures.[24]

On one occasion Maude unwisely agreed to take Getey to a Wagner concert and has left a memorable account of the experience:

Went to the Richter with Getey in the evening. She was such a bother. First she didn't want to go in by the Piccadilly entrance because she said it smelt of dinner. Then she gave a halfpenny instead of a half sovereign for her ticket and then protested that they must let her in without paying. I persuaded her at last to give her address. Then she would sit next to me, and so I had to turn a man out of his seat for her. After that she insisted on taking his book and kept it entirely – till the horrid idea occurred to her to send him for another book in the middle of the music. I protested in vain but fortunately the man's good nature stopped at this and he refused to move. It is certainly rather a trial to take aristocrats to concerts. Nevertheless I enjoyed my evening because we had nothing but Wagner. I sat next to a man who talked with the greatest enthusiasm of *Judith* asking me if I had heard Lloyd in it etc. At last I told him who I was which covered him with confusion.[25]

Parry's expanding musical career augmented their financial situation and gave Maude domestic breathing room but it had little impact on her social status. Parry's pupils and his academic associates rarely became members of her social circle. The exceptions were Grove and Dannreuther, Plunkett Greene and Fuller Maitland. Discussions were more often about theatre than music: 'Fuller talked of Ibsen with the greatest enthusiasm. He says Miss Adamson is just like Mrs. Stanford who of course is just like a doll.[26]

Mary Gladstone's reminiscences give an indication of how the Parrys entertained: 'Spenser Lyttelton and I used often to dine alone with the Parrys on a leg of mutton and a pudding. On the sideboard there was bread and beer and sardines to fill up the chinks. The meal did not take long and the evening was devoted entirely to music. I remember one night of Wagner only – suddenly he stopped 'Oh let's have something healthy, and he broke into Bach. He put life into everything he touched. His spirits touched the stars, they were so madly high.'[27] On another occasion Mary Gladstone mentions walking to Maude's 'for dinner and putting the little girls to bed ... She [Maude] was very ill, but full of pluck and a burning politician.'[28]

The transition from her courtship role to a more mature one cannot have been easy for Maude. In this respect Sir William Richmond's 1888 portrait is an intriguing study. She is portrayed with dramatic effect in a dress of intense scarlet trimmed with white against an almost black background. The face captures her mature beauty at 37. The pose is enigmatic and quintessentially regal, and the portrait prompts comparison with contemporary studies of Elizabeth of Austria and Princess Alexandra of Wales, whom Richmond also painted. These comparisons certainly provide a clue why the vagaries of her moods inspired Parry with a mixture of fascination and awe. Her bullying, contradictions and obsessions only ensured she never lost her hold on his affections.

Parry's diary testifies that she remained as unpredictable as the weather and usually he refers to her like the weather, with her own attendant vocabulary: 'Maude in wild state of thrill' or 'Maude badly out of sorts again all day. Seems to me she must be taking too much veronal' or even 'Maude still dilapidated.' Her reactions never ceased to interest him:

After dinner Maude came with me to horseshow. She was bored with the four-in-hands but much amused with the double jumping competition – and especially delighted when Frenchmen did better than Englishmen.

By this time (1912) they were both over sixty but Parry's description could have been written thirty years before.

From their reading lists, diary entries and theatre-going, it would appear that Parry and Maude became keenly aware of the latest psychological observations on marital relationships, and the arrival of Ibsen's *The Doll's House* in 1889 exercised a profound impact within their social milieu. They went to see the play on 27 June. Parry declared it was 'the most interesting modern play I ever saw, and supremely true to human nature whatever it may be in the truth of the special application of its social and moral principles'. He continues:

> People seem inclined to over-estimate the direct purpose of the dramatist, as if he meant that directly one of a couple find him – or herself unsuited, he or she ought to cut and run. While the larger problem and thesis that it is everybody's duty to clear their truths for themselves is thoroughly acceptable. If Ibsen has a moral and didactic purpose, at all events it made him true to human nature and human situations in this case.[29]

Avid debate over the play's significance continued, as we know from Lady Maude. Her brilliant account of the dinner party at the Richmonds two days later remains the *pièce de résistance* of her diaries, a testament to her powers of observation and to the bold ferment of ideas that animated late Victorian society. Maude's considerable command of the English language is all the more impressive for being free of Victorian literary cliché. It is surprisingly contemporary in style and feeling:

> June 29, Saturday
> Dinner with the Richmonds. Sat next to W. Morris who made such a noise that he nearly deafened me. A German lady on the other side apparently irritated him so that he bawled more than usual. We talked of Ibsen's *Doll's House* wh. Morris admired immensely. The German lady thought Norah should not have left her children. "Why not screamed Morris her husband was a cur why should she stay with him". "No woman has a right to leave her children" returned the German. "But a man may" returned Morris "For any national cause or duty, & a woman is an individual just the same therefore she may". I tried to show them that Ibsen felt that Norah was not morally fit to bring up the children, & that the nurse was. The German maintained that the husband was no worse than the generality of men wh. if I believed I should cut my throat at once.
> But I found most people agreed with her. One man said indeed that he was not at all a bad man, but a kind good fellow, & that it was a great want of gratitude in Norah to leave him.
> Mrs. Richmond said she thought the play so immoral that she wdn't go & see it. And that Norah must have been either a fool or a knave, wh. showed how little she knew about it. Afterwards Morris talked of Bismarck. He said he felt him to be the most unmitigated rascal in the whole history of mankind & that the Germans were a most immoral race to stand him.
> Here the German lady vigorously protested. She said Bismarck wasn't a rascal, & that Germans were a very moral race, though she thought them wanting in individualism, & character. She defended Bismarck's system of mouchards, & said the Empress was the most indiscreet, & traitorous woman possible, and that as she was most intimate with her, & saw her nearly every day sh. was bound to know. I would say "defend me fr. my friends". Then she asked Morris if he approved of the new German socialistic law of providing for poor people in their old age, & said it was very bad for trade.
> "If it is bad for trade" replied Morris "I should certainly approve of it; anything that is bad for trade is a blessing. I look upon all trade as thieving. Everybody steals, all

capitalists are thieves. The judge who condemns the poor man for thieving, is a greater thief himself. As a boy I did not think it very wrong to steal, & I think it less wrong now". I said of course that I felt that if a poor person were in want of food they were justified in stealing. Morris agreed, & quoted an old saying that the English were a better race than the French because so many more hundred men were hung every year for stealing. "When an Englishman wants a thing he has the pluck to take it". I asked Morris how he wd like to live in a common house sharing with everybody alike. "Not at all" he had the honesty to reply. He defined himself as a parasite feeding on the rich, as the poor couldn't afford to buy his goods. Then he stated the startling paradox that the labourer ought to be better paid than the skilled artisan because we could live without the latter, but not without the former. The German lady here remarked that there were plenty of arguments to be adduced on the other side. "Yes" he replied "but I sha'nt stop to argue with you neither will the labourer he will just cut yr. throat that is what he will do – he wo'nt stop to hear all your arguments".

Here fortunately strawberries & cream arrived wh. calmed Morris's ardour a little. He grunted at intervals "we must all eat – the labourer just as much as you what is the use of this bottle" catching hold of Mrs. Richmond's elaborate water jug. "We can do without the man who made this but we can't do without the labourer". He says socialism is increasing. He approved of Cooperation but does not think it will do everything.

And he seems to be all against poor people saving.

Any interpretation of Parry and Maude's marriage has to proceed from the premise that they were sufficiently intelligent to 'clear their truths for themselves'. It was not a marriage where either party was forced to 'cut and run' and Maude's faith in husbands did not collapse to the point where she was prompted to 'cut my throat at once'. Judged superficially, Maude was not the ideal marriage partner for Parry but highly intelligent complex people, like Hubert and Maude, choose each other on the basis of deep, perhaps unconscious needs. Had he waited and married a young singer willing to play a supportive role, his emotional equilibrium and his creativity might well have benefited. But in all likelihood Parry would have become bored in a way that marriage to the temperamental Maude totally precluded. For her part, the limitations of her education and status left only a conventional aristocratic alignment as the alternative. In a later age she might have been happier as a freer spirit where her interests in women's suffrage, politics and the theatre could have found more rewarding expression.

In the last part of her life Maude's uneasy *détente* with life and marriage suffered as a result of a car crash – she also shared Parry's enthusiasm for motors – and, though she recovered, doctors unwisely prescribed veronal for her nerves and soon she became dependent. The symptoms were violent changes of mood and erratic judgement. However, Parry's diaries suggest that as they grew older most days still ended with 'read to Maude and so to bed', but veronal ensured that Maude remained alarmingly unpredictable to the last.

Contrary to medical logic she outlived Parry by fifteen years and became a plague on her son-in-law Arthur Ponsonby. In desperation, when Maude decided to leave a substantial endowment to his dissolute but attractive daughter Elizabeth on her marriage in 1929, he investigated the possibility of having her declared insane, comparing her mental state to that of a character from an Edgar Allan Poe story.[30] Finally a series of major strokes rendered her inarticulate and tragically immobile for the last years of her life.

Maude inspired others, apart from her son-in-law, to ponder on the paradoxes of her character. Sir Harry Johnston (1858–1927), African explorer and first Commissioner of Central Africa, was a valued friend and neighbour, keen supporter of women's suffrage, and endowed with a strong literary facility. He published numerous books and penned the following priceless verses on Lady Maude. Sir Harry (also married to the daughter of a lord, the fifth Baron Boston) gave a humane and sharply witty portrait of Sir Hubert's wife in action:

Mrs. ARTHUR PONSONBY AND Mrs. PLUNKETT GREENE
(A Hint to the Unwary.)

Our Lady Maud is fickle: I dare say you have seen
That her manner changes instantly from sombre to serene,
And equally from intimate to haughtily aloof,
While confident encroachers meet an indirect reproof:
For if they speak of 'Doll' and 'Gwen', a change comes o'er the scene,
And it's 'Mrs. Arthur Ponsonby' and 'Mrs. Plunkett Greene'.

She sat with fifty factory girls and lightly passed the time,
The while she chatted easily and read in prose and rhyme,
Of 'Dolly's' favourite shape in stays, 'Gwen's' love for chewing gum,
And 'Gladys'' (Lady Ripon's) skill in language deaf and dumb.
But when the sound of wheels was heard and a heed-less lassie asked:
'Expectin' "Gwen" and "Gladys"?' the Aristocrat unmasked
Replied in freezing accents, 'I don't know what you mean;
It's my sister, Lady Ripon, and my daughter, Mrs. Greene.'

But it's rather with the highly-placed one sees the steely tip
Of the claw between the velvet if they chance to make a slip;
For instance, Mrs. Asquith, glaring hard at Daisy Jones,
Asked 'How's your cousin Eddie, Maud?' and heard the icy tones
'My cousin, Prince Edgardo, is suffering somewhat more
Than usual, Mrs. Asquith, and your car is at the door.'

'Your daughter Dorothea' is the nearest that *I* get;
I once said 'Mrs. Gwendolen' – half whispered it – and yet –
The one brief look that followed from the dark-fringed Russian eye
Made me glad I was in England, in a land of libertye.

This is only one of several amusing poems Sir Harry wrote before the war about Lady Maude, and gave to her as a present. She plainly treasured them and after his death she granted his sister permission to publish some of them in her biography of Johnston; significantly this book appeared in 1929 when Margot Asquith was still very much alive.[31]

On balance Lady Maude remains a fascinating creature. Her surviving letters, many undated, and her diaries demand a study in their own right before we can arrive at a complete assessment. Men are rarely objective about their mothers-in-law and Ponsonby was no exception. Rather than to characters out of Poe, Lady Maude bears several similarities to Bette Davis and Gloria Swanson, not simply as she appears in *Sunset Boulevard* but as the sophisticated actress who played her. Amongst the wives of composers there are no English comparisons, in fact the unforgettable Pauline Strauss is the only other name that comes to mind.[32]

3 The Ambivalent Road to Dr Parry and Sir Hubert

'Tis good; though music oft hath such a charm
To make bad good, and good provoke to harm.
(William Shakespeare, Measure for Measure)

The pleasure of everything beautiful, the consolation afforded by art, the enthusiasm of the artist which enables him to forget the cares of life, this one advantage of the genius over other men, alone compensating him for the suffering that is heightened in proportion to the clearness of consciousness, and for the desert loneliness among a different race of men.

(Arthur Schopenhauer)[1]

The transformation from Mr Hubert Parry, city underwriter in 1872, to Dr Parry, Director of the Royal College of Music in 1895, required him to make a series of subtle compromises to his natural development as a composer. They clouded his 'clearness of consciousness' and resulted in a series of creative lapses, several of them perceptively exposed by George Bernard Shaw. These lapses are evidence of his ambivalence as a man and a creative artist. Why was this so? It is as if the blossoming academic, the public servant and even the great teacher were a series of masks to cover Parry's fundamental inability to put his creative life first. We could say these were compromises of the 45-degree order but their cumulative impact on his creative development was frequently more severe. The only 90-degree compromise he made professionally was his agreement to work at Lloyds. This decision became unpalatable; but it took more than five years to free himself.

However, working in London brought compensations in the form of the Crystal Palace concerts and 'The Pops': these gave him the opportunity to become familiar with the orchestral repertoire especially Beethoven, Schubert, Mendelssohn and Schumann. His musical acquaintances increased and he met Stockhausen, Joachim and Broadwood. He came into contact with Mme Schumann and her daughters 'whom I revere hugely as the wife and children of one of the highest of my ideal composers.'[2] As Parry cast about for a way forwards Schumann provided something of a model: the romantic idealist, family man, writer and creative artist. His attributes provided Parry with a concept of the bourgeois composer acceptable to both the Gambier Parrys and Herberts alike, though Parry's concept always remained more formal than Schumann's life would imply.

Early in his marriage, he was still seeking composition lessons in an attempt to rekindle the process ruptured by his failure to return to Pierson. There is evidence he studied with Sterndale Bennett and attempted an approach to Brahms, through Joachim. This interesting idea was thwarted by the latter's lack of encouragement and Parry's lack of self-confidence. In the event, he was destined never to meet the composer he came to revere as 'a living master worthy of being numbered with the greatest'.[3] In 1875 his search concluded with a series of lessons in strict counterpoint from Sir George Macfarren, head of the Royal Academy of Music. As C.L. Graves explains, he found these fatiguing: 'a more or less aggravating lesson from the kindly old man'.

But composition and the dedicated life offered no economic solutions. Once the Pembrokes had become his domestic centre, creativity was required to fit round the exigencies of family life. In the early 1900s Parry admitted to Graves that in the previous 20 years he had earned only £25 from his compositions. The comment contains an element of self-justification, as though the committed path of the creative artist was an inadmissible option. Parry was not built in the heroic or the tragic mould and the spectre of Clinton's wayward life, together with Lady Herbert's warning, helped to ensure that Parry never risked the security of his family for his art. One wonders however, if Maude, the political radical, might not have risen to the challenges, had Parry required her to put his creativity first, thus revealing unsuspected dimensions to her character.

The price of safety was a life that never focused around composition. He was forced to exist, often awkwardly, in several compartments at the same time, of which the most obvious were a domestic life dictated by family responsibilities, an academic career necessary for financial stability and a creative life fitted around the demands of the other two. Over time he would extend this process through the creation of numerous sub-compartments that frequently argued with each other for his over-stretched attention. Nonetheless the influences crossing between these were sometimes rewarding.

Highnam in 1896 added a further compartment and he should have been forced to choose between his academic career and running the Highnam estate, since the added burden retarded his compositional development for more than a decade. But any choice between the Royal College of Music and Highnam was inadmissible since George Grove was demanding the first and Lady Herbert the latter for the sake of 'Maude and her children.[4] The unwitting by-product was that Parry appeared greedy, materialistic and inexorably wedded to class, particularly in the eyes of self-consciously artistic composers such as Bax and Delius giving them grounds for later regarding him as 'The Old Fox.'[5]

The decision to study with Dannreuther may have been prompted by his intention to build a career as a pianist. This is born out by his regime of practice which continued until 1880. Dannreuther decided to institute a range of study that encompassed Beethoven's C minor and Liszt's A major concertos, solo compositions by Mozart and Brahms, and the piano quintets by Schumann and Brahms. They also worked on *Don Giovanni* and Cherubini's *Medée*. However, his lack of early training prevented Parry from achieving the degree of technical excellence necessary for a career as a pianist – as Dannreuther commented in the *Musical Times* in 1898:

He can play an Adagio of Beethoven's very beautifully, his accent is so good and true. As you can imagine he came to grief now and then in the allegros when his impetuosity literally outran his technical facility.

Reluctantly he must have abandoned the possibility of making a career as a pianist. But Dannreuther as mentor was crucial for Parry's renewed self-confidence as a composer. His house in Orme Square was a meeting place for artistic, political and social leaders such as the Gladstone, Balfour and Burne-Jones families, Lord Leighton and Alma-Tadema, but its focal point was Dannreuther's Chamber Concerts which continued into the 1890s These provided Parry with the encouragement to compose and the opportunity to hear an extensive output of chamber music.

Orme Square enabled Parry to build up an important range of contacts; and one gave him the key to escape the commercial strait-jacket. This was George Grove, whom he had met several years previously but in 1875 acquaintance ripened into friendship. Grove published six mild poems by Parry in *Macmillan's Magazine*, and in July he invited him to become a contributor, along with Dannreuther, to his forthcoming *A Dictionary of Music and Musicians*. His first assignment was the article on 'Arrangement', but in November 1875, Parry wrote in his diary that 'Grove asked me to take a larger share in the work of the Musical Dictionary and to help him to edit it'.

Thus it was his powers as a writer, not as a performer, which provided the 27-year-old composer with an entrée into the music world. Grove was a generation older and single-handedly he shaped Parry's academic career and ensured that he succeeded him as Director of the Royal College of Music. He became a powerful complement to Dannreuther, in effect a surrogate father who trained Parry to follow in his own literary and academic footsteps.

The *Dictionary* was a principal source of income for the next seven years, augmented by private tuition, and it enabled Parry to wind up his business at Lloyds in 1877. Despite the close association, Grove did not always confide in his younger assistant: when his most ambitious project, the inception of the Royal College of Music came to fruition, Parry was left uncertain as to whether Grove would give him a post, much to Maude's irritation. However we know from a letter from Grove to Mary Gladstone, dated 6 October 1882, that he had made up his mind some time before any announcements:

> As to Parry *of course* I shall have him – but not as Professor of Harmony, but as Prof. of Musical History and Literature. *Counterpoint* – I am not prepared with a name for that yet. Composition and orchestration will go to Stanford.

Grove's letter of appointment arrived on New Year's Day 1883: 'I write by desire of the Prince of Wales to ask if you will assist him in his great experiment by taking the Department of Musical History with a seat on the Board of Professors.'[6] Remuneration was the 'low rate' of '15/- an hour', but with Highnam suffering from the agricultural depression of the 1880s Parry was more than grateful at 35 to land a secure professional position.

By May, when the College opened, Parry had already been appointed an examiner at Cambridge and in March 1883 he received an honorary doctorate from the same university. In time Oxford and Dublin would follow suit. Soon Grove encouraged him to become a musical jack-of-all-trades at the College where despite his reputation as a composition teacher, his greatest influence was as a music historian and writer. It was at this level that Parry articulated for English composers a definition of their role: a role at once elevated, even idealistic, and yet essentially practical. Once Parry's ambitious streak had found this acceptable outlet the determination to advance ensured his progression to Director of the College on Grove's retirement in 1895. The overlay of the Oxford Professorship in 1900 in succession to his old friend Sir John Stainer, plus seats on numerous committees and *ad hoc* lecturing responsibilities were all the inevitable outcome of his constant need to direct his energies outwards. Activity became a crutch to avoid introspection and to find distractions from the creative artist's 'desert loneliness among a different race of men'.

He was aware that the knighthood he received in 1898 was a political recognition for the Director of the Royal College, not an honour for the composer. Nonetheless, 'When I went down to find out if the Prince [of Wales] wished me to accept I was made to see he would be the reverse of pleased if I didn't' and Queen Victoria evidently enjoyed herself at the investiture: she 'laughed all the while she was dubbing me in the most genial manner!'[7] A few years later Edward VII elevated him to Baronet but his reputation was already in decline and no more honours followed. Yet it would belittle his powers as a teacher and historian to consider these honours empty: the testimony of his pupils alone is a refutation.

Success as a writer had other compensations: it enabled him to counter Pembroke's accusation in 1875 that 'I was indolent and lived upon Maude's money instead of making it as he said I ought'. Moreover it enabled him to establish a household structure that remained in place for the rest of his life. In December 1879 he bought land by the sea at Rustington (near Littlehampton, Sussex) and soon he was supervising the building details of Knight's Croft, even involving himself with the welfare of the workmen. He hired a well-known architect Norman Shaw (designer of Scotland Yard), and engaged the best decorative artists of the time, in particular wallpapers designed by William Morris and tiles by De Morgan. The result, though modest in scope, was charming and airy; Maude adored it. Parry's diary provides entertaining accounts of their early domestic struggles with malfunctioning chimney flues,[8] tree planting, gales, and the arrival of 'a terribly cumbrous and ugly revolving bookcase, generously meant but fearfully unendurable in my room.'[9] Occasionally there were gifts of a more 'delightful' order, in particular the arrival of a new telescope. Parry describes his excitement in unpacking the instrument and his first 'bout with the stars'. 'I went on looking again and again with a sort of feeling of amazement akin to the feeling one has when someone tells a thing beyond the range of experience.'[10]

It took him some time to become attuned to the 'isolation' of Rustington: 'I get so musically depressed in the complete loneliness here with not a single soul to speak to on a musical subject that I get almost demented.' Self-reflection often induced a melodramatic caste of mind. His birthday always depressed him and in 1880 he described it as 'that sad day which so forcibly recalls to my mind the relentless haste of years, and the stay of the prisoner who daily saw the walls of his prison contract'. These typical comments point up the melancholy that often accompanies his reflections on his existence. His sense of loneliness persisted even when surrounded by wife, family, friends and servants, and buffered by artistic success. He continued to look without for a solution to a haunting which could be quieted only from within.

In 1886 the move from Lower Phillimore Place to 17 Kensington Square was an improvement in his London existence. Kensington Square was the home of his old friend Robin Benson, the art collector, at No. 18, and Burne-Jones, of whom he continued to see 'a good deal', had resided at No. 41. In the same year he purchased the seven-ton yawl *Hoopoe*, named appropriately after the prince in *The Birds* who prefers to become a bird. The yawl vastly expanded his sea going yachting. The evident improvement in his financial situation, whether from work, a family inheritance or another source, has yet to be explained. George Bernard Shaw, as early as 1887, went out of his way to remind his readers that Parry was a man of independent means.[11] Thus the material structure of his existence was firmly in place by the time he was 38 and before the success of *Blest Pair of Sirens* and *Judith* brought him national fame. The inheritance of Highnam was superfluous and only caused intense family acrimony with his half-brother Ernest, as well as Clinton's children, so that Maude not surprisingly came to dislike it intensely.

During these years Dannreuther's support was crucial. Dorothea has remarked that her father was always at his most calm after Dannreuther's visits to him. From 1873 until his death in 1905, Parry showed him every composition and in most instances heeded his advice. Unfortunately Dannreuther did not develop his own compositional abilities; eventually in 1895 he accepted the post of Professor of Piano at the College, working under Parry, and wrote several musicological books. In the later years of their friendship there is evidence that he was insufficiently critical to be an effective mentor, indicated in his untempered enthusiasm for *Guinevere* and *Job*. I would argue that Parry' greatest music was written after Dannreuther's death; to apply Dorothea's dictum, Dannreuther was too supportive. Without his help, however, it is doubtful whether Parry would have escaped the creative vortex he was in by the early 1870s. He ensured that Parry developed a solid Germanic technique by writing chamber works in most of the major forms. Parry was fortunate that Dannreuther could provide a prestigious venue for performances in Orme Square where a remarkable number of new works from Europe were also introduced. In their first four years, Parry produced *Variations on an Aria of Bach*, *Four Sonnets* (Shakespeare), Violin Sonata in D Minor, Großes Duo for Two Pianos, Piano Sonatas in F Major and A Major, *Theme and Nineteen Variations for Piano*, Piano Trio in E Minor and Nonet for winds. His technique develops consistently through these pieces but there is no evidence of the English voice that would follow later. *Concertstück* for Orchestra (1877) is the first work of interest, and still worthy of performance.

The culmination of their early association was the programme put on in 1879 at Arthur Balfour's house in Carlton Gardens. The concert was devoted to Parry's compositions and featured the first performance of the Piano Quartet, the first composition to display a consummate technique combined with a personal (English) voice. Parry had at last arrived as a serious artist in the eyes of his peers. Mary Gladstone has left a perceptive first hand account:

London, *Tues. Ap. 1* ... Afterwards came off the great and eventful Hubert Parry Concert. Enjoyed it quite enormously, and Spencer did sing splendidly 'On a day' and 'Fill me, boy.' Pianoforte trio in [E minor] opened the Concert, the 1st movement specially vigorous and broad. I like the trio decrescendo to the end. A double p.f. duet finely played by Hubert and Mr. Dannreuther, with exciting fugue and main subject. 14 variations on a lovely theme of Bach's (Hubert alone) and P.F. Quartet in [A flat] (with a few more songs) completed the prog. The latter a remarkable work indeed, the passion- ate, slow movement specially; Dannreuther played enthusiastically throughout, sup- ported by Strauss, Lasserre and [Jung]. A rum audience consisting of H[ubert]'s relations and musical connoisseurs. It was great fun and a huge success and wonderfully appreci- ated, and supper after for the million.[12]

Parry brought his compulsion for success to his role as composer; however, he paid a high price for his involvement in so many other activities – the muse is stern. As over-activity became a panacea for unresolved and emotional conflicts, compo- sition was forced awkwardly to fit in with all the competing demands placed on his time. These conflicts forced Parry to achieve an apparent synthesis by evolving the concept of the bourgeois composer and musician. For the brother-in-law of Lord Pembroke, to make music a career necessitated turning, in Victorian times, a demeaning job into a gentleman's profession. To his credit Parry succeeded in elevating the role of the composer in British society, he gave it social acceptability and through its academic functions, financial viability. However, by becoming the working model for the British composer–academic or, far more deadly, for the British academic composer, he paid a very high price. Parry the composer belongs to both categories; like Madame Curie who discovered radium and later died from its effects, he almost destroyed his own creativity.

Conformity carried a degree of artistic hypocrisy since it precluded creative freedom.[13] The successful composer was expected to subscribe to the Victorian values of respectability and religious convention as prescribed by the Deans and Chapters of Hereford, Worcester and Gloucester. The composer's artistic vision was not considered. Did these restrictions encourage Parry to set up Bach as his idol? The annual festival cantata mirrored the eighteenth-century *Kappelmeister's* requirement to produce a constant flow of church cantatas. Parry felt morally obliged to shape his output around commissions, although in those days the composer, as public servant, rarely received a commission fee. This resulted in a creative crisis which was most acute, from 1887 to 1894, when his reputation was at its height. His academic career and social responsibilities allowed insufficient hours in the day for him to become an efficient composer on demand.

His finest music from the period is notable for its sensitivity and not least its intimacy. Parry spoke of the soprano solo in *The Lotos-Eaters* giving expression to the 'inner spirit', and a similar elusive lyrical yearning distinguishes the high string passages in the slow movement of the English Symphony. Unfortunately, all too often his music fails to connect with the 'inner spirit', which is usually unlocked by the feminine aspect of a man's psyche[14]. It remains obstinately stuck in pedestrian rhythms and prosaic syntax. During this period, Parry's diary demonstrates that he allowed a demanding academic schedule to preclude opportunities for contempla- tion. Paradoxically the rare opportunities he allowed for self-reflection often induced melancholy, the frequent separations from his family left him lonely and the quality of his music rarely pleased him.

In 1884 on the heels on the dual success of *The Birds* and the Cambridge Symphony, Parry planned the most ambitious composition of his life, an opera based on Malory's *Morte D'Arthur*. It was the last time he conceived a large-scale work without an assured performance. Years of assiduous opera-going, an intimate acquaintance with Wagner's art, his refined literary tastes and the recent experience of writing for soloists and orchestra in *Prometheus Unbound*, should have augured well for an opera. However, 1884 was also the first year Parry had to contend with a full-time academic position. His responsibilities at the College had attracted additional duties: lectures at Birmingham, examining at Trinity College, and other lectures at Cambridge and Oxford where he was appointed Choragus. Work on the *Dictionary* was still taking up time, so he was now doubly responsible to Grove.

In these circumstances it is not surprising he acquiesced to Grove's recommendation that the young daughter of the writer Sir Henry Taylor should furnish him with a libretto. Although a published novelist, Una Taylor had no stage experience and Parry would live to rue this compromise. He subsequently wrote of Una as 'one of the most singular miniatures of cleverness and silliness' he had ever encountered and he declared her company was 'thoroughly uncongenial'.[15] They rarely met and the numerous revisions were mostly conducted by correspondence. The libretto is witless, dull and dramatically stillborn. Yet Una Taylor's reminiscences of the experience, sent to Graves shortly before her death in 1922, are not without perspicacity and their style is superior to anything in the libretto; they remain a perplexing addendum to what Dannreuther absurdly called 'the real English Opera for which we have waited so long.'

As the winter of 1884 set in, Parry's health deteriorated: 'Felt desperately tired', he wrote and his heart condition returned. To distract himself from the opera he engaged on the first two collections of *English Lyrics*: settings of Keats, Scott, Shelley and Shakespeare. In April 1885 he suffered severe heart disturbances and, after a depressing visit to Highnam, Dr Black ordered him to 'knock off' all exercise and stop smoking. The disturbed state of his equilibrium is confirmed by his diary and Una Taylor's reminiscences. He was rebelling against the drudgery of academic life with vocal students that 'look such idiots with their mouths wide open howling nothings,' and failed Bachelors of Music, 'people not yet wedded to their art'. Even correcting band parts 'drove him crazy' affecting the action of his heart. The doctors insisted he should be removed from all temptation to work, so Robin Benson arranged for him to take a three-month sea voyage to South America with the ailing Sedley Taylor (Taylor was a musician, composer and friend of Robin Benson and Hugh Montgomery, who was still in touch with Parry in the 1900s.) as a less than congenial travelling companion.

On 13 June 1885 Benson gave a dinner party in his honour and three days later Parry first saw Lady Maude off at Victoria: 'It was grievous. I watched the train till it disappeared with a horrid ache in my throat and a miserable morbid dread in my mind.' Then, in the evening he journeyed to Liverpool to board the *Aconcagua*; his cabin was 'the worst and the noisiest on the entire ship.[16] Throughout the voyage he composed nothing and remained constantly homesick, and it effected no improvement to his health. Had he listened to the promptings of his unconscious (in this case a simple dose of intuition), the combination of his abject reaction to Lady Maude's departure capped by the dire circumstances of his cabin, should have convinced him to abandon ship immediately.

After his return he still felt no improvement so Dr Clarke's advice to him that 'work is good for me and that I should not keep well without it' came as a surprise endorsement of hyperactive tendencies. He returned to College and to *Guinevere* with renewed vigour. The four-act opera was completed by May 1886. Dannreuther, and Stanford who thought it 'quite superbo', took it off to Carl Rosa in the hope of an English production, but Rosa promptly turned it down. Further attempts by Stanford to secure a foreign performance resulted in failure and Parry decided to put it 'into the drawer for good'. An examination of the score in the Royal College of Music library says much. Parry worked on *Guinevere* for two years but no more than a perfunctory vocal sketch with the merest indications of scoring remains. The final order is unresolved, so Parry plainly broke off in mid-revision. The opera is notable only for its Wagnerian imitations; its high tessitura for soprano, in a style reminiscent of Brünnhilde, noisy but without Wagner's intensity. It also contains the worst libretto I know. Although based on Malory and Tennyson's *Guinevere*, lines like Guinevere's 'My Lord and King, or to the painful stake or to thy throne the way thou bid'st me I will take', are totally unsuitable for operatic purposes.

Una Taylor sheds some interesting light on Parry during the opera's composition, in particular:

> My impression at that time was that his ignorance of the practical requirements of the stage was almost as great as my own. I remember asking if we had not best call in a stage carpenter to help. But he had Dannreuther behind him, under whose supervision every page was rewritten. Hubert Parry had absolute confidence in his judgement. . . . I should say . . . that he was working under very strong emotional stress. In fact I should have said aesthetic emotionalism was one of his most characteristic gifts, balanced, or should one say distracted, by his absorbing interest in literature and life at large.[17]

She gives credence to the view that Dannreuther's influence was not always beneficial and of course he too had no experience of writing an opera. He also failed to channel Parry's concentration onto the matter in hand, a point she duly notes.

It was unfortunate that Parry did not fight to overcome the initial failure of *Guinevere* and attempt to secure a première. He made no further effort to revise it, either with Una Taylor, or with a more experienced librettist. He allowed the experience to remain negative and over time it prejudiced his views on opera as an art form. The deadly repercussion was that he used the failure as an excuse to fall back on the well worn road of oratorio and festival cantata. Parry, who could write the tenor aria in *Invocation to Music*, the witty choruses in *The Birds*, and the dramatic setting of Ezekiel's 'Vision of the Bones' in *The Soul's Ransom*, was capable of composing an effective opera. Despite the effectiveness of *Blest Pair of Sirens* and The English Symphony the opera's failure narrowed his range and slowed down his development. Worst of all it encouraged his decision to write *Judith* in 1888.

Graves devotes considerable space to Parry's deliberations over the Birmingham Festival Commission. Following the success of *Blest Pair of Sirens* and the revised

Cambridge Symphony in 1887, Parry was confronted by three commissions simultaneously: a Jubilee Overture for Richter, a large work for Birmingham in 1888 and an extended choral piece for the 1889 Leeds Festival. In a splendid piece of self-contradiction, Parry turned down the Overture, which on the basis of the March from *The Birds* he could have done extremely well. 'I really can't. The idea is disgusting!' he spluttered in a letter to Lady Maude putting it on a level with the production of Jubilee cups and other festival ephemera; luckily Elgar in later decades would not take such a snobbish attitude. The Birmingham request was different, the most ambitious commission to come his way. In fairness Parry wrote to the Committee that he wished to adapt Wagnerian music drama for the concert hall environment and offered to work with a leading contemporary poet (Robert Bridges?). To their detriment the Festival committee turned down this interesting proposal. Sadly Parry immediately acquiesced and agreed to write a biblical oratorio. 'Don't swear', he writes nervously to Dannreuther, though it is unlikely the over-supportive Dannreuther ever swore at his friend.

Once this initial compromise had been accepted he abandoned any attempt to incorporate modernist tendencies. He constructed a conventional oratorio to his own text from the stories of Judith and Manasseh, a safe two-act construction with little trace of Wagnerian influence. Its composition is marked by dissatisfaction, 'having to smite it out bit by bit', he moans, 'stuck fast in middle of a stupid chorus' and 'whacking it out'. 'It's poor stuff, sugary and thin, I am too done up to do better.' In later life he accused the work being dull 'old fashioned stuff', and Graves recounts an amusing incident with the Royal College singer and close friend, the Hon. Norah Dawnay, which occurred in the early 1900s:

> When Miss Norah Dawnay was once going to sing 'The Lord is long-suffering' to some friends in the billiard room at Highnam, Parry came in and there was a tremendous tussle, which ended in his throwing *Judith* out of the window.[18]

In 1914 Parry recorded one meeting of the 'Royal Choral Society at Albert Hall. Had to take the chair. Bridge proposed to do *Judith*, but I said "Not while I am on the Committee." However Parry was given his reward for this arrant example of compromise: the work was judged a great success. When the hastily written *Ode to St Cecilia's Day* enjoyed a similar public reaction at Leeds it was inevitable that he would become the doyen of the regional festivals until Elgar displaced him irrevocably to the status of a supporting composer.

Two years later, while writing *Job*, another task Parry took upon himself was the composition of incidental music to Aristophanes' *The Frogs*. Before and during the Oxford University performances in February 1892 his diaries and letters reveal him at his most unreflective. The immersion in the undergraduate world of amateur dramatics and adulation were a welcome antidote to *Job*.[19] At the band rehearsal on 16 February, 'Things sounded well and I came away feeling happy.' On 24 February he conducted the first performance and 'Even the overture was vigorously applauded'.[20] On 4 March, in a letter to C.H. Lloyd he wrote: 'I wonder how those dear Frog people are! What a wildly jolly time it was and what a nice lot of fellows they were.'[21] In contrast to his usually masculine persona Parry often sounds childish during this period. For example a misrepresented comment reported in the *Pall Mall Gazette* on 16 February asserted that 'the critical people of Oxford express disappointment at Dr. Parry's music.' In the face of this mild disparagement his ego crumbled 'it did upset me sorely and I had a bad night of it.'

His 44th birthday, on 27 February, fell during the run which continued until 1 March. We have three accounts, first a letter from Parry to C.H. Lloyd (who conducted the second performance on 25 February): 'It must have gone very well indeed. I can't think what a welcome birthday letter yours was. It was a dismal day: six hours hard work and Lady Maude ill at home, but your note put some shine in it.'[22] Parry's diary entry reads more pathetically:

> I have had some wretched birthdays but none to come close to this one for thorough misery. . . . When I got home I found Maude very unwell with cold and in a most irritable humour which worked on my weariness so desperately that though I was fit for nothing in the way of work I had to go to my room by myself. For it was no use even by silence to stop her bullying me. She couldn't stop herself being out of health, so the only thing was to remain apart.

Yet by 1 March he can look back on his month with *The Frogs* and declare 'I never had such splendid fun in all my life', evidence that Maude's admonishment had little lasting effect on his mood.

Maude's diary, reproduced in full, provides a further perspective:

> February 22nd London. Went to W. Mitchell's play with Phil., Lady Rayleigh, Lady Violet Treasure. Saw heaps of friends and nearly all the leading actors and actresses. February 23rd to Criterion. Feb. 24 Bad Cold. Feb. 25 worse. Feb. 26 Still worse. Feb. 27 Worse. H says The Frogs has been an enormous success. Feb. 28 No better. Feb. 29 To Oxford. The Frogs was most amusing so well acted and the music quite lovely. Tremendous enthusiasm. Mar. 1 Very dead. March 2 Hubert returned full of glory.

Maude, true to form, makes no mention of 'bullying' Parry but clearly her cold wrecked the week's social fabric. Since Parry was running back and forth to Oxford, the Royal College and Rustington he had little time for Maude's cold or his birthday until he finally ground to a halt on Saturday night, 27 February. In addition to conducting *The Frogs* on 26 February he was 'at *Job* again and got to the end of his lamentation', 'caught the early train to London' and 'off to College where we examined for scholarships from 11 till past 10 at night. Very exhausting work.' On Saturday 27 February he put another six hours into College work before he returned weary to Kensington Square. The reprimand he received from Lady Maude was understandable, though perhaps she should have appreciated by then the muddled situations into which the manic aspects of his personality could lead him.

For Parry the creative artist this constant misuse of his energies caused his output to be far more unequal than his talent and effort deserved. However, he was too astute not to realize that inactivity and contemplation had a psychological impact. After the trip to South America in 1885, he wrote this revealing passage:

> But the strange feeling is present all the while since landing that everything is so exactly the same as when I went away. The people just on their ordinary course, places just as if I had left them yesterday. More and more it is as if I had squeezed a long queer dream in between yesterday and today and yet the inner being is not quite the same. The experience makes some effect though it cannot alter constitutional indolence, hastiness and irritability.[23]

The South American experience however was not entirely forgotten for there is evidence that he used his annual sea voyages from 1896 to 1914 as therapy to counter the negative effects of overwork. It still took a further two decades of experience, increasing ill health and the onset of old age before the conflicts that wracked his equilibrium were partially subdued by life itself.

The passage suggests that at this stage of his life, Parry was beginning to grasp the emotional implications of various levels of consciousness. In referring to the three-month voyage as a 'queer dream' in between yesterday and today, he recognized that time is elastic, dependent on the intensity of experience or number of events experienced within a given span of time. He knew that the experience had changed the 'inner being'; however, it is obvious from the last line that he underestimated the profundity and relevance of his reflective observation. He minimizes it, not appreciating that the cliché 'Rome was not built in a day' was really the apposite retort to his conclusion that such an experience could not change his character.

Nor does Parry relate the experience to the creative process, which could be described as a little like a sea voyage. Whether it be like Beethoven practically disappearing from sight in Vienna for nearly a year to finish the Ninth Symphony or like Mozart writing the Overture to *Don Giovanni* in a single evening, one might say the process is concentrated self-removal from everyday life. If Parry had taken his observation as an experience central to his growth as an individual, his music might have avoided the sharp deterioration in quality apparent from 1898 to 1905; this was due primarily to overwork outside the creative realm.

4 'Beethoven's business' – Parry the Symphonic Composer[1]

[The Orchestra] is capable of almost unlimited complexities of rhythm and figure, of varieties of colour which are countless, in power of tone it is tremendous, in depth of expression infinite. To venture to put such an engine of power into motion at all seems to be courting responsibility.

(Hubert Parry Style in Musical Art)

The orchestra, in the present sense of the word, like the virtuoso, is finished. Therefore orchestration, as we call it, must revert to its original meaning; must become part and parcel of the substance itself. From this it follows that Rimsky-Korsakov was a poor orchestrator and Brahms a good one. The composition itself is the orchestration.

(Edgard Varese[2])

In contrast to his later reputation, Parry's predominant interest between 1867 and 1887 was not choral music but an 'instrumental art on the grandest and broadest lines' which had found its 'perfect revelation' in Beethoven. He evolved his technique cautiously through the series of experimental chamber works which culminated in the Piano Quartet of 1879 and the Cello Sonata of 1880. The sonata contains fine themes and an altogether thoughtful slow movement. The solo line is a little limited in demonstrating the capabilities of the cello, but considering how few exceptional cello sonatas have been written by English composers, it should be in the repertoire. The Piano Quartet however is a

Ex. 1   from the piano part 1st Movement: Piano Quartet

genuine masterwork. In the big A flat tune for piano solo, which opens the first movement (Allegro), we hear for the first time since Purcell an authentic English voice. Parry thought highly of the piece and revised it in 1882 and 1884. From a technical standpoint it remains a Parry *tour de force* comparable to the finest chamber music of Brahms and Elgar.

In the same year Parry's most ambitious orchestral work to date, the Piano Concerto in F Sharp, was premièred by August Manns, with Dannreuther as soloist. The work is a disappointment even in the 1895 revised version.[3] It lacks melodic distinction, harmonic inventiveness or an imaginative handling of the solo instrument. This is surprising in the light of the majestic piano writing in the Piano Quartet. But working on the piece with Dannreuther did provide a valuable preparation for the First Symphony.

Symphony No. 1 in G

Composition of the First Symphony started in December 1880, a month after Parry heard Brahms's First Symphony, 'altogether much finer than his second'. By then Mendelssohn had been dead for 33 years and Schumann for 24, but it was these composers to whom Parry was most indebted as a symphonist, especially Schumann whose emotional world had such strong affinities with his own.

There were no English models. The symphonies produced by the previous generation of English composers, such as Sterndale Bennett, Prout and Benedict, lacked the strength of their Schumann and Mendelssohn originals and failed to create an English idiom. Parry was consistently critical of these attempts; however, he was familiar with the concert overtures of Pierson, and they may have acted as a bridge to the two German masters. By 1880 he had already gained some experience in writing for the orchestra, with the *Intermezzo Religioso* (1868), the lost overture *Vivien* (1873) and the *Guillem de Cabestan* overture (1879).

These attempts are disappointing. The *Intermezzo Religioso* is a slight salon piece of no consequence. *Guillem de Cabastan* was rightly disliked by August Manns; it is harsh to the point of crudeness and the echoes in the thematic material of Beethoven's Pastoral Symphony make matters worse. In 1981 this overture was scheduled to complete the first recording of Parry's English Symphony and *Concertstück*. However, after two playthroughs with the Luxembourg Orchestra, everyone agreed it was too weak to be included; but greater composers than Parry have made worse false starts writing for orchestra. Two works of greater importance, the *Concertstück* (1877) and *Prometheus Unbound* (1880) are heavily influenced by Wagner; but Parry chose not to become a post-Wagnerian symphonist, despite a slight influence on his instrumentation (the brass writing becomes heavier, grander than Mendelssohn or Schumann). Surprisingly traces of Dvořák are discernible before the influence of Brahms appears.

Throughout the 1880s Hans Richter and August Manns ensured that an unprecedented array of new music was performed in England; at their concerts Parry encountered the latest symphonies and concertos of Tchaikovsky, Dvořák, Raff and Brahms. The experience helped to clarify his conception of an English sym-

Ex. 2   the opening of Symphony No. 1

Ex. 2   concluded

phonic idiom, capable of expressing 'great and noble traits of character and thought' as he said in *Studies of Great Composers* (1887).

The First Symphony occupied him throughout much of 1881. Richter agreed to produce the première and after several delays – welcomed by the composer, since 'I felt I had a reprieve' – it went into rehearsal on 13 June 1882. Graves recounts that 'it was an unlucky day and number. Many of the band were absent and after a struggle, in Parry's words, "Richter couldn't make it go and it was given up. Some of it sounded well but the men were tired and shirked their work".' The première was delayed until the Birmingham Festival on 31 August when it proved a success.

[Parry, who conducted] was especially moved by the approbation of old Sir Julius Benedict 'who after all was the pupil and familiar of Weber and often saw Beethoven and Schubert in the flesh'. The best Germans in the band were equally kind; Gounod 'buttered' him to the skies though not very acceptably.[4]

This was sufficiently encouraging for the symphony to be brought to London.

A second performance followed under August Manns at the Crystal Palace in April 1883. This had a similarly inauspicious start with a poor Monday rehearsal for which Manns gave Parry a memorable explanation. 'He says the men are always in bad order on Monday morning: they smoke too much and kiss their wives and sweethearts so much that the lips of the woodwind players are all out of order'.[5]

Maude came and 'sat in the corner in the Gallery and I held her hand nearly all the time. That was sweet.' He dedicated the symphony to his 'dearest wife' which emphasized its links with his concept of the 'bourgeois composer'. Parry, like Elgar, was deeply drawn to Schumann's Rhenish Symphony, perhaps because it was the first great symphony to espouse the bourgeois ideal: middle-class, 'homely' sentiments and moods are set alongside the more abstract art of the Haydn–Mozart symphony, and the universal archetypes which unfold in the expansive symphonic structures of Beethoven.

The first movement, Con fuoco, opens with a vibrant extended theme, the first part strongly reminiscent of the Rhenish, the second already characteristic Parry. But for all its lively charm the first movement exposition is a loquacious affair so that Parry fails to achieve a contrast with the quite elaborate development section that follows. The tentativeness of this structure is not repeated in the second movement, Andante (quasi adagio). Whilst Beethoven, Schumann and Mendelssohn again provide the formal models, the harmony and instrumentation show how well Parry had digested early Wagner. But the movement is more than the sum of its influences; the melodic ideas, the cut of phrase and the way the music moves are Parry's own. That distinctive combination of intimate emotion and pastoral evocation which was to become a hallmark of English music makes one of its first appearances in this movement.

If the Scherzo (marked *presto*) has touches of Dvořák and the Russian nationalists, the Trio–with its subtle references to the first and second movements–captures an unequivocally English atmosphere. The finale, Allegretto, molto vivace, begins with a vigorous tune again reminiscent of Dvořák; it is amusing to hear it anglicized as Parry moulds it through a finely proportioned, thematically inventive movement. The broad second subject is the first successor to the great tune in the first movement of Parry's Piano Quartet, and the high-spirited coda is the first of Parry's many skilful orchestral perorations.

After 1883 the First Symphony languished unpublished and unperformed for 107 years.[6] Yet this fine symphony bears comparison with initial attempts by many nineteenth-century composers long accorded a place in the CD catalogue and which achieve revivals. It would be difficult to overestimate its place in the development of British orchestral music.

Symphony No. 2 in F (The Cambridge)

In the 1880s it was Wagner who still dominated Parry's horizons (if not his style) and on 21 June 1882 he set out for Bayreuth to attend the first performances of *Parsifal*. 'As a work of art it is the very highest point of mastery', he concluded. He and Dannreuther attended a sumptuous reception at the Villa Wahnfried 'crowded with all the notabilities and the nullities', where 'Mme Wagner did the royal person' and 'Wagner looked like a lively irrepressible boy'. One morning they explored the theatre where they experimented with the *Parsifal* bells which 'could be made to sound all right if played properly'.

On his return to England, with *Parsifal* 'still ringing in my ears', he resumed his private teaching and his work as Sub-Editor on the *Dictionary* for George Grove – often after they had lunched on oysters, porter and cigars! By the autumn of 1882, Parry had already commenced work on his Second Symphony. Inspiration did not flow and he complained of working 'against the grain' and 'wrastling' with it. The symphony was completed in April 1883. The Cambridge Musical Society première conducted by C.V. Stanford in June was an 'excellent performance', Parry noted, and it attracted appreciative notices. Four years later he subjected it to a thorough revision and recomposed the outer movements, as we know from Willeby.[7] Hans Richter gave the première of this new version on 6 June 1887 in London. It was an unequivocal success, 'the band being specially loud in rattling their bows'. The Second Symphony remained one of Parry's own favourites, but a publication in 1906 incorporating further revisions did not prevent it from total neglect after the First World War.

This Second Symphony is an advanced example of cyclic form, of which Brahms's great String Sextet No. 2 in G Major is the most obvious precursor. There are several examples in Parry's early chamber music and cyclic elements occur in the other symphonies, especially the First and Fifth. The Second Symphony is an accomplished sonata structure that has no more to do with Cambridge than the First Symphony has with Birmingham: these were merely the locations of their first performances. It was Stanford, not the University of Cambridge, who promoted Parry's music in that city.

The symphony's introduction, Andante sostenuto (in F minor) is not mysterious but ambivalent and the main theme of the Allegro moderato is uncomfortably reminiscent of the end of Mendelssohn's Scottish Symphony. One of the motifs derived from this expansive Allegro moderato foreshadows the fiery opening theme of Elgar's *In the South*, and—with Strauss' *Don Juan*—it is a notable influence on that work. This motif, scored with élan for the brass, enlivens a movement that otherwise lacks the sharp emotional focus necessary for a great symphonic statement. The gently flowing second subject and energetic development section lead to a recapitulation and coda devoid of real surprises; but regardless, this is enjoyable music of undoubted sincerity and commitment. Parry paid the price for his gain in technical mastery with a temporary loss of his 'English' voice so apparent in the rhapsodic charm of his First Symphony.

The Scherzo – almost a sonata rondo, in D minor/F major–shows too clearly the extent to which Parry enjoyed Dvořák's 'delightful' D major Symphony Op. 60.[8] The droll chromaticisms of the opening theme, scored for woodwind with staccato strings, lead to an outburst for full orchestra, jaunty and memorable; but what is the nationality of the composer who wrote it? The transitional material between these ideas and the trio-like second subject echoes the first movement's themes, again providing a link between the Adagio of Mendelssohn's Scottish Symphony and the central section of Elgar's *In the South*.

The B flat Andante is the finest movement of the work, and a precursor to the noble elegiac slow movements of Parry's last three symphonies. The usual influences are still apparent; note the trill in the tenth bar as in the Schumann Second Symphony but the stately ample paragraphs use themes derived from the first movement with a terseness and surety of touch. One senses a change in this movement; the personality is now Parry's own. With a mounting intensity quite new to British music, the Andante builds to a splendid craggy climax; for the remainder of the movement Parry concentrates on presenting the lovely opening melody in various attractive orchestral guises.

This important transitional work concludes with a broad sonata rondo finale that skilfully combines all of the principal melodic material. The second half has its longeurs and occasional nods to Brahms and Wagner, but towards the exuberant close its sound world overlaps with Charles Ives' Second Symphony. Like the Ives, the coda is a head-on romp – the final bars land on a delightful cadence that would take English music, half a century later, straight into Hollywood.

Symphony No. 3 in C (The English)

The successful première of the symphonic *Suite Moderne* at the Gloucester Festival 1886 encouraged Parry to produce a sequel, which he sketched in 1887. Graves, who had access to Parry's 1887 diary (now lost), states that he finished the first movement of a 'Symphonic suite' in the Easter holidays at Rustington and mistakenly assumes this is the *Suite Moderne*. However, this was probably the lost draft of 'the small symphony' which Parry diffidently offered the Philharmonic Society for their 1888/9 season.[9] Uncertainty about its scope – he felt the term 'sinfonietta' too affected – suggests that it was conceived as a second suite. After further rewriting it finally earned the title 'symphony'. By this time he was engaged on another symphony for Richter – the Fourth. Thus work on the two overlapped through 1888 and early 1889.

Ex. 3   from the andante of Symphony No. 2

Parry's creative reputation was at its height when the Symphony No. 3 in C 'The English' was introduced on 23 May 1889, with the composer conducting. Maude commented 'The Symphony was done by the Philharmonic and very well received. Getey was there and enjoyed it. It was a first rate concert if it hadn't been so hot.' It won immediate favour and for the next twenty years was the most frequently performed symphony by any English composer. It remains his most characteristic orchestral masterpiece on a large scale. Parry achieves perfectly what he sets out to do: create an ebullient English equivalent to the Mendelssohn Italian and Schumann Rhenish Symphonies. The structure and developmental procedures resemble the Italian, with nods to Beethoven's fourth and eighth symphonies, but the themes are all thoroughly English in their rhythmic cut. The symphony in the 1907 published version is scored for normal Romantic orchestra (in an 1895 revision Parry added trombones).

The dance-like open-air quality of the first movement, Allegro energico, and the third, Allegro molto scherzo, shows Parry's mastery in building terse symphonic structures which give the listener a sense of large-scale architecture achieved by his adroitness in handling his musical paragraphs. (Dr Dibble in his biography of Parry, *Hubert H. Parry: his Life and Music*, Oxford: Clarendon Press, page, 278, ends his disparaging assessment of the movement by stating that 'it is thematically dull'.[10] I disagree; so it seems did Ralph Vaughan Williams who in 1924, with Parry's entire orchestral output to choose from, quotes one of the scherzo's main ideas as a refrain in the first movement of his Concerto Accademico for violin and string orchestra.) This technique develops into an almost Beethovenian expansiveness in the finale, built up through an engaging set of variations. The last three sound positively Elgarian. Indeed, with their expansive rolling *nobilmente* they were the greatest influence on the extrovert side of Elgar's orchestral vocabulary. Elgar was also influenced by Symphony No. 4: he was in the audience for the première of the original version (1889). But it was 'The English' that gave the language and the impetus to the whole tradition.

The second movement, Andante sostenuto (in A minor), is the heart of the symphony. The introductory theme stated on the oboes sets the mood of introspection tinged with melancholy; this dissolves into a magnificent yearning melody immaculately scored for divided strings, and the whole movement expands with a Brahmsian richness both in harmony and orchestration.

George Bernard Shaw's condemnation of 'The English Symphony'[11] is most unfair and difficult to understand. Shaw's prejudice, which he admitted in his justifiable review of *Job*, shows most clearly here. Parry was composing just the kind of music Shaw had advised. The score is epoch-making in the history of English orchestral music. Shaw should have heard better, but then he also said: 'There are some sacrifices which should not be demanded twice of any man; and one of them is listening to Brahms's *Requiem*'.[12] The English Symphony is inspired and well wrought in every detail: it has the 'inevitability of the classics'.

SYMPHONY in C.

I.

C. Hubert H. Parry.

The Symphony was originally written without Trombones, which were added, on request, for a special performance.

Ex. 4 the opening of Symphony No. 3

Symphony No. 4 in E Minor

We know from his diaries that Parry began work on the Symphony No. 4 in E Minor during the summer of 1888. On 21 September he notes that being short of rest he lay down to sleep in the afternoon. 'When suddenly a new version of the Symphony I lately started for Richter came into my head, and I wrote away for about an hour at a good pace.'

It was completed in April 1889 and the first performance took place soon after The English on 1 July 1889 under Richter's baton. Parry noted that parts of it 'come off pretty well' though most of it failed to please him. He remained displeased and, despite repeated requests from Richter, refrained from writing another symphony. Finally in 1910 he re-wrote the E minor for a Philharmonic Society performance and added a new scherzo. Much of the thematic material remains similar in the other movements but the structure and orchestration is greatly elaborated. The resultant style is closer to the symphonic *Ethical Cantatas* (1903–8) and the Symphony No. 5 (1912). In a letter to Napier Miles[13] in March 1910 Parry commented:

> I'm glad you thought well of the Symphony. I suppose it is a bit stern as you say. On the whole I'm glad you thought so. Just at this time of day it seems to me inevitable though it militates against its acceptance. It seems to me it said what I wanted it to say – but it's not likely to be taken in at a first hearing and as generally happens in such a case it may be a good while before it gets another.[14]

This proved a fateful prophecy: after 1911 the E minor remained unplayed until the Trust–Chandos recording eighty years later in which Parry's subsequent revisions were heard for the first time; several performances have followed.

The opening movement, Parry's most expansive and personal, is an elaborate sonata rondo structure with elements from the concerto grosso. The splendid extrovert opening motif in 3/4 time, marked *con fuoco*, is used as the movement progresses to change tack, like a yachtsman in a headwind on a rough sea. Parry was an intrepid and inveterate sailor and the movement evokes a dark-hued blustery seascape. The exposition culminates in an augmented version of the main theme which prefigures Elgar's First Symphony with its rhythmic hesitation and dashing waltz-like lilt. In contrast the wistful second subject on the clarinets offers a subtle foil. The grand sweep of the coda, full of fine harmonic shifts and thematic interweaving, proves not to be the end, in the 1910 version, but a preparation for a closing *tranquillo* passage of extraordinary beauty, an evening sun breaking through the clouds. This is the most poignant page of music in all Parry's symphonies.

It heralds a shift in mood: like Brahms's First Symphony, the last three movements hint that this opening is not tragic but heroic. The slow movement, Molto adagio (in C major), is a sonata structure; its roots lie in the piano music of Chopin and Liszt. The string figurations employed display an elaboration which points the way to Elgar's Second Symphony. The music speaks of starry nights and the inward sea of dreams. After a superbly controlled climax this mood of elegiac restraint dissolves into an engaging third movement scherzo, Allegretto, in 3/8 time. It reveals Parry's knowledge of the complex cross-rhythms of the Burgundians and

Ex. 5   from the finale of Symphony No. 4

early Baroque. This masterly construction is superior in every way to the conventional, pretty 1889 scherzo.

The symphony concludes with an expansive, proclamatory finale in E major, both a summing up and a return to the nautical mood of the opening. This is suggested by a first theme based on the descending intervals that are the symphony's unifying force. It is a skilful neo-baroque variation on the opening motif. Parry attended the 1887 great naval review and in the evening rowed about the Solent among the fleet of yachts and warships to see the fireworks and illuminations. The movement's thematic arrangement suggests such a kaleidoscopic sequence of impressions, highlighted by scoring that is brilliant without being blatant. Halfway through the movement in the 1910 version Parry introduces a euphonious new theme which forms the basis for the most memorable of his inimitable perorations.

The first performance of the Fourth Symphony in 1889 (score and parts for this earlier version still exist) proved a watershed in Parry's compositional career: despite the fact that 'it was much better received than I expected', he was unable to discover a satisfactory route forward as a composer of symphonic music. In the next eight years he wrote only the anaemic *Overture to an Unwritten Tragedy* of 1893 (a fifth symphony *manqué*), but he did produce several major compositions for soloists, chorus and orchestra. Possibly he needed the catalyst of a text to fire his creativity, and certainly he used these choral works to expand his orchestral technique; in the early 1890s he turned down several Philharmonic Society commissions. Elgar's development was similar: the *Froissart Overture* was his sole symphonic contribution before the *Enigma Variations* in 1899.

Symphony No. 5 in B Minor

Parry's final symphony, in B minor, written in four linked movements, was first performed at a Philharmonic Centenary Concert on 5 December 1912, conducted by the composer. Several performances followed including a repeat in Balfour Gardiner's concert series under Parry at the Queen's Hall in November 1913 – 'a really wonderful performance', he concluded. In 1922 it was published with the title *Symphonic Fantasia 1912*. The titles of the movements, 'Stress', 'Love', 'Play', and 'Now', relate the symphony to Parry's ethical views.

Parry supplied extensive ethical/moral programmes for the revised Fourth Symphony, Fifth Symphony and From Death to Life. Regrettably, it is questionable whether such abstract descriptions as 'the recognition of tragedy in the light of human love becomes the token of healing', for the climax of the *Fifth Symphony's* final movement, aided the original audience's understanding of the music.

It should be noted that in 1911 Parry wrote to Herbert Thompson who was writing the analytical notes for his coronation *Te Deum*, disclaiming the value of such programmes: 'the older I get the more intolerable it is to me to try to explain what I mean in any musical work I attempt'. He goes on to explain that:

> Every moment in Art ought to look several ways at once. Mere symbolical references are but one aspect of it. They also have their places in the design – psychological as well as

Ex. 6 from Symphony No. 5

objective, but it is no use. I can't set-to to appraise my doings like a commercial traveller to a customer.[15]

Early Romantic composers had experimented with one-movement sonatas and concertos that retained aspects of the four-movement sonata structure, but Schumann was the first composer to create a one-movement symphony with the revised version of his D minor. Schoenberg followed Schumann's example with his own Chamber Symphony No. 1 in 1906. Parry admired Schoenberg enormously and would have known both this and his other early 'four-in-one' compositions, such as String Quartet No. 1 and *Pelleas und Melisande*.[16] In September 1912, according to Boult he attended the English première of Schoenberg's *Five Orchestral Pieces* under Henry Wood in the same month that he had begun his final symphony. This Fifth Symphony, with its ingenious combination of brevity and complexity, like *The Soul's Ransom* goes forward to meet Beethoven.

The first movement, 'Stress', opens (*slow*) on a bare rocking figure which stems out of Brahms. It is used throughout the linked movements to achieve thematic unity. The main motif of the symphony follows immediately, a dark brooding statement on woodwind and horns which Parry submits throughout the movements to a resourceful sonata-style development and Lisztian thematic transformations. The exposition introduces two more motifs and builds to a powerful statement–in the manner of Beethoven's Ninth–for full orchestra (Allegro) relocated to one of Parry's blustery English seascapes. A terse development, recapitulation and coda, based on the main motifs, closes the first movement.

The *lento* movement, 'Love', in D major, contains the most glowing music in the symphony, quintessential Parry, its mood crossing over the Adagios of Elgar's First and the opening of the Lento assai of Beethoven's last string quartet. The material is a subtle blending of three principal themes and culminates in a passionate recitative, marked *feroce*, which surely alludes to the Gretchen movement from Liszt's Faust Symphony. The Scherzo, 'Play', in G major (*vivace*) contains Mahlerian echoes of the Austrian Ländler, while the Finale, 'Now', in B major (*moderato tranquillo*) opens with a wistful nod to Strauss as solo strings and winds dovetail to the accompaniment of harps, whilst at the climax the reference is to Tchaikovsky's *Pathétique*. Parry raises the art of allusion to a principle of almost Ivesian proportions, but these are subtle references which he assumed his audience would appreciate. The Finale, remarkably, continues to develop the same themes that form the kernel of the symphony without any falling off in freshness and invention. It concludes with a majestic expression of pre-war affirmation, heartfelt and musically convincing. This is a symphony in beige and brown, the dark harmonic colouring offset by a masterly orchestral sheen.

Other Orchestral Music

Throughout his career Parry composed orchestral works in various forms, and the most memorable considerably enrich his symphonic achievement. In addition to the compositions discussed below, Parry wrote elaborate incidental music for five Greek plays: *The Birds* (1883, revised 1904), *The Frogs* (1891, revised 1909),

Agamemnon (1900), *The Clouds* (1905) and *The Acharnians* (1913). These are elaborate affairs, each having an overture, entr'actes, and choral numbers, some highly developed. Like all of his works in a genre their quality varies enormously. But the liveliest is the score written for *The Birds*; the March, still occasionally played in the version Parry arranged for full orchestra, is a miniature masterpiece. The tune itself has a melodic swagger and the structure is so well appointed that it bears comparison with Elgar's *Pomp and Circumstance* series, which it certainly influenced. Parry enthusiasts should enjoy the quotations from other composers which Parry sprinkles throughout these sincerely felt scores for Aristophanes' brilliant comedies. Unfortunately the score for Aeschylus' *Agamemnon* requires more forbearance than could be expected of any Strauss lover; it is bleakly thin in musical ideas, rather than stark and dramatic like the subject.

Parry also wrote an elaborate score for Stuart Ogilvie's melodrama *Hypatia* in 1892–3, from which he hastily fashioned a suite for the Philharmonic Society, and in 1899 he produced an overture and incidental music for Pearl Craigie's one-act play *A Repentance*: this score is not sinful enough for repentance, and not interesting enough for performance. Parry was more successful with orchestral works not related to the stage.

In 1973, among the incomplete works, sketches and fragments in the Royal College of Music, I noticed there was a movement for orchestra entitled *Concertstück* bound with some sketches for piano and orchestra that evidently pertained to a different piece. In fact the work was complete except for one section, where the music stopped altogether for a few bars and some places where the supporting harmony and orchestration had not been filled in. To make a performing version I added only the minimum required to complete the score. Editing was also necessary; Parry had written out alternative versions to the principal string lines in several passages and accompanying figurations were sometimes incomplete or ambiguous. In places the tonality is so unstable that it is unclear whether, for example, a passage is in C minor or G minor.

Although the manuscript is undated it is obviously the *Concertstück* in G minor for piano' 'of which no trace remains' (as Graves mistakenly wrote) and written as a composition exercise for Dannreuther in September 1877. The work has yet to receive a concert première, although it was recorded in 1981 by Leopold Hager and the Luxembourg Radio Orchestra and also included in the Chandos series.[17] *Concertstück* was written immediately after Parry and Lady Maude, in company with George Eliot, attended Wagner's 1876 London Concerts. Dannreuther was the founder of the Wagner Society and the Wagners stayed at his home. Parry's German was sufficiently competent for him to become friendly with the composer and Cosima Wagner. The principal, indeed the overwhelming, influence on *Concertstück* is Wagner. Although references to the Beethoven and Weber Overtures and the tone-poems of Liszt are apparent, *Concertstück* is not an overture but, as the title accurately states, a concert piece. Despite the revised date (I originally had hazarded 1884)[18], I still adhere to my opinion that the piece is strongly influenced by the piano works of Liszt's old age. Since Liszt was in London in the 1870s and Dannreuther saw him in Germany, it is quite possible Liszt may have played or shown Dannreuther some pieces in draft form.

For a work so deliberately an essay in the style of another composer, *Concertstück* is an exhilarating and fascinating composition. Whilst the melodic material and much of the instrumentation are totally Wagnerian, the development strays far from Wagnerian music drama. We are in the tragic–heroic atmosphere of *The Ring* but the sense of movement is closer to *The Flying Dutchman* and *A Faust Overture*. This accounts for part of the intensity: the back-to-front effect of late Wagnerian thematic ideas, with their slower pace, being worked out in the classical momentum we find in these two earlier overtures. Add to this a slow contrapuntal section which is similar to Bruckner, and an intense fugal passage clearly derived from the scherzo and instrumental double fugue in the finale of Beethoven's Ninth Symphony, and it is remarkable that the piece does not explode, a tribute perhaps to Parry's natural gift for composition. It is interesting to contemplate the implications for future English music if Parry had built his style on this curiously avant-garde work.

In 1886 Parry wrote the *Suite Moderne* for the Gloucester Festival and revised it in 1892. It is not a bad piece, but Parry stored these ideas better elsewhere. No. IV, 'Rhapsody', is the finest movement: it moves along with plenty of energy, and it may have begun life as a planned symphonic finale. School and youth orchestras would learn much on how to play the classics by studying this suite.

In 1893 he furnished a one-movement 'orchestral piece' for the Worcester Festival. The following comment from his sparse 1893 diary says much: 'Vile rehearsal at St. Georges Hall, my new Overture seemed a wretched failure. Quite not what I wanted'. The addition of the title (to *an Unwritten Tragedy*) and subsequent revisions did not help and it remains the feeblest of his mature works for orchestra – a failure indeed.

The year after this stodgy, gloomy music, Parry composed the charmingly suave and expert *Lady Radnor Suite* in F major for strings. It was premièred on 29 June 1894 at St James's Hall, with Lady Radnor conducting her 72-piece string orchestra. Of its six movements the third, 'Sarabande', and the fifth, 'Slow Minuet', stand out for their heart-warming qualities. The Sarabande with its downward grave phrases foreshadows Elgar's *Introduction and Allegro*. The pastiche element is well managed: rather than Handel taking off his wig and donning a Victorian frock coat, Parry dons Handel's wig. If one of the great 'nineteenth-century German masters' had composed this suite in the English style it would be commonly played. As the first cousin of The English Symphony it deserves to be heard more regularly.

In 1897 Parry returned to orchestral music with the skilful *Symphonic Variations*, in E minor. For several decades this set of 27 'symphonic' variations remained his only orchestral work to be given the occasional performance.[19] Greatly admired by Tovey, Joachim and Elgar, it remains an effective orchestral showpiece, though no more his masterpiece than the *Haydn Variations* are Brahms'. The 'symphonic' structure implied in the sonata-style divisions of tempo and key, gave Parry the opportunity to explore and enhance his technical resources: it was a lesson that bore fruit in his later symphonic cantatas. The result is not an academic exercise but a minor classic which no academic composer could have written. The first performance was given under the composer's baton at a Philharmonic Concert on 3 June 1897. 'The band played up like bricks and it went capitally.' It was taken up in America under Theodore Thomas and in Europe, where performances continued into the 1920s. Its echoes found their way into Korngold's score for the 1939 film *The Private Lives of Elizabeth and Essex*; This is particularly noticeable in the *Overture* Korngold, composed for the premier.

The death of Brahms on 3 April of the same year affected Parry profoundly. He put aside all creative work and by 29 May he speaks of 'taking every moment' to get on with the orchestral *Elegy for Brahms*. 'The great heroes of the world are so rare that it is fortunately but seldom in the brief spell of our lives that we have to try and realise what parting with them means', said Parry at the time of Brahms' death.[20] He never released the *Elegy* for performance. It was a private tribute. The première was given at his own memorial concert in 1918, conducted by C.V. Stanford, in a revised version. The work was not heard again. In 1975 I showed the score to Alasdair Mitchell who conducted the first performance of the original version with the Edinburgh Camerata on 5 March 1977. The *Elegy* is a splendidly proportioned symphonic movement in A minor, which owes as much to Liszt as to Brahms. The sonata-style seams are clearly evident to the eye but the inspirational flow of the music strikes the ear more as an improvisation. One suspects Parry created his own programme in which the psychological argument prompted the technical solutions.

There are several references to Brahms' music. The lilting second subject in E minor is surely purposely reminiscent of the second subject in Brahms' A minor string quartet and the passionate development section is based on the famous C major tune from Brahms' First Symphony, but plunged into the minor to achieve the inverse of the original's mood of optimism. Parry uses the romantic orchestra with delicacy to convey his own sense of hollowness and loss. The work culminates in a radiant coda, which in its last upward gesture recalls Strauss's *Tod und Verklärung*.

One of the most splendid aspects of Parry's late self-renewal, was his return to the orchestra; the glowing Fifth Symphony, following the expansive revision of the Fourth Symphony led to a final orchestral work, *From Death to Life*. This 'symphonic poem in two connected movements' bear the mottoes 'Via Mortis' and 'Via Vitae'. It was written for the 1914 Brighton Festival and first performed on 12 November; at the invitation of Percy Pitt the second performance, with some revisions, took place at a Philharmonic concert on 18 March 1915. Parry shared the platform with Elgar who concluded the concert with his own Second Symphony. 'To Queen's Hall at 10.30', Parry noted; 'Very good rehearsal of *From Death to Life*, Band played up most amiably'. In the evening, '*Death to Life* went capitally, but I could feel it was not a success'. There is no record of any subsequent performances. Parry's unpublished manuscript is, in several places, quite a labyrinth and I found editing the score a delicate operation. I suspect there was a copyist score, which contained revisions made by Parry during the last rehearsals and performance in 1915; if so, it disappeared with the original orchestral parts.[21]

Written during the first months of the Great War, it takes on from *The Vision of Life*, revised earlier that year and also subtitled 'A Symphonic Poem'. Parry referred to the work in his programme, as the spiritual triumph of life – earnest and also joyful – over Death, arm in arm with Fate 'who walks ever in our midst'. The title gives the hint: essentially it is a work about mourning and readjustment that wisely eschews the tragic. This is the only late work to absorb the light music styles, marches, pastiche (even a reference to *Cockaigne*) that Parry normally reserved for his incidental music to Aristophanes' plays. Earlier that year Parry had responded enthusiastically to a number of Russian pieces – 'I enjoyed Stravinsky's *Rossignol* immensely' – and *From Death to Life* captures something of their vitality.

The first movement, in B flat minor, begins with a Fate–death motive very reminiscent of the Tomb Scene in *Aida*, which metamorphoses into a slow waltz lament. This is followed by a lovely folk-song inspired melody and Parry builds a series of grand and subtle paragraphs on these themes. In the second movement (B major), Parry's 'Return to life' tune is an ingenious combination of the waltz lament and folk melody from the first movement. The music is boisterous and joyful, but he did not live to see the Armistice and the undertones give the listener a feeling that Parry was biting hard on his lip when he composed this music.

From Death to Life suggests he was in the process of renewing every aspect of his compositional technique. If Symphony No. 5 is a summation, this score – like a late Rembrandt self-portrait – reveals the emergence of a new approach to realizing ideas. Orchestral effects which look doubtful on paper are startling and successful in performance. The superficial similarity of the melodic ideas to those in No. 5 only highlights the difference between the two works and his new treatment of the late romantic orchestra. It is the aesthetic precursor not to *The Songs of Farewell* and *Jerusalem* but a possible Sixth Symphony in an imaginary world after the Great War.

After the War, Parry's five symphonies (and other orchestral works) were dismissed cursorily as a side issue even to his own choral music. This opinion was unfortunately founded on ignorance, for there is not a single movement which does not possess the controlled expansiveness of the true symphonist, especially the finales, the place where greater composers than Parry have faltered. Understandably it has been the revival of the Fourth Symphony which has generated the greatest critical acclaim, perhaps because it is Parry's most overtly late romantic work (the early symphony Elgar could have written?). On balance I consider The English is Parry's most original contribution, the most perfectly proportioned and thematically integrated of the symphonies, historically the most influential. The terser Fifth Symphony remains his most mature expression for full orchestra and like the Third and Fourth deserves a re-admission to the concert hall.

The neglect of Parry's orchestral music was due to several reasons. He was the first composer in England to write complex symphonic music, but unfortunately in the 1880s there was no automatic system for commercial publication of successful new orchestral works, as there was in Germany. It is even questionable, at that time, whether there was a solid core of critics capable of evaluating and informing the public on modern orchestral music. Certainly Graves' comments in his biography support this theory. By the time conditions improved, during the Edwardian era, Parry had not written a major symphonic work since the first version of the Fourth Symphony in 1889, almost twenty years before Elgar's First Symphony appeared in 1908. However, the situation in England only became comparable to

Nº 1 - Via Mortis

Ex. 7   the opening of *From Death to Life*

the Continent after the First World War had come and gone and with it Parry's last symphony, after a gap of 23 years.

In the 1920s, although the war had ended, anti-German sentiments in England remained extremely strong, and even composers of the order of Beethoven and the contemporary Richard Strauss were criticized in print for being Teutonic, something Shaw strongly disapproved of. Everything in French culture, especially music, became the fashion. For the English musical establishment, music – after Brahms and Wagner – had to be French or French influenced. Even Schumann, a vital link as a symphonist between Beethoven and Brahms, was known primarily through his piano music and songs, and his musical architecture and orchestration were dismissed as too un-French. Yet it was Schumann and Mendelssohn whom Parry rightly considered Beethoven's successors and his own principal models. The chief champion of Parry's earlier orchestral music, Hans Richter, left England in 1911 and like Parry he was dead before war ended. He had no successor to create and expand a tradition for performing Parry. Elgar himself was creatively dormant after the Cello Concerto in 1919, in which curiously there are nods to *The Soul's Ransom*, and soon he too went into eclipse. Parry's entire symphonic output was almost unplayed; only the *Symphonic Variations* hung on precariously.

One would have thought that with the restitution of Elgar's music, which began in the late 1950s, Parry's symphonies would have been re-evaluated at the same time. However, the absence of a complete performing edition, including miniature scores, available from one publisher, and the total lack of enthusiasm for Parry's music generally, were responsible for this not happening. The situation was further undermined by the fact that no performing material survived at all for the revised Fourth Symphony, *Concertstück, Elegy for Brahms, Proserpine,* or *From Death to Life*.[22]

Parry suffered the fate often given to a precursor or founder of a tradition. The great Haydn is still more talked about, in relation to Mozart and Beethoven, than played. One hundred years later, Parry fulfilled a similar role in English symphonic music that Haydn had played for European symphonic music in general.[23] The qualities which Parry personally espoused, honesty, integrity, generosity of spirit and above all creativity and caritas – have always been the preserve of an enlightened minority. If earlier times seem richer in these qualities it is precisely because viewed from a distance they represent hope in every age. Today these values are so scarce they are almost revolutionary. Parry's symphonies are valuable not only for intrinsic musical merit but at their best they impart these ideas and feelings to the listener.

5   What Shaw Understood

Man, if thou knowest what thou dost, thou are blessed; but if thou knowest not, thou
art accursed and a transgressor of the law.

(Apocryphal Gospel of Luke, VI, Codex Bezae)

But the recognition of deficiencies need not necessarily imply disparagement. Human
beings with deficiencies and inequalities of character often become the more subtly
interesting. When the difficulties are surmounted something of a special kind may be got
out of them which could not be got out of simpler conditions.

(Hubert Parry, Style in Musical Art)

In 1893 George Bernard Shaw reluctantly attended the Middlesex Choral Union
performance of Parry's short oratorio *Job*. His devastating review appeared in *The
World* on 3 May. It did not affect public opinion but when *Job* lost its popularity
and Parry's reputation declined, the review became a classic. Shaw, with critical
acumen and biting satirical wit, had exposed all the oratorio's grave defects.

Perhaps it was divine justice that, as Shaw's creative reputation grew, his attack
on *Job* became all the more notorious, for he was the only important contemporary
artist to confront Parry's creative problem head on and diagnose the problem early
enough for Parry to act on it, had he chosen to. Shaw's criticisms invite a few
comments on Parry the composer and Parry's relationship to *Job*.

By the time Shaw's review appeared the industrious Parry was already engaged
on yet another subject, that would have 'taxed to the utmost' as Shaw said in the
review composers of greater genius, Browning's mythical–psychological labyrinth,
the narrative poem *The Pied Piper of Hamelin*. He designed it for similar forces
and on a comparable scale to *Job*. Significantly, after its belated premier at the
1905 Worcester Festival, it went on to become a popular if transient success. In my
opinion it too is an 'utter failure' and it is useful to consider the works together
because they shed different lights on the same problem.

Shaw had given Parry a severe but not unfair review of *Judith* in 1888, praising
some of the final sections. However Parry did not take his criticisms to heart, and
he should have expected the worst:

I take Job to be, on the whole, the most utter failure ever achieved by a thoroughly
respectworthy musician. There is not one bar in it that comes within fifty thousand miles
of the tamest line in the poem. This is the naked, unexaggerated truth. Is anybody
surprised at it? Here, on the one hand, is an ancient poem which has lived from
civilisation to civilisation, and has been translated into an English version of haunting
beauty and nobility of style, offering to the musician a subject which would have taxed
to the utmost the highest powers of Bach, Handel, Mozart, Beethoven, or Wagner. Here
on the other is, not Bach nor Handel nor Mozart nor Beethoven nor Wagner, not even

Mendelssohn or Schumann, but Dr. Parry, an enthusiastic and popular professor, forty-five years old, and therefore of ascertained powers.[1]

Shaw points out that it is irrelevant to praise the professional virtues of a work, if the author lacks the creative intensity to match his subject. He puts his finger on the crux of the problem by analysing Parry's inept characterization of Satan and Job:

> The first conspicuous failure in the work is Satan, who, after a feeble attempt to give himself an infernal air by getting the bassoon to announce him with a few frog-like croaks, gives up the pretence, and, though a tenor and a fiend, models himself on Mendelssohn's St. Paul. He has no tact as an orator. For example, when he says: "Put forth thine hand now and touch all that he hath, and he will curse thee to thy face," there is not a shade of scepticism or irony in him; and he ineptly tries to drive his point home by a melodramatic shriek on the word . . . "curse". When one thinks – I will not say of Loki or Klingsor, but of Verdi's Iago and Boito's Mefistofele, and even of Gounod's stage devil, it is impossible to accept this pale shadow of an excitable curate as one of the poles of the great world magnet.
>
> As to Job, there is no sort of grit in him: he is abject from first to last, and is only genuinely touching when he longs to lie still and be quiet where the wicked cease from troubling and the weary are at rest. That is the one tolerable moment, in the work; and Job passes from it to relapse into dullness not to rise into greater strength of spirit. He is much distracted by fragments of themes from the best composers coming into his head from time to time, and sometimes cutting off the thread of his discourse altogether. When he talks of mountains being removed, he flourishes on the flute in an absurdly inadequate manner; and his challenge to God, Shew me wherefore Thou contendest with me, is too poor to be described.

Shaw makes the salient point that 'it is the old academic story – an attempt to bedizen a dramatic poem with scraps of sonata music' and for good measure concludes his review with a telling sideswipe at one of Parry's academic associates, the unsuspecting Alexander Mackenzie:

> Dr. Parry reads, The walls are broken down: destroyed are the pleasant places; and it sounds beautifully to him. So it associates itself with something else that sounds beautifully – Mendelssohn's violin concerto, as it happens in this case – and straightaway, he rambles off into a rhythm suggested by the first movement of the concerto, and produces a tedious combination which has none of the charm or propriety of either poem or concerto.
>
> For the sake of relief he drags in by the ears a piece of martial tumult – See! upon the distant plain, a white cloud of dust, the ravages come – compounded from the same academic prescription as the business of the dragon's teeth coming up armed men in Mackenzie's *Jason*; and the two pieces of music are consequently indistinguishable in my memory – in fact, I do not remember a note of either of them.

If the 'dramatic poem' did not enlighten Parry about the nature of the subject, William Blake's illustrations should have caused him to stay his hand. Here was another Englishman who had created works of genius on the same subject and in a related field, a field with which Parry was very familiar.

Blake was a double genius, poet and artist, and a genuine mystic. Nearer to our own time C.G. Jung wrote his seminal 'Answer to Job' (1951), a psychoanalytic interpretation of this story, 'because The Book of Job is a landmark in the long historical development of a divine drama'. Jung viewed the Book of Job as a prefiguration of the coming of Christ. The story of Job's sufferings was, thus far in Judaic history, the most dramatic confrontation between God (Yahweh, Jehovah) and individual man. Jung felt that despite God's long justification at the end of the drama, citing his own omnipotence and omniscience, he was morally suspect. He thought so for two reasons: Satan was clearly still part of the divine entourage and under God's authority, and secondly God allowed Satan to tempt and nearly destroy a man of whom God himself approved.

Because God's self-justification is suspect to himself he must experience being a man himself. Therefore one could say simply that while Christ was destroyed by mankind, Job was almost destroyed by God. There could hardly be a more profound or tragic subject, including Greek Drama. Jung analyses the story as a turning point in the ongoing process of God becoming more conscious of himself and man, like the Buddha, becoming more aware of the divine nature of consciousness and therefore his own cosmic dignity. The relationship between man and God is irrevocably changed by their confrontation in the Book of Job.

Shaw himself recognised that Job was an archetypal story, a landmark, 60 years before Jung's awesome study, 'a subject that would have taxed to the utmost the highest powers' of the greatest composers who ever lived, as did every other contemporary composer except, it seems Hubert Parry. It is a subject that requires the composer, in Shaw's opinion, 'to have the powers to let us hear the morning stars singing together and the sons of God shouting for joy'. The glibly extrovert Parry takes no notice of these dimensions and, as Shaw says, Satan is reduced to 'an excitable curate' and God to speaking through the accents of Brixton and Bayswater which make up the Middlesex Choral Union.

Much of the humour of Shaw-on-Parry is that he sets up Parry as a composer unequivocally in control of his own destiny, a 'composer of ascertained powers' faced with artistic choices, especially the choice to leave alone subjects like Job and stick to writing 'absolute music with no more than one pedal point per page.' Parry, in contrast, often presents himself as a composer not in control of his compositional output.

The request for a short oratorio for the 1892 Gloucester Festival had come some eighteen months earlier and within a matter of weeks Parry took on a further four commissions, all demanding chorus and orchestra, and all due for completion before the oratorio.[2] It meant that somehow in the midst of this ceaseless production Parry had to look around for a suitable oratorio subject.

With all this distraction it was ill advised to consider setting the archetypal story of Job. Not that I suggest that in order to compose *Job* or any major work a composer has to be in a constant state of romantic angst or Wordsworthian elation. But it does require hours of concentrated work every day, for months or years, not the endless distraction of overwork in non-creative areas. The following quotation from Jung's *Freud and Psychoanalysis* defines what was wrong with Parry's life:

> But we must not believe that we can save ourselves permanently from the compulsion of libido by forced efforts. Only to a very limited extent can we consciously set tasks for the libido; other natural tasks are chosen by the libido itself because it is destined for them. If these tasks are avoided, even the most industrious life avails nothing, for we

have to consider all the conditions of human nature. Innumerable neurasthenias from overwork can be traced back to this cause, for work done amid internal conflicts creates nervous exhaustion.[3]

In addition to composition, only two of Parry's work activities were not counter-productive to his creative output: his writing on music and his teaching activities. His work as administrator, squire, Justice of the Peace and committee man, could have been executed by dozens of other men in his social position. It could even be argued that he spent too much time writing books and lecturing. Parry had such a consuming love of composing and performing music it is obvious this was his destiny. There is plenty of evidence from his diaries that he would not have suffered from constant bouts of ill health if he had controlled his workload more intelligently.

No doubt William Blake Richmond reminded him that in 1887 he had suggested Job as a possibility for his first oratorio. Richmond had at that time recommended Browning as the librettist, not Parry himself! The subject was close to Richmond's heart (his father George Richmond the painter was at William Blake's deathbed and had the honour to close the artist's eyes). By 1891 Browning was dead and Parry foolishly decided to chance his own limited poetic skills. It is not surprising he experienced considerable aggravation in fashioning his libretto and soon had doubts about the whole project. But he wanted to be acknowledged as a great composer and it was more important to meet the deadline for this prestigious commission than to take the time to discover the precise reasons for his doubts.

By January 1892 Parry was 'Hard at *Job*' and on the 24th 'took a lot to Dann in the afternoon. Never saw him so enthusiastic'. However, a week later 'Frank [Pownall] came after tea and sang from *Job*. But it doesn't seem to come off as I meant it.' As the work progressed his criticisms become more intense: 'It's flabby and wanting in vitality', he stated abjectly to Dannreuther. The writing was on the wall but Parry refused to act on these warnings. He continued, partly because of the encouragement from Richmond and Dannreuther, partly to fulfil his commission obligations. Yet only a week before the première on 8 September Maude noted in her diary 'Hubert returned [from rehearsal] very low about *Job*, says it is a dreary business.'

Parry would have known how long Beethoven had to wrestle with the creation of the *Missa Solemnis*; the Archduke Rudolf of Austria was already installed for three years as Archbishop of Olmutz before Beethoven presented him with the requested score. Parry unfortunately was not willing to experience the total absorption often necessary to produce a large-scale masterpiece on a sublime or cathartic subject.

Instead he regressed and soon used literally schoolboy language about his subject: 'Poor old Job doesn't get much chance' he complains in the midst of a self-inflicted crowded agenda and 'I thought old master Job would come totally to grief'. Parry was unconsciously afraid of his subject – and rightly so. Parry never admitted any conscious fear of his subject matter in his diary, but he acted in numerous ways to reduce his creative responsibility towards his subject matter. He took on more commissions in a short period than he would ever do again, he took on additional college duties, additional pupils, and as stated he made no attempt to reduce his demanding social agenda. When all these conscious actions are coupled with his curiously regressive use of language regarding *Job*, and his concurrent creative dissatisfaction, one is forced to conclude that this was a definite case of unconscious fear.

The September 1892 Gloucester première in the event was a triumph, Lady Maude concluding 'It did sound so splendid in the Cathedral'. Privately however Parry continued to have his doubts. Sedley Taylor wrote to him in July 1894 voicing one of the few general criticisms, namely that the scene of Job's comforters should have been included. In reply Parry wrote 'that human efforts must always be imperfect in some respects and all we can do is the best we can. I often squirm over my own deficiencies – but I have to brave them as best I can. In the case of *Job* the scheme is too complicated to revise without complete rewriting and recasting.'[4] It is indicative that Parry defends *Job*, by objectifying it and distancing it: he talks further on about 'the grand scheme', necessities of 'development and balance', 'materials available' and so on, terminology better suited for an engineer.

Shortly after Shaw's review appeared, Parry manifested his laudable concern for other members of his profession: he discovered that his pupil Richard Walthew was also working on a setting of *The Pied Piper*. In deference Parry put his own version aside until 1905.

Unfortunately, even in the final version which he orchestrated in 1905, *The Pied Piper* fails to do justice to the text. Browning's fascinating but grim tale has all the dark ambiguity found in the best children's stories; a tale which is really a precise psychological allegory[5] along the lines of Christ's parables about the corruption in society. On the surface (a key word of failure), Parry has written a cogent, fluent quasi-symphonic cantata – entertaining in a somewhat blatant way. For even on this level the work has its faults. There is a 'breathless romp' quality about much of the fast music as Parry struggles to get through the complex text in the shortest possible amount of time. The music in slower tempi, though mildly *nobilmente*, lacks atmosphere, that 'once upon a time quality' appropriate for even the lightest fable.

The mysterious *Pied Piper* is reduced to a 'boisterous' (as *The Times* described it) light-hearted Cantata suitable for the competitive music festivals of Surrey, Hampshire, Sussex, Devon and Wales where it continued to linger on into the 1920s. It is questionable whether Parry's judgement was right in attempting a choral setting at all. The poem suggests a programmatic orchestral work, a Berlioz overture or a Strauss tone-poem. It could even be used as the basis for a one-act opera such as *L'Enfant et les Sortilèges*. The genius of Strauss or Ravel would have been especially suited to this subject. It is extraordinary that Parry had so identified with his persona, as the official composer, that 'The Pied Piper', like the Book of Job, is relegated to serve the conventional demands of Victorian choral societies. He studiously avoids coming to terms with either the profound or the tragic in this text, just as he failed to in *Job*. Why?

Parry possessed a brilliant intellect, almost renaissance in its sharpness, wide-ranging comprehension, and ability to realize his creative aspirations. The problem lay elsewhere; in his own emotional immaturity. As was discussed in Chapter 1, the lack of the maternal influence appears to have caused a serious retardation of his unconscious feminine side (anima). This aspect of his personality lagged behind the overly dominant male intellectual, and throughout his career his inspiration was often short circuited.

In 1892 Parry was vulnerable in another vital area: his teenage daughters were beginning to form romantic relationships; indeed both their future husbands, Arthur Ponsonby and Harry Plunkett Greene were involved in Parry premières in that same year, respectively in *The Frogs* and *Job*. Both daughters retained a strong emotional attachment to their father and it is perhaps symptomatic that they married men who were friends of their father, performers of his music and defenders of his ideals. Indeed Plunkett Greene became the leading interpreter of Parry's baritone solos for a whole generation. But in 1892 Parry was more aware that there was suddenly competition for their affections. For example Philip Burne-Jones was banned from the house after he made advances to Dorothea; a forlorn letter of apology survives in Shulbrede Priory.

There were other problems. A question mark hangs over the relationship between Parry's treatment of Job and his own religious faith. In December 1873 Gambier Parry formally decided to leave Highnam Court to Hubert rather than to his elder brother. The decision was prompted by Clinton's dissipation, but religious disagreements also played a part since Clinton had rejected orthodox christianity in contravention of Gambier Parry's High Church allegiances. Parry defended his brother in a letter to his father setting out his own religious credo and asserting his own agreement with Clinton's non-conformity.

The kernel of Parry's belief is contained in the following sentences: 'I believe in religion, but one so pure and simple that its chiefest maxim is "strive after virtue for itself". I believe that the theological part of Christianity and all dogmas connected with it are a mistake ... I believe in God, and I believe that he is good, and I think that is the one form of "faith" that will always stick to me. Beyond that I believe we can know nothing of him'. In another part he makes some theological assertions that throw an equivocal light on his reaction to the Book of Job:

> I ceased to believe in the theory that we are all punished for the sin of our first progenitors, as altogether contradictory to the theory that God was good and beautiful; as I conceived very early that no being called good would punish other beings whom he himself brought into existence for sins they had nothing to do with. Along with this naturally went the idea of Hell – which I early thought an unfit conception for any rational being.[6]

He rejects Genesis, the 'early history of mankind', as the 'poetical conceptions of a barbaric people in a very early stage of development'. Graves concludes that in essence Parry never deviated from this rationalist, Darwinist viewpoint and his later ethical views can be seen as a logical humanist development of this early credo. However, it could be argued that when it came to *Job*, these views left Parry in a theological wasteland, caught between Christian belief and the advent of modern psychology. In effect it robbed him of a *sine qua non* for the task and robbed his characters of the necessary dramatic force.

Though Parry's religious views distressed his father, they never diminished their strong mutual affection and Gambier Parry persisted in leaving Highnam to Hubert, despite the fact that Clinton had two sons. As stated in Chapter 1, Parry identified with and fashioned himself on his father in many respects; in terms of Victorian society he became a model family man. But Victorian England adopted such high ideals of personal and social morality, that the moral weakness of the age became a widespread and self-righteous form of hypocrisy. The jingoistic imperialism of late

Victorian and Edwardian England is too well known to discuss here, especially as manifested in the upper classes, where lack of self-reflection and indolence (an indolence often forced on women) were considered proper modes of behaviour.

To be fair to Parry he became a vociferous critic of Victorian hypocrisy, but like his age he appears to have been unconscious of his identification with the upper classes and perforce with so many of their traits. As well as his very conscious desire to marry Lady Maude Herbert, his close friendships were all with members of the aristocracy or even royalty and heads of state. The only exceptions were the self-made artists such as Burne-Jones and Richmond, but they were already famous when he met them. Parry always kept his pupils at a social distance and there is no evidence that he had any friends from the lower classes – not that he should have been required to – but it forced him to be part and parcel of an establishment with whom he frequently felt out of sympathy.

These difficulties did nothing to assuage his frantic hyper-activity and certainly contributed to his breakdowns in health from nervous exhaustion. For Parry activity became a justification in its own right, a moral assertion against the apathy and indolence he saw around him. But it caused him to exist in a daylight world where he did not set aside the regular periods of reflection necessary to produce creative work of the highest calibre. In his middle years the constant overwork almost killed him and his creativity altogether. At a lesser level it caused a certain glibness in his relationships and a nervous irritability displayed on many occasions: witness his behaviour on his birthday in 1892 (see Chapter 3).

It is difficult at this stage to assess Parry's exact financial status or needs, but the fact that he could support Rustington, Kensington Square and run the *Hoopoe* when he was only Professor of Music at the RCM and relatively unknown as a composer, leads one to conclude that the willingness to take on ever increasing responsibilities sprang from motivations other than the financial.

It is not surprising Parry's fine intellect hit the proverbial blank wall when he mistakenly decided to come to grips with *Job* and *The Pied Piper*. Shaw does not deny Parry's 'powers' as a composer of 'absolute music', but when he asks: 'Has the author been able for his subject?' the irrefutable answer is no. Shaw contends rightly 'that Dr. Parry has left his subject practically untouched' in his 'dreary ramble' 'through the wastes of artistic error'. The epic, the poetic and indeed the tragic dimension of Job's story lie outside, in Shaw's words, 'the limits of those powers'.

From his diary and the fact that he went on to write *King Saul* in 1894, Parry was apparently unconscious that he was acting arrogantly and wilfully in tackling these subjects at all. It was his lack of reflection on the relationship between his chosen subject and his own creative ability that led him into committing an unintended artistic hubris. His diaries confirm he was only too aware of his lack of inspiration, but he was determined to succeed, if necessary by effort alone. Like the former Eton football player he would win the cup, no matter what the cost. The cost was artistic failure, and devastating public criticism by a man destined to become one of this century's leading playwrights.

To create art which mirrors tragic catharsis requires an emotional depth of character and a capacity for spiritual development beyond analysis: it requires a profound modesty towards the great creators and the masterpieces of the tradition in which the artist is working. This teaches the artist his true direction, and the knowledge of his own limitations. For all Parry's many faceted gifts – his warmth, generosity, exalted nobility of feeling, and his grasp of musical history and European philosophy – he lacked the heart of darkness necessary to create tragic art. His acknowledgements of his own limitations now appear suspect; he lacked the self-reflection and creative modesty which would have kept him from committing the hubris apparent in his *Job*. This is what Shaw understood.

Shaw compares Parry's Satan to Verdi's Iago and Parry writing *Job* at all to Shaw himself – absurdly – writing a tragedy on *King Lear*. At the time Shaw would have been unaware of Mascagni's observation of Verdi's modesty in a delightful and touching reminiscence:

> 'Maestro why have you not composed King Lear?'
> Verdi closed his eyes for several seconds, perhaps to remember, perhaps to forget. Softly and slowly he then replied: 'The scene when Lear is alone on the heath terrified me!'
> I sprang to my feet with wide open eyes. . . . The colossus of music drama, had felt fear . . . and I . . . and I . . .
> Never again in my life did I speak of King Lear.[7]

In 1894 Shaw was still persisting with his critique of Dr Parry the composer. He concludes his generally favourable review of *The Art of Music* with a sound piece of advice:

> The future is bright however: Dr. Parry's latest composition is an "overture to an *unwritten* drama"- precisely the right sort of drama for an absolute musician to write an overture to. In process of time he will see that his particular "art of music," though a very noble art, has nothing to do with tragedies, written or unwritten or with Jobs, or Judiths, or Hypatias, or anything else of the kind.[8]

6 'As befits an Englishman and a democrat' – the Creation of a Modern Choral–Orchestral Tradition

> There is nothing more ideally suited to the inward nature of music than the presentation in the closest and most characteristic terms, of great reflective and dramatic poems and odes by genuine poets.
>
> *(Hubert Parry, The Art of Music, 1893)*

The one important factor which acts as a thread through Parry's thirty works for chorus and orchestra is contained in the above quotation. The poetic element inspired him and when it was not present in the text his creativity remained unkindled. Like a long-distance runner of old the great poets offered him the torch anew for each creative journey. Because of the gruelling demands of this genre and in accepting the role of festival composer, he took hold of the torch only intermittently.

The sixteen works for chorus and orchestra that Parry produced between *Prometheus* (1880) and the six *Ethical Cantatas* (1903–8) fall into three broad categories: settings of Church texts, several in Latin; three oratorios to biblical texts fashioned by himself in English; and eight choral odes, to poems by English poets. These works call for large performing forces and the majority feature one or more soloists. In my opinion there are seven which deserve a place in the repertoire: the *Invocation to Music* (1895), lasting just under an hour; *The Lotos-Eaters* (1892), *Magnificat* (1897) and *A Song of Darkness and Light* (1898), all featuring a solo soprano and approximately half an hour in duration; and finally three single movement settings, *Blest Pair of Sirens* (1887), *Ode to Music* (1901) and *I was Glad* (1902).[1]

All have certain attributes in common. Once Parry's inspiration is sparked, two related processes occur. These are manifested in the above works, where his technique, normally more than professional, intensifies to the point where he becomes a master. Hand in hand, his musical personality expands: the tinge of genius appears. It pertains to the 'inward nature' mentioned by Parry and the awakening of his emotional nature. These seven works are written for large orchestra and chorus but retain an intimate quality which links them to each other. The intense emotions Parry experienced in response to the texts are imparted to the listener, which is why they all deserve to be revived. Significantly the four longer settings give a prominent role to the soprano – for Parry, invariably the voice of the 'fem inspiratus'. After 1900 Parry returned only once to the specific combination of solo soprano, chorus and orchestra; the outcome was his masterpiece, the 1912 setting of Dunbar's *Ode on the Nativity*.

Other intimate factors are also at work. *Blest Pair of Sirens, Ode to Music* and *Invocation to Music* are poems addressed directly to the muse of music; the great Dirge in the *Invocation* was a tribute to Lord Pembroke and the *Ode to Music* celebrated the College. Even *I was Glad*, a text familiar from Purcell's setting, was written for the coronation of Edward VII, a long-standing friend, president of the College and supporter of Parry's aspirations. It has to be emphasized that the commission element is a secondary matter: the personal element dominates. (Parry was almost never paid to write his choral works, only guaranteed a performance.)

In the other choral works the intimate quality appears either occasionally, fleetingly, or not at all. However, Parry rarely writes bad music: it remains professional. When the seven masterpieces are regarded in tandem with *The Soul's Ransom* and the *Ode on the Nativity* it is a remarkable number of successful works in this demanding genre; that they represent only a third of his choral orchestral output does not mitigate its truth. A look at his great and greater contemporaries abroad confirms the statement. It is necessary to go back to Handel or Haydn, whom Parry resembles in so many ways, to find such prodigality.

It will be many years before readers can test my assessments; twenty years ago only *Blest Pair of Sirens* was available on recording. At the time of writing a mere six have been recorded and only two or three others have achieved a recent performance. They remain the most inaccessible branch of his considerable *œuvre*.

Parry's precocious first essay in the genre was a biblical cantata heavily derivative of Handel and Bach, and also S.S. Wesley; *Oh Lord Thou Hast Cast Us Out* (1866) written for his degree at Oxford. It is a genuinely interesting work scored for soloists, chorus and piano duet doubling strings. It was considered an outstanding success by his professors at Oxford and the critic of the Eton College chronicle. Its Biblical text on the subjects of forgiveness, repentance and thanksgiving would remain a philosophical prototype that Parry returned to throughout his life.

There was an interval of fourteen years before he wrote his second essay, a large scale setting of scenes from Shelley's *Prometheus Unbound* (1880). Family connections may have prompted the Gloucester Festival commission; Parry had conducted an 1867 performance of *Oh Lord Thou Hast Cast Us Out* in the Cathedral and *Intermezzo Religioso* had been premièred there during the 1868 Festival. By 1880 it was a different matter: the success of the 1879 concert music put on by Arthur Balfour had 'taken him out of the category of mere amateurs'.[2] The September 1880 Gloucester première of *Prometheus* was the culmination of a fruitful year in which the Cello Sonata, String Quartet No. 3 and the Piano Concerto had all received first performances.

It was probably the Wagnerian elements in the score that annoyed the critics and baffled the majority of its first listeners. Yet for the sophisticated, here at last

Ex. 8   from the score of *O Lord Thou Has Cast Us Out*

was a well composed work which moved away from the pathetic imitations of
Spohr and Mendelssohn which English composers had been writing for the previous fifty years. Prosper Sainton, who led the orchestra, commented on 'the deep,
very deep impression *Prometheus* has made on me.'[3] Rivers of ink have been spilt
over its merits. The experience of attending the BBC revival in the early 1980s
made it clear that *Prometheus* and *Blest Pair of Sirens* are the precursors of the
whole tradition Parry created, but *Prometheus* is not strong enough to be convincing today.

For the next Gloucester Festival in 1883 Parry was asked to contribute a short
choral piece, either sacred or secular. Significantly the invitation came in a letter
from his father, still one of the Stewards. He composed his setting of Shirley's
funeral ode, *The Glories of Our Blood and State*, during the summer of 1883.
Vaughan Williams was fond of it, saying it was 'a bit Brahmsy but very fine'. The
original score is preferable to the revised version of 1908. Parry's revisions rob the
work of a raw virility. Although less subtle, the original has a lean, untamed
vigour, much more in keeping with its youthful 35-year-old composer.

By a stroke of irony it was Stanford's desire to perform *The Glories* in the Bach
Choir Golden Jubilee concert which prompted *Blest Pair of Sirens*. The committee
raised objections to Shirley's poem: 'Crown and Sceptre tumbling down' was not
felt to be appropriate for 1887, Victoria's Golden Jubilee year. Instead they commissioned a new piece of similar length. With the miseries of *Guinevere* behind

him and the move to Kensington Square completed in December 1886, Parry approached *Blest Pair of Sirens* with renewed vigour. Work began over Christmas 1886 at Wilton. Though Parry had toyed with this seminal ode since the 1860s, it was Grove who suggested it for the Bach Choir commission.

Blest Pair of Sirens[4] resounded throughout the English music world of 1887; it was 'quite uproariously received', Parry commented. The critics were less impressed: both the *Athenaeum* and the *Musical Times* discussed its Brahmsian influences while failing to hear its English originality. However, choral societies avidly took it up.

A work of this originality and mastery was totally unexpected, though Parry had laid the groundwork better than people realized. The extended choral writing in *Prometheus Unbound* and especially in *The Glories of Our Blood and State* is closer to *Blest Pair of Sirens* than it sounds on first listening. It is the new concept of form and the genius of Parry's principal melodic idea, combined with the flow of Milton's mighty line, which is the essential difference. The rondo-like structure is a perfect vehicle for Milton's pindaric verse. The first performance, on 17 May, was a major event in the history of British music.

Parry based the work on sketches dating back to that fertile year 1867 and made rapid progress; he only complains of 'getting stuck fast' on the last line. Even at the rehearsal on 29 March, the chorus were 'vociferous and at the end G[rove] jumped up and wrung my hand with tears in his eyes'. *Blest Pair of Sirens* proved to be the most popular of all his works for chorus and orchestra, the only one to hang on at the fringes of the English repertoire.

This spacious setting in E flat major of Milton's 1633 ode 'At a Solemn Music' for eight-part chorus and orchestra is the apogee of his *nobilmente* style and Elgar took due note. Parry developed this style from the legacies of Handel, Bach, Schumann and Mendelssohn. But Brahms' *German Requiem* and most of all *The Song of Destiny* and the *Nänie* were the models. *The Song of Destiny* is one of the most perfect works ever conceived for the medium; the *Nänie*, though less well known, is equally inspired melodically while containing paragraphs of such length and complexity, that even today it is rare to hear a satisfactory performance. Parry learned from both. (In 1882 he sang in The London Musical Society performance of the *Nänie*.) Remarkably, *Blest Pair of Sirens* does not sound Brahmsian, but late nineteenth-century English: Parry had become the first personal English voice in music for two hundred years.

Vaughan Williams was fond of quoting Parry's assertion that 'style is ultimately national', the outcome, in Parry's view, of a communal sifting to find 'the thing that suits the native taste'.[5] *Blest Pair of Sirens* is the outcome not just of sifting but synthesis. Parry's style absorbs the accents and contours of national song, from street songs to sea shanty, folksong to hymn. He taps the common melodic roots that run through all these modes of popular expressions, which, as always, are influenced by the speech rhythms of the country's language. The achievement of *Blest Pair of Sirens* is that the essence of these national traditions is wedded to the powerful forces of chorus and orchestra; Parry's music is as English as Milton's verse.

Tunes come out of people and people come out of landscapes. Parry was the eldest of that remarkable group of composers, including Elgar, Howells and Gur-

Ex. 9   from the piano reduction of *Blest Pair of Sirens*

ney, who grew up in the charmed landscape of Gloucestershire and the Malvern Hills. But ultimately the appeal of the wide-spanned, upward-moving melody in *Blest Pair of Sirens* is that it gives perfect expression to Parry's own personality; his qualities of aspiration, sincerity and idealism.

In his own mind, Parry was building on the work of S.S. Wesley and his friend John Stainer. He always held *The Wilderness* in great affection and commented on its Englishness. *Blest Pair of Sirens* rolls along with a majestic splendour, the wide-arched melodic paragraphs are bridged seamlessly, the choral and orchestral sound combined and interwoven like dramatic cloud-landscapes of Constable. Some ears find the texture too thick. I disagree: at no point is the score crowded. What critical ears really sense is that Parry's orchestration has not reached maturity, his clouds don't always have silver linings, or the wind-blown trees enough shimmering light diffusing through them.

Blest Pair of Sirens employs varied numbers of vocal parts, from unison to eight-part harmony, adding contrast to the presentation of the words – a technique he would return to later, especially in *The Lotos-Eaters* and the *Ode on the Nativity*. As late as 1950 Ralph Vaughan Williams, surveying the history of English music, concluded that '*Blest Pair of Sirens* is my favourite piece of music written by an Englishman.'[6] Like Elgar, Vaughan Williams was profoundly influenced by its style and tended to overestimate its place in Parry's output. But its splendour and historical significance are incontrovertible.

In Vaughan Williams's opinion, Parry did not represent a break with the past but another stage in the evolution of 'the great English choral tradition which Tallis passed on to Byrd, Byrd to Gibbons, Gibbons to Purcell, Purcell to Battishill and Greene and they in their turn through the Wesleys.'[7] The modern reader may blink at the significance of Battishill and Greene, but for Parry and Vaughan Williams they were essential links in a living heritage. This statement of Vaughan Williams is an important refutation of the misnomer that 'English' means 'modal', a mistake that Vaughan Williams repeatedly corrected. Parry is rarely modal. Vaughan Williams considered that Parry 'derived largely from S.S. Wesley' and 'I remember even as a boy, my brother saying to me that there was something, to his mind, peculiarly English about his music'.

Parry's knowledge of English music from the sixteenth and seventeenth centuries was formidable, and this enabled him to develop the medium of voices and orchestra into a wonderful vehicle for English poetry, both secular and sacred. He extended its expressive range to include the tender and wistful as well as the opulent and grand, while his highly developed technique enabled him to harness the resources of the late nineteenth-century orchestra. He gave English choral music a new vitality stamped with his own personality.

New choral works followed quickly and during the next two years Parry took on the unfortunate *Judith* and the *Ode On St Cecilia's Day*. This extended setting of Pope's ode, featuring soprano and bass soloists, was written for the 1889 Leeds Festival. The première a 'wonderful' performance in October, was a major personal success, and over the next decade numerous performances followed. It crowned a year which had seen the Third and Fourth Symphonies and his Violin Sonata in D major. In addition to his heavy teaching schedule he miraculously found time to read Zola's *La Curée* and *La Fortune de Rougon-Macquart*, Machiavelli's *The Prince*, and Tolstoy's *Sebastopol*. At the theatre he and Lady Maude encountered Ibsen's *The Doll's House* and Verdi's latest opera *Otello*.

The *St Cecilia Ode* is well written from every standpoint, its melodic material, harmonic world, bright orchestration and sensitive word setting are all to a high standard. But it lacks the large-scale opulence and glorious writing found in the *Invocation to Music* or the powerful emotional appeal and succinct formal structure which distinguishes the *Ode to Music*, the two works it most resembles. It is in fact their precursor. With odes to St Cecilia by Purcell, Handel, a very find neglected one by Liszt, and several distinguished modern settings, there is little hope for this version as repertoire, but a recording would be welcome.

In 1890 Parry returned to Milton with *L'Allegro ed il Penseroso* for the Norwich Festival. The work received Dannreuther's approval and that of Shaw who wrote in *The World* on 10 November 1890: 'This new cantata of his is happy, ingenious, as full of contrapuntal liveliness as *Judith* was full of contrapuntal deadliness, and genuine in feeling throughout'; it has always had advocates among Parry's admirers. While some of the solo songs have melodic beauty, the work lacks variety and the riveting orchestral backdrop which would give this nineteenth-century version a *raison d'être*. Like his Cecilian Ode, it is a precursor to *Invocation to Music*.

In 1891 he composed two works which need detain no one. His setting of Swinburne's 'Eton', a short piece for the 450th anniversary of that College, shows no advancement in technique and emotionally is very low voltage. *De Profundis*, commissioned by G.R. Sinclair, a grandiose setting of Psalm 130 in Latin for soprano, chorus and orchestra, was premièred on 10 September 1891 during the Hereford Festival. In spite of Vaughan Williams strong advocacy the work is a disappointment. The highly elaborate choral writing, often in 12 parts, fails to come alive because of banal melodic material, conventional harmonic progressions and undistinguished orchestration. There are conventionally impressive passages, but reviving this work, like reviving the oratorios, would only make the enemy blaspheme – Parry was indeed out of his depth.

In the autumn of 1891, on completion of the music to *The Frogs*, Parry happily gave us *The Lotos-Eaters*,[8] a genuine masterpiece. He set the 'Choric Song' from Tennyson's *The Lotos-Eaters*, his 1833 poem about the followers of Odysseus, in response to a commission from the Cambridge University Musical Society. Of the many secular works he composed before the turn of the century it was his favourite. The Cambridge première on the occasion of the installation of the Duke of Devonshire as Chancellor of the University was conducted by Parry on 13 June 1892. It 'went finely' and the audience 'seemed to like it well enough'. But the critical reaction was disappointing. 'I suppose they have made up their minds what sort of music I ought to write and object to my trying to widen my field'. But further performances followed; in 1896 The Bach Choir under Stanford gave the work in London and there was a performance in Milwaukee, USA. Elgar chose it for a Worcestershire Philharmonic concert which he conducted in May 1902 together with the *Pomp and Circumstance Marches No. 1* and *No. 2* and in 1912 Vaughan Williams revived it while Parry was working on the *Ode on the Nativity*, but after the First World War *The Lotos-Eaters* was rarely heard.

It is one of the finest examples of the purely secular aspect of Parry's art, an aspect that found eloquent expression in his twelve sets of English lyrics. Whatever the intended moral, the composer, like the poet, became seduced by the atmosphere of the subject. Through the languid but troubled musings of the drug-addicted mariners, Parry gives voice to the hedonistic and rhapsodic leanings in his own character, which are rarely apparent in his music. Tennyson's own reaction was equivocal. 'After breakfast', Parry wrote, 'I also had to play him my version of *The Lotos-Eaters*. He did not understand much of it but was quite amiable and then we went for a short walk'.[9]

The eight stanzas are presented within a one-movement structure in which the solo soprano is given the prominent role of ballad singer: she gives voice, as Parry noted, to what the 'inner spirit' sings (Choric Song, second stanza). No other composition before the *Ode on the Nativity* offers such an effective demonstration of his sensitivity to the possibilities of choral colour and nowhere is he more adventurous in his harmony and melodic contours. He synthesizes Wagner (*Parsifal*), Liszt, Brahms and Gounod into a personal language which in places looks forward to French Impressionism and the sunset of German Romanticism – the later Strauss and Pfitzner.

The 16-bar D major orchestral introduction contains the three main motifs of the work. The mood of floating lightness and eroticism is enhanced in the opening chorus by omitting the bass voices. Until the final section only the settings of the second and fourth stanzas use the full choir. The third, fifth and seventh stanzas are given to the soprano solo while the greater proportion of the eighth is presented by the solo soprano, male choir and the female choir separately.

The choral paragraphs are built on the opening melodic and rhythmic ideas but Parry uses variation techniques and tertial key relationships to give each stanza a sharply differentiated quality. The work gives a dramatic presentation of the poem; it is not a mere exercise in mood painting.

He tells us so much about his life and personality in this masterly evocation. For instance his setting for male chorus of the sixth stanza's final flowing line, 'There is confusion worse than death', ending 'and eyes grown dim with gazing on the pilot stars', is a confession. The daily struggle in living helped divert him from inward turmoil, yet everything ends in confusion; but confusion is dissolved momentarily by the night sea and stars. The final words bring forth two four-bar phrases of such exquisite beauty that I am tempted to say they are the loveliest music ever written for male choir. Parry modulates out of and back into G major via B flat major in a magically seamless way. The mood is enhanced by the subtle positioning in the last four bars. Holst may have had this passage in mind for a similar, haunting moment in *Ode to Death*.

Typically and sadly, Parry – in spite of balking at the adverse critical reaction from Fuller-Maitland, Graves and others – began to doubt his achievement. *The Lotos-Eaters* had no direct successors though its influence is felt in several later works and in the pellucid texture of Vaughan Williams's early *Garden of Proserpine*. We can only regret that a nineteenth-century Valéry was not on hand to tell him:

Ex. 10   from the piano reduction of *The Lotos-Eaters*

Ex. 11   excerpt from the male chorus in *The Lotos-Eaters*

'You mustn't hesitate to do what will lose you half of your fans and triple the affections of those who remain.'

For the Ralph Vaughan Williams Trust – Chandos recording, it was necessary to add some dynamic markings to the last few pages of the choral parts. The climactic phrases seemed to sit back on themselves. With the addition of *crescendo* marks the problem was solved. In general the orchestral passages benefit from a little *tempo rubato* in the French operatic manner.

Accolades for *Job*, criticisms for *The Lotos-Eaters* and the failure of *L'Allegro*, in part explain Parry's decision to accept an oratorio commission for Birmingham in October 1894. In May that year he produced *Hear My Words Ye People*, an anthem for Salisbury Cathedral scored for soloists, chorus, organ, brass and timpani. The piece begins impressively but inspiration and technique fizzle out after the opening section; even the choral finale, a still popular setting of 'Oh Praise Ye the Lord', is no salvation.

But much of the year was taken up with his last oratorio, *King Saul*. Every criticism which can be applied to *Job* can be levelled with increased force at this ultimate creative aberration. At this point in his development there was no excuse for it. Considering his doubts about *Job* and the publication of Shaw's criticisms, he would have honoured his higher self by withdrawing from the commission. What 'abaissement du niveau mental' (Pierre Janet's term in *Les Névroses*, page 358) made him choose a subject which Handel had already immortalized in one of his supreme dramatic creations defies even a lengthy analysis. Parry would have worn out the upholstery on Freud's couch. Since he was the son of an eminent painter and avid visitor to art galleries, perhaps if he had stared at Rembrandt's violently intense, psychological double portrait in oils on this very subject[10], he might have desisted; there was no such luck. One only has to compare Parry's setting of the *Witch of Endor* scene with his Saxon predecessor's to see the trouble. Handel's music is both magisterial and genuinely spooky; one can feel the hoar-frost as the witch raises Samuel from the dead. Parry's limp Victorian melodrama would not have frightened his little nieces, or raised one of his cigars off the table. Creative *embourgeoisement* – the equivalent a hundred years ago of today's 'making it acceptable' – can be worse than total incomprehension.

In 1895 Parry made amends and wrote *Invocation to Music*.[11] He had written in *The Art of Music* (1893), that Purcell 'was saturated with the characteristic English tunes of his day and possessed an instinct for the true relation between the accents of musical melody and declamatory recitative, which has never been surpassed by any composer of the same nationality'.

In the second half of the nineteenth century there was a major re-evaluation of Purcell's music: the Purcell Society was founded in 1876, editions of his works were published for the first time since the seventeenth century, and the bi-centenary in 1895 prompted a host of concerts. For example, Stanford conducted the first staged performance of *Dido and Aeneas* in modern times with the young Vaughan Williams and Holst in the chorus.

Parry responded with the ode *Invocation to Music*, his third Leeds Triennial contribution and written 'In Honour of Henry Purcell' (The 1892 Festival had featured a 'splendid' performance of *De Profundis*). The première took place on 2 October 1895, conducted by the composer. The evening concert provided an appropriate setting: Weber, Overture *Der Freischütz*; Parry, *Invocation to Music*; Mozart Symphony No. 41 in C (the 'Jupiter'); and Mendelssohn's *The First Walpurgis Night* – a programme that would not disgrace a festival today, if any had the opportunity to mount a concert of this length.

Purcell's own ceremonial 'Welcome' odes – and their successors such as Handel's *Alexander's Feast* and the *Ode for St Cecilia's Day* – provided the blueprint for this spacious neo-baroque cantata set out for soprano, tenor, bass, chorus and full orchestra, including bass clarinet, double bassoon, harp and organ.

Robert Bridges (1844–1930), the future Poet Laureate, remained a lifelong friend and this was the first of their four collaborations for chorus and orchestra. His poem is a curious mixture of seventeenth-century pastiche and passages of great poetry, though today it compares favourably to the similar efforts of Dryden, Shadwell and Tate, who were Purcell's principal collaborators.

Parry was 'most grateful for the parts in which he [Bridges] turned out such noble lines and thoughts as in the Dirge', and he composed the music for this elaborate tripartite section in memory of Lord Pembroke, who died aged only 45

Ex. 12   from the vocal score of *Invocation to Music*, 'Rejoice ye Dead'

in June 1895. This magnificent nineteen-minute inspiration forms the heart of *Invocation to Music* and displays Parry's sensitive response to Bridges' memorable stanzas, 'Man, born of desire' and 'Rejoice, ye dead'. In 1930 Parry's pupil Gustav Holst set these same lines in the *Choral Fantasia*, dedicated to the memory of Bridges; Holst had also become a close friend. The melodic cross-connections between the settings are clearly intentional and they would make an interesting coupling.

If there was any work which was to exercise a lasting influence on English composers it was *Invocation to Music*, in its peculiarly English vocal style, its breaking down of the traditional cantata divisions and its finely poised use of symphonic elements. This is particularly noticeable in the 'Man Born of Desire' section. Parry admitted to the Leeds Committee in 1887 his dislike of the cantata 'which has become such a regular hackneyed resource', and certainly he was the first English composer since Purcell who was responsive to the musical implications of English poetry.

The vocal style, in its unforced lyrical outpouring stems directly from the English school of the seventeenth century – Locke, Blow, Purcell – and this gives the solo writing a new found emotional directness and the choral writing an extended range of expression which clearly separates it from the German nineteenth-century choral tradition.

The compositional processes employed develop tendencies discernible in *St Cecilia* and *L'Allegro*; he blends the closed baroque cantata forms into a large-scale structure which is only a step away from Elgar's *The Dream of Gerontius* and which exercised an overt influence on the *Coronation Ode* (1902), since there are direct quotes. This is one of Parry's strongest scores, beguiling the ears with a protean stream of lyricism from the first bars of the prelude to the grand sweep of the final chorus. The premise that the muse of music had abandoned the British Isles struck the contemporary critic Joseph Bennett, who wrote the bloodless analytical notes, as (in his word) a 'bold' conception. But the musical achievements of succeeding decades lend credence to the notion that the 'enchantress of the air' was indeed moved by Parry's heartfelt invocation to return to the isle and make again 'our Graces three'.

The ideas in the surging paragraphs of the opening prelude and chorus are used throughout to create a cyclic form which Parry would use but not over-use. For example in the 'monstrous sea' chorus, at the words 'Return, O Muse!' he brings back the 'invocation' music from the opening chorus and this device is employed subtly throughout the work's four main choral sections.

The melodic charm of the rapt tenor aria is more evident on repeated listening as are the felicitous details of scoring, notably the lovely clarinet counterpoints to the tenor line; like so many aspects of this work the aria had an impact on tenor arias for the next sixty years including Vaughan Williams' 'Bright Portals of the Sky'. The duet and trio reveal the beneficial influence of Gounod and flow with a mellifluous ease for which Parry is rarely credited. Indeed there are no weak links throughout the work's fifty-five minute span.

Invocation to Music, written when Parry's reputation was at its height, is a seminal work of the English musical renaissance and the concluding statement of his early style. From the entry of the dirge, through the majestic march 'Man Born of Desire', Parry proceeds to build a paragraph of soprano and chorus which mirrors the final peroration in *Blest Pair of Sirens*, but with firmer structural control, clearer textures and greater melodic distinction. A powerful series of harmonic gear-changes culminates in a telling choral unison 'Now Have Ye Starry Names', before the music dissolves into a codetta of yearning beauty for solo soprano and chorus where the orchestration becomes suitably tinged with the 'hues of the rosy fingered dawn.' Vaughan Williams either emulated or half remembered this passage when he composed the final soprano line at the end of *A Sea Symphony*, 1910.

The late romantic solution would have been to end the work at this point, but Parry adheres to the baroque antecedents and shapes *Invocation to Music* as an arch, concluding with a celebratory trio and a choral finale that harks back to the 'invocation' mood of the opening. Of all Parry's choral works before the *Ode on the Nativity*, 1912, *Invocation to Music* is the score which should least be relegated to the position of precursor to the later acknowledged English masterpieces. Whilst it influenced both *The Dream of Gerontius* and *A Sea Symphony*, it is as unlike those two masterworks as they are each other.

The score heralded a four-year period of consistent creative achievement. The fact that it coincided with his assumption of the Directorship of the college and cessation of his tuition duties cannot be coincidental; his rate of production slows down and the output diversifies. The year 1896 was mostly devoted to a set of English lyrics, choral songs and some part-songs, several to poems by Tennyson, Bridges and A.C. Benson.

The musical landscape was changing and he was now familiar with Dvořák's *New World* Symphony, Strauss's *Till Eulenspiegel*, MacCunn's *Jeanie Deans*, Elgar's *King Olaf* and music by Gabriel Fauré, 'Some of it delicately and artistically good. Very sensitive stuff'.[12]

And sensitive is the word for Parry's setting of the *Magnificat* for soprano, chorus and orchestra produced for the 1897 Hereford Festival. Parry for once disagreed with Bach. He felt a different kind of music was suitable for this ancient text and produced a setting which captures some of the intimate inward feeling he thought appropriate. He had a special appreciation of the young Virgin Mary as she thanked her God in a spirit of awe for choosing her for the 'incarnatus est'. There are some fine melodic paragraphs featuring an appropriate solo violin obbligato, some very personal harmonic progressions and many examples of lovely orchestration.

The whole prelude is an almost unending series of resolving suspensions – a typical Parry device turned here into a structural principle. The real harmonic surprise is the entry of the solo soprano on the word 'Magnificat' marked *lento expressivo*. Parry opens the windows of his chromatic F major and lets in the light with a D major dominant 7th (V of VI) and several unexpected modal inflections. This is viewing Wagner as Pfitzner did nearly twenty years later in *Palestrina*. The music's spontaneity suggests its roots lay in an inspired moment of improvization. Parry's musicological survey of the sixteenth century enriched his own musical language. The piece deserves a revival.

Parry was asked to write a large-scale work for the Gloucester Festival of 1898. He discussed the idea of a sequel to *Invocation to Music* with Robert Bridges, who supplied Parry with *A Song of Darkness and Light*, an elaborate philosophical poem in seven sections. Bridges, anticipating the need for recasting and revisions, insisted on an organized schedule of meetings which proved unnecessary, for the composer was delighted with the poem.

The score was completed in August and rehearsals went sufficiently well for Parry to reward everyone with a party at Highnam the day before the 15 September première. 'The Chorus went to the Pinetum and all the band came over to the garden where I had a marquee for them and whiskeys and sodas and fruit and cigars'.

The titles suggest the dramatic all-embracing quality Parry wanted the text to embody: 'Mystery', 'Terror', 'Peace', 'Toil', 'Art', 'Tears', 'Faith'. (In 1926 Holst preceded his setting of 'Man Born of Desire' with 'Toil'). The poem is reminiscent of Shelley's *Prometheus Unbound*, and Parry produced a masterly score which contains some of his most complex forward looking music. There are some bold progressions which unfortunately he rarely used again.

Ex. 13   from 'Terror', *A Song of Darkness and Light* vocal score

And the following, which appears eight measures later, became in many versions an Elgar fingerprint:

Ex. 14   from piano reduction *A Song of Darkness and Light*

It is worth noting that *A Song of Darkness and Light* was his most recent published score when Elgar began *The Dream of Gerontius*; and Elgar was present at the première.

The prelude is one of Parry's boldest orchestral creations, a successful English essay in Liszt's harmonic idiom; *Tannhäuser* is also an influence. Parry handles the transitions between the poem's sections with a deftness not hinted at in *Prometheus*. Rhythmically too, Parry is at his most adventurous, approaching Strauss in activity within the beat, increased use of two against three and the occasional complex figuration. This gives greater life to the music's flow and fluidity to the paragraphs. He creates 'new' music for the various sections of the poem, but carefully links each section with thematically organic symphonic bridge passages. The work's formal structure may well look back to Schumann's song cycles with their instrumental interludes.

The scoring is imaginative and full of subtle technical details, for example the use of harp and bass drum. The harp part is the most elaborate he wrote. The brass writing is more developed and independent of the string band than ever before. The winds too (in the prelude) are more often thrown into relief. Berlioz, Liszt and Wagner's orchestral innovations are being integrated in a positive way. The main limitation is the melodic invention, which is intermittently not first-rate. There are lovely ideas in 'Tears', for example, but they never quite rise to the level of *The Soul's Ransom* or the *Ode on the Nativity*. Nevertheless, the work deserves a good recording and the occasional live performance. (It would go well with Bruckner's Mass in F Minor). It is perhaps the most important stepping stone to *Gerontius*. There was no false modesty in Elgar saying of Parry that 'he is our leader'. Performances lingered on until the 1950s when apparently it was revived at the King's Lynn Festival of 1952.

Ex. 15   from 'Tears', *A Song of Darkness and Light* vocal score

These innovative orchestral developments should have reached their apotheosis in the large-scale thanksgiving *Te Deum* produced for the 1900 Hereford Festival (the première was on 11 September). It is historically interesting because it relates back to *Oh Lord Thou Hast Cast Us Out* (1867), where the Baroque style is based on a modern adaptation of Purcell, Bach and Handel, unlike the Mendelssohnian Baroque employed in his three oratorios. In this respect it paves the way for one stylistic aspect of *Ode on the Nativity*. Unfortunately the wonderful old liturgical text failed to inspire Parry, so feelings of genuine grandeur and divine joy are not achieved. Ten years later he was invited to write the *Thanksgiving Te Deum* for the Coronation service of George V (11 June 1911). Again the text did not spark his imagination; Parry produced a score which shows his impatience with the task at hand. The result is crabbed in structure and uncertain in style. He may have been trying to move on from 'I was Glad' but he failed to compete with his masterpiece of ceremonial music.

In contrast the *Ode to Music* written to inaugurate the New Concert Room at the Royal College of Music in June 1901 is a delight. Parry gave the College a new organ which was being heard for the first time. A.C. Benson supplied Parry with a fine ode in four stanzas. The language, though very much of the period, has a burning sincerity and a masterly use of poetic imagery, which lifts it above the ordinary, and Parry produces one of his finest minor scores. The prelude plays a game usually associated with Ives – quotation and self-quotation, blended superbly to create a new fabric – alluding to Handel of the Chandos anthems, the Rhine motif from Wagner's *Ring*, and 'Love to Love Calleth' from *Invocation to Music*. But the result, rather than pastiche, is a seamless flow of silver-tinged orchestral harmony worthy of the poem's transcendent subject. Elgar, despite Parry's misgivings (because the work was written for the College), programmed it in the 1913 Leeds Festival. Parry sustains the mood throughout and there is not a dull moment.

As usual with Parry at his best, the harmony is enhanced by an unusual number of appoggiatura chords, secondary dominants, and general enrichment of the harmonic texture, particularly in the upper middle registers. Exceptionally fine is the choral passage (derived from the prelude) for choir and organ in D flat beginning 'The mighty organ wakes from sleep' and leading with great changes of texture to the very noble 'In no light fancy, no inglorious mirth. But strong to labour striving well to set the crown of song up on the brow of earth'. Parry piles it on here. His letter to Elgar suggests that he was somewhat embarrassed by his overt emotionalism. He need not have worried, for Elgar knew that people of all ages would respond. With the paucity of good late romantic works in this genre, this piece should be played constantly in youth concerts throughout the English-speaking world. But it has received barely a handful of performances.

Parry contributed two works for the Coronation of Edward VII; the hymn 'God of all Created Things' and the anthem *I was Glad*[13] which has been sung during the monarch's entrance at every subsequent Coronation. He was in Westminster Abbey for a rehearsal when the Bishop of London announced the deferment of the 1902 Coronation and 'the necessity of the King's undergoing an operation'. He ended 'with an appeal to all to join in a litany. The choir joined in with a most superb tone and produced an effect I have never experienced before – so solemn and pathetic. A few kneeling figures on the floor of the chancel. The sunlight streaming in on the ancient recumbent figures on the tombs and the thousands of empty seats'.[14]

Ex. 16   from *Ode to Music* vocal score

I was Glad is Parry's most successful essay in the monumental manner, especially in his own night-sky orchestration, not to be confused with the brightly
conventional Gordon Jacob re-orchestration played today. The structure consists
of four sections. The expanded 1911 version opens with a ten-bar orchestral
introduction followed by the opening double chorus marked *maestoso*. The second
section, *animato*, heralded by fanfares from the brass introduces the traditional
declamation of the 'Vivats'. This fades into a *più lento* for the orchestra which
modulates into the beautiful third section, *dolce* (in G flat) for semi-chorus. The
work concludes with a magnificent nineteen-bar peroration, *alla marcia*, for full
choir, which ends triumphantly in the home key of B flat.

Parry's harmonic fingerprints are discernible in the use of tertial key relationships, a practice he learnt from Beethoven. But under the late romantic panoply of
sound the work manifests a connection with Purcell, Schütz and the choral styles
of the seventeenth century. There are harmonic analogies with Purcell's setting for
the Coronation of James II in 1685 and the use of dotted rhythms is common to
both works. But the mood here is more intense. Time has tended to reveal the
extraordinarily private emotion that wells up through the music. Parry tapped a
mood of profound intimacy, a lump-in-the-throat quality and the effect now is not
jingoistic but personal, dark and already elegiac; bearing in mind Mary Magdalene's
aria in Elgar's *The Kingdom* one might say it is more 'the sun goeth down' over the
Empire.

By 1902 Parry felt he had exhausted the manifold traditional forms for chorus
and orchestra he had been working with for over twenty years. The advent of *The
Dream of Gerontius* would have confirmed this view. He wanted to move on and
create something new in this most difficult of genres. But perhaps Elgar was the
only man – much more than Parry himself – to realize how significant and splendid

an achievement already lay behind him. Parry had prepared the groundwork for three generations of English composers on how to write for chorus and orchestra, and his seminal creations had given back to England her musical voice.

7 *The Soul's Ransom* – Parry and the Ethical Cantata concept

There is no goodness except the possession of a good soul, – which may be seen in all things, from which one need not seek to hide.

(Ludwig van Beethoven writing to Bettina von Armin, 1812)

It illustrates the just view of the Teutonic composer that music deals with the inward man and not with what is external to him, with the mood induced by the external and not with the external itself.

(Hubert Parry in his 1902 analysis of the Symphonia Sacra, 'Saul, Saul was verfolgst du mich?' by Heinrich Schütz)

For many years Parry had wished to create a new choral–symphonic form to supersede the nineteenth-century oratorio. Perhaps Elgar's *Dream of Gerontius* confirmed that the structural concepts he had began to formulate in *Job* and carried further in the single-movement design of *A Song of Darkness and Light* (1898) were the most propitious for realizing this ambition.

There are two important points regarding *Job* which had little meaning for Shaw. The work did attempt to create a terser more symphonic concept of oratorio by eschewing separation between recitatives, arias and choruses; *Parsifal* is an obvious influence here. Secondly, although the orchestral writing and the orchestration are not especially imaginative, the orchestra does have a more independent role than in the earlier cantatas. Therefore the best moments provided a hint to Elgar and Vaughan Williams about creating an English dramatic musical idiom. Elgar never lost his enthusiasm for *Job* and Vaughan Williams continued to perform it regularly at the Dorking Festival into the 1940s. In *A Musical Autobiography* (1950), he states 'but I still thrill to the magnificence of *Job* and *De Profundis*'. It must be said that Vaughan Williams's loyalty to these two dreariest examples of Parry's art continued to fuel the ire of those who shared the opinions of Shaw and helped to retard the re-evaluation of Parry's major works. Shaw was right in every biting criticism, but English composers were happy to grasp at straws because there had been nothing to follow since Purcell.[1]

Although Elgar created a supreme masterpiece in *Gerontius*, he did not seem to be entirely conscious of what he achieved in terms of structural concepts. Only in *The Kingdom* would he partially carry on the idea of dramatic scenes built on large-scale symphonic structures. Unfortunately Parry's own concepts did not reach the stage of a creative revelation (such as *Gerontius*) or a concrete musical dramatic principle he could put into practice. The all-important gestation period needed to bring a new form into being never took place because of Parry's usual hyperactivity. Following *A Song of Darkness and Light*, the Director of the RCM and squire of Highnam Court began writing *The Music of the Seventeenth Century*, became President of the ISM Orphanage in 1898 and of the International Music Society, British Branch in 1900, he became Chairman of the People's Concert Society, Professor of Music at Oxford University and Member of the London University Commissions (all in 1900), and then in 1905 he took on the duties of a local magistrate.

His usual composing practice of 'hit or miss' carried over into the creation of the Ethical Cantatas. That he felt the necessity to attach sub-titles (indicating the type of musical–dramatic form) to the six works points to a half-realized concept. It was symptomatic that he finally sat down to serious creative work only six months before the scheduled première of the first Ethical Cantata.

The cycle occupied him from 1902 until 1908, the set of six (with their first performances) being *War and Peace* – Symphonic Ode (3 April 1903, Royal Choral Society, Albert Hall), *Voces Clamantium* – Motet (10 September 1903, Hereford Festival), *The Love that Casteth Out Fear* – Sinfonia Sacra (7 September 1904, Gloucester Festival); *The Soul's Ransom* – Sinfonia Sacra (12 September 1906, Hereford Festival); *The Vision of Life* – A Symphonic Poem (26 September 1907, Cardiff Festival – revised for the 1914 Norwich Festival but never performed); and *Beyond These Voices There is Peace* – Motet (9 September 1908, Worcester Festival). All six are scored for soprano, baritone, chorus and orchestra except *The Love that Casteth Out Fear* where he substitutes a contralto for the soprano. In duration they last between 45 and 75 minutes approximately, except for *Voces Clamantium* which is under 30 minutes. Parry wrote the free-verse text himself for *War and Peace*, where A.C. Benson provided some initial assistance, and for *The Vision of Life*. For the other cantatas, he assembled the texts from the Bible with some original lines to shape the structures.

Two are complete failures: *War and Peace* is the weakest score Parry ever composed for chorus and orchestra, and *The Love that Casteth Out Fear* is hopelessly banal, with little of Parry's musical personality in evidence. *Voces Clamantium* begins impressively, but tails off into conventionality after the first half. *Beyond These Voices There is Peace* has attracted strong advocacy: Herbert Howells, Gerald Finzi, Ivor Atkins, W.G. Whittaker and even Vaughan Williams liked all or parts of the score. (Because of this advocacy, it should be revived.) Certainly it contains fine music, and some sense of dramatic momentum, but I find it manic and inferior in many respects to *A Song of Darkness and Light* which it resembles. Both works show a concern for dualism, contrasting material for darkness–light, 'voices'–'peace', encompassed in a broad single movement design and both are unusually brooding and dark in instrumental colouring. They share a preoccupation with Lisztian harmony and thematic transformation and in each case the mood dramatically shifts in the final chorus of triumph. *The Vision of Life* will be discussed later in this study. *The Soul's Ransom*, until recently the least known, is in my opinion his experimental masterpiece, and the only way to reach an understanding of the musical–dramatic principle Parry wished to create is by examining this work.

In an interview with Ingmar Bergman, Jonas Sima quoted Eugene O'Neill, who is supposed to have said: 'Drama that doesn't deal with man's relationship to God is worthless'. Bergman replied: 'Yes, and I have often quoted him; and have been thoroughly misunderstood. Today we say all art is political. But I say all art has to do with ethics, which after all comes to the same thing. It's a matter of attitudes, that's what O'Neill meant'.[2] Parry, like Bergman, realized that, when spiritual faith is absent and religious dogma rejected, ethics becomes the central guiding force behind civilized behaviour. Parry's well known comment to Vaughan Williams 'compose choral music as befits an Englishman and a democrat', becomes a more personal, deeply felt statement, when thought of with this understanding.[3]

Parry's last two published books became increasingly concerned with the ethical implications of music. He saw Bach and Beethoven, his greatest musical heroes, as symbolizing in their attitudes to life and in their creative work, what the composer should represent in society. But though he avidly read the great nineteenth-century philosophers, especially Spencer and Nietzsche, they did not displace the Bible as his main source of ethically inspired poetic prose. The King James Bible could be described as the rose window of English Literature. Like the history of most peoples, it is filled with power politics; and with ethical tracts which counterbalance the decadence and bloodshed caused by politics. It was the prophet's business to set ethical standards, though he claimed this right by divine appointment.

Parry's intense dislike of organized religion did not blind him to the central position which biblical words held in English culture, and he did not see those words as antithetical to his Victorian idealism or the modern philosophy he admired. He manages to combine the humanist concept of man as a developing species, with a firm belief in the essential divinity of man's nature. Despite his agnosticism he was in agreement with the central Christian doctrine that God is a spiritual being, and he builds a memorable choral climax to section two of *The Soul's Ransom* on Christ's assertion to the Woman of Samaria that 'God is a Spirit and they that worship him must worship him in spirit and truth'.

He wanted the text in each work to have a specific philosophic–ethical meaning. This constellation of thoughts was intended to guide the entire composition. Unfortunately his choice of words may have satisfied his moral intellectual concepts but too often it failed to fire him creatively. He remained unaware, to the end of his life, that it was only great poetry which inspired him. It was not his intellect that controlled this process but his half-conscious emotional and intuitive functions which made that all-important decision.

Fortunately, Parry constructed a text for *The Soul's Ransom*[4] that displays a surprising poetic flair and coherence and vividly reflects his profound immediate humanism. This 'Psalm for the Poor' (as it was subtitled) was a challenge to the complacency of Edwardian society and is still apposite today. For once the shaping of the biblical passages (not sourced in the vocal score) and his own poetry bears testimony to Parry's philosophic erudition and literary sensitivity. I have compiled the sources detailed below from the King James Bible and the Old Testament Apocrypha; biblical scholars may be able to cite alternative references.

THE SOUL'S RANSOM
A Psalm for the Poor

CHORUS
Who can number the sands of the sea   *Ecclesiasticus 1:2–5, 26*

BASS SOLO
Hear ye this, O ye people   *Psalm 49*

CHORUS
We look for light   *Isaiah 59: 9–10*

SOPRANO SOLO AND CHORUS
Why are ye so fearful   *Matthew 8: 26 and 5:3*
                                             John 6:63
                                             Matthew 5:6
                                             Matthew 4:4
                                             Matthew 5:11–12
                                             1 John 5:6 and John 4:24

BASS SOLO AND CHORUS
The hand of the Lord was upon me   *Ezekiel 37:1–14*

SOPRANO SOLO
The people that walked in darkness   *Matthew 4:16; Isaiah 49:10, 13*

CHORUS
See now, ye that love the light   *Parry*

The text is remarkable for the fluency with which it moves from the Old Testament Apocrypha, via the Psalms and the Prophets (Isaiah, Ezekiel), to the Beatitudes and the Gnostic-influenced Gospel of John, to shape a cogent central message that man exists as an emanation of the divine. Parry believed man's moral purpose was a humanist task, 'to rate the tempting world aright.' Though he insists on the spiritual nature of the Soul, there is no assertion of individual immortality in the final attainment of 'harmony . . . with that which was and is.' The dualistic thinking which he adopts in *A Song of Darkness and Light* and the earlier *Ethical Cantatas* gives way to a more Eastern concept of all things coalescing into a 'limitless oneness' which 'binds us together', as he describes it in *The Vision of Life*, – nirvana – cessation of the play of opposites, inducing a blissful state. This can also be related to St Paul's *caritas*, 'To crown all there must be love, to bind all together and complete the whole'.

The earlier cantatas structure their musical argument, with varying success, round the opposition of negative and positive conditions, such as darkness–light, war–peace and love–fear. The resolution is achieved by the positive winning the conflict. *The Vision of Life* in this respect develops ideas propounded in the final chorus of *The Soul's Ransom*, 'Where trust is there is love! Where love is there is heaven!' Later works, such as *Beyond These Voices* and *From Death to Life* return to the earlier concept of the play of opposites.

It is evident in the musical structure of *The Soul's Ransom* that Parry wanted to create formal principles on which the Ethical Cantata concept could be based; to achieve this he gathered together stylistic and formal elements from the seventeenth, eighteenth and nineteenth centuries. By 1906 he was an authority on seventeenth-century music and could see cross-connections between tendencies developing in the early German Baroque, towards a mixing of instrumental and vocal style-forms as found in the *Sinfoniae Sacrae* of Heinrich Schütz or the *Geistliche Symphonien* of Andreas Hammerschmidt, and more developed use of similar techniques by the nineteenth-century masters Brahms and Liszt. The two most important influences from the seventeenth century are first, that the text sets the mood, therefore suggesting the various tempi for the compositions (not so obvious a point as it might seem), and second, the use of instrumental transitions, interludes, and short instrumental movements between the vocal sections. The seventeenth-century influence is further emphasized by Parry's adoption of 'Sinfonia Sacra' and 'Motet' as subtitles. With the exception of the fugue, 'The Word of the Lord Most High', in section one of *The Soul's Ransom*, the eighteenth-century forms such as sonata and rondo, are only tangentially alluded to, and even this fugue has seventeenth-century aspects to the movement of its inner parts.

In *The Soul's Ransom*, Parry comes close to creating his new form, not a purely musical one like sonata form, or a dramatic form like Wagnerian music drama, but something akin to *Ein Deutsches Requiem* and Liszt's *Psalm 13*. Of course these two works came into being through sheer force of inspiration and their musical–dramatic structure was born out of immediate necessity (though the evolution of the final version of the Brahms proved a long-term affair). Parry combines techniques employed in these works and carries them a step further by creating a terse, highly organic symphonic poem in four sections. The orchestral interludes and postludes linking the sections serve in the same way as a seventeenth-century ritornello, while the harmony and orchestration are often richly late romantic. But there are many passages where a true twentieth-century starkness is displayed; emphasized by prominent parts for violas, bass clarinet, double bassoon and bass trombone. *The Soul's Ransom* moves from the late seventeenth and early twentieth centuries to an historical and stylistic centre – to meet Beethoven. Before he began work, Parry attended a performance of the re-scored *Voces Clamantium* at the Leeds Festival in 1904 where Beethoven's *Missa Solemnis* 'impressed him more than anything else'.[5] Considering the enormous increase in quality from *The Love that Casteth Out Fear*, it is possible the experience of hearing Beethoven's very symphonic *magnum opus* led him to revalue 'all life and all thought'. His creativity was renewed. *The Soul's Ransom* displays a considerable advance in his symphonic technique.

The tonal scheme is the most complex and subtle of all the *Ethical Cantatas*, perhaps of his entire *œuvre*. Cherubini's monumental *Requiem in C Minor*, Beethoven's Ninth Symphony and *Missa Solemnis*, Wagner's *Parsifal*, Elgar's *Gerontius* and Parry's finest earlier scores form the comprehensive historical backdrop to its harmonic world. Parry was able to assimilate the personal language of *Gerontius* since he had prepared the way for it harmonically in *A Song of Darkness and Light*. If Parry found the less surcharged idiom of *The Apostles* more congenial, his unconscious was drawn into the *Gerontius* orbit where the extreme points in his own style (Mendelssohn *contra* Wagner) were integrated for the first time. The work's title comes from the line in *Gerontius* when the angel sings 'dearly ransomed soul'.

The superb opening section of the prelude (measures 1–42 in the vocal score) contains most of the harmonic-relationship prototypes that Parry develops throughout the score. Here he employs F minor and A flat major with important secondary dominants on G flat major and D major, a liberal use of suspensions and altered chords to construct a wide-ranging harmonic momentum, enhanced by a bold, constantly changing orchestral tessitura and deft contrasts of texture and tempi. The opening of the first chorus with its lilting triplet accompaniment is immediate and magical; it continues to explore the harmonic relationships of the prelude and sets the style for the choral writing throughout. The concluding fugue is a wonderful machine. It is augustly solemn, but its tightly interweaving lines and finely judged harmonic shifts give it plenty of momentum. The short orchestral interlude before the words 'If thou desire wisdom' is one of the most memorable moments.

Section two is the slow movement of this quasi-symphony. Like the other sections it is in two parts, a bass solo which functions as a dramatic introduction and a fine aria for soprano and chorus which concludes with the powerful setting of 'God is a Spirit' mentioned above. The third section functions as a complex and very dark scherzo for bass solo and chorus. There are several telling programmatic strokes such as the music which follows 'in a valley that was full of bones'; several fine modulations and the whole has a Handelian mastery and sense of inevitability.

These extended recitative–ariosi for the bass-baritone in the second and third sections are the dramatic kernel of *The Soul's Ransom*; multi-faceted and serving

Ex. 17   piano reduction from Prelude, *The Soul's Ransom*

Ex. 18   from opening chorus *The Soul's Ransom*

Ex. 19 orchestral interlude from *The Soul's Ransom* piano reduction

to drive forward the narrative and thematic development of the music. The soprano complements with two arias of operatic dimensions; the second, a setting of 'The People that Walked in Darkness' (famous from Handel's *Messiah*) which opens the fourth section, is one of Parry's high points, a radiant passionate outpouring which leads into the final chorus, the concluding compositional triumph. Its seraphic main idea, perfectly wedded to the text, is organized rhythmically in a pastoral, lilting slow 6/8, but Parry creates an innovative structure by employing extreme changes of texture and unusual phrase lengths which gives it a panoply of Dantesque perspective. The orchestration too is unusually glowing for Parry. He has understood the closing music from *Parsifal* and that most marvellous movement for chorus and orchestra, the Sanctus and Benedictus from Beethoven's *Missa Solemnis*.

When the final chorus of *The Soul's Ransom* is performed at the tempo recommended to June Aberdeen by Sir Adrian Boult (who at 92 was making his first acquaintance with the work), it is a moving and original music experience. If rushed, the perfectly judged architecture implodes and a sense of anti-climax is inevitable; it is not a romp but a profoundly reflective meditation. There is evidence that Parry, who as a conductor tended to rush things, fell into this trap at the final rehearsal before the première.

Many of the ideas he tried to implement in the *Ethical Cantatas*, especially *The Soul's Ransom* and its successor, his would-be testament the symphonic poem *The Vision of Life* were remarkably innovative; for example, that musical techniques of the distant past can integrate with contemporary developments has become an established practice in the twentieth century (as in Stravinsky and the Italian Renaissance). Parry might have been surprised to learn that the forms he created have a curious resemblance to hypothetical musical compositions found in Thomas Mann's *Dr Faustus*. Mann has his Nietzsche/Faust-like hero Adrian Leverkühn compose large symphonic cantatas whose structures show the same musical antecedents as those stated above. Adrian's last masterpiece, a 'Symphonic Cantata' called *The Lamentations of Dr Faustus*, is certainly a very Parry-like concept.

Parry wrote his own non-biblical text for his most Faustian, almost existential conception *The Vision of Life*. This proved fatal: whilst the work took further strides towards his conception of a new art form, his short-breathed prose poem, which reads like rejected lines from Goethe's *Faust*, Nietzsche's *Zarathustra* and Hardy's *The Dynasts*, doomed the result. As he stated after conducting the final rehearsal in Cardiff: 'Thought it rather tedious'.[6] His inspirations had fled – though Elgar was highly impressed, and always remained so.

For all its literary shortcomings the text speaks well of Parry's crusading humanity with its attack on the 'Empire of the Proud Ones' where the free 'As slaves shall they slay one another.' Indeed it is no optimistic vision where:

> The World is brooding, and we go stumbling
> Through wrecks of ancient learning.

and, as stated earlier, there is no conventional Christian consolation in:

> Limitless oneness binds us together
> Passing on life from one to another.

Elgar was right when he wrote that 'Your Cardiff "Vision" was, I conclude, too strong for the Church[7] and neither the Three Choirs nor the Leeds Festival were ever to take it up.

On balance, the work deserves a sensitive modern performance. Parry expanded the orchestration and recomposed the final chorus for the aborted 1914 Norwich Festival. The heavier orchestration may not improve matters: *The Vision of Life* is meant to be a philosophical meditation not a choral orchestral *tour de force*. So it is to *The Soul's Ransom*, that we must return.

The Three Choirs Festival première took place in Hereford Cathedral on 12 September 1906. The composer conducted with the French-Canadian soprano Marie Albani and the Irish baritone Harry Plunkett Greene (Parry's son-in-law). Typically there was only one orchestral rehearsal on 10 September, when they 'went just straight through, no time for more – went fairly well but finale evidently a failure'. Parry wrote laconically in his diary. The performance itself allayed some of his fears: 'The chorus pulled themselves together grandly in The Soul's Ransom and it went splendidly, barring one accident by Harry and a strange aberration of Mme. Albani. People seemed pleased.' It is doubtful, however, whether there was a second performance.[8] *The Times*, in a generally favourable review remarked that 'the instrumental introduction is most impressive and finely scored' and after a 'series of noble choral numbers' concluded that the finale 'seems at first hearing the most successful part of the work'. This comment would suggest Parry resolved the problems that had dogged the rehearsal.

It is not surprising such a splendid score as *The Soul's Ransom* has an important if unrecognized place in English music: it is one of the first successful works to move away from nineteenth-century oratorio and it foreshadows the mature compositions of Parry's own pupils, Vaughan Williams, Holst and Howells. It is arguably the link work between Elgar's *The Dream of Gerontius* (1900) and Vaughan Williams's *A Sea Symphony* (1909).

8   The People who Knew Parry – and the People Parry Knew

Skating on the river at Richmond continued for some weeks; Hubert Parry, Fred Verney, Lord Archie Campbell, and my brothers were all proficient – Hubert reckless, a passionate performer, but he did nothing slowly, he put joy and go into everything he did, were it teaching, composing, conducting, or friendship – at the last he was an adept.

(W.B. Richmond, The Richmond Papers)[1]

I can see him striding into the hall on the first morning of the College Term, a carnation from Highnam in his buttonhole, a slip of paper on which a few notes were scribbled in his left hand, and his right hand free to grasp that of any boy or girl who greeted him in its enveloping grip. Sometimes the right hand was used to deliver to some unsuspecting youth that smack on the back which was his favourite token of recognition and which has made many of us still associate a sharp pain between the shoulder-blades with the glow of the Director's presence.

(H.C. Colles, College Addresses)[2]

After Parry's death, the ramifications of his social interconnections, his artistic circle and his academic status were soon clouded by an obscurity that became all-pervasive. The isolated biography, or volume of reminiscences, covering the period was naturally concerned with a specific individual; little or no attempt was made to depict the complex centrifugal structure in which those individuals existed. Studies of Arthur Balfour, Robert Bridges, Burne-Jones, Morris, the Pankhursts, Isadora Duncan and others, rarely stopped to consider the implications that most of them knew each other and they *all* knew Hubert Parry.

There has never been a comprehensive investigation into the cultural significance of this late Victorian society whose protagonists all met in the country houses of a select, interlocked group of the aristocracy. At its edges it entertained the monarchy, drew in the military, explorers, philosophers, designers and social reformers. Not since the reign of Elizabeth I, had such a cultural–political convergence occurred in English Society. Unfortunately its influence was doomed to be short lived. By the time the country re-emerged from the holocaust of the First World War, the majority of its leaders had died, not just the older generation, but many of the heirs to those country estates: Charterises, Wyndhams, Asquiths, Grenfells, and Gladstones were felled to waterlogged graves in the trenches, where, as Ivor Gurney described it, 'Sheer hideousness is the prettiest thing.'[3] Never again could an English composer claim to be friends with six successive Prime Ministers: Gladstone, Salisbury, Rosebery, Balfour, Campbell-Bannerman and Asquith.

Parry's alarming capacity to live several lives in tandem ensured that he connected with a bewildering spectrum of society ranging from the famous to the infamous, the venerated to the obscure. Who now can judge whether dinner with Princess Louise, an intensive session skating in Regents Park where he learned 'some new dodges' from 'the cracks', an hour with Harold Darke playing over his chorale preludes or taking the 'Brownies' canoeing was the more meaningful social encounter? The surviving evidence suggests all were meaningful expressions of his life, though his diary implies that he was never comfortable in any of them for long periods; therefore each facet fulfilled a complementary need. The result was a life rich in diversity and remarkable for the light it brought to so many people's lives, not just his family and pupils, but the myriad of forgotten folk who could also claim they knew Sir Hubert Parry.

Throughout his life Parry encountered people from every walk of life; however, the number who could claim to know him intimately was extremely few. Moreover they do not form a composite group, and we can only hazard theories about the distinction between friend and acquaintance. For his enthusiasm ensured that he frequently exerted a memorable impact. The fact that he was prompted continually to fill the void of loneliness does not mitigate the significance of his engaging role as a restless kindling spirit moving across the hierarchies of complex social structures.

Gambier Parry's status ensured that Parry moved with ease in a country house environment where there was a fluid mix of the educated classes. At the centre were the extended families of Gambiers, Fynes Clintons, Majendies, Bakers and Lears. Isabella's mother 'Granny Clinton' lived on until Parry was twenty-two and the round of visits to relatives at Bayfordbury (near Hertford), Bishopstone, Hedingham and Salisbury formed the nexus of his domestic circle; Graves observes that Parry was 'a very good family man'.

Parry was particularly fond of his cousins Willie Baker and Lewis Majendie, thirteen years his senior. The Majendies owned Headingham Castle which became a second home to Hubert. Just across the River Severn from Highnam, at Elmore Court, was his childhood friend Anselm Guise, whose family originally owned Highnam, but Anselm died in 1863. Parry's sister recounts that 'he always spoke of him in a peculiarly gentle voice'.[4]

In terms of easy camaraderie, it was his cousin Edward Hamilton (1848–1907) who could claim to know him best. His father was Bishop of Salisbury, much beloved by Parry, and married to Ethelinda's sister Mary. As mentioned in Chapter 1, the cousins were the same age and both members of Evans House at Eton, from which they went to Oxford together, Parry at Exeter and Hamilton at Christ Church. Known at Eton as 'Flab', Hamilton was an able musician who shared Parry's love of Bach and his religious scruples. His grandfather, the Revd. Lear, was a one-time tutor of Baron Herbert and, as Lady Maude reminded him in 1895, Hamilton was George Pembroke's best friend.

Pembroke was only one of several members of the aristocracy with whom Parry was familiar. For example, Lord and Lady Sherborne were regular visitors to Highnam and Lady Sherborne, a fine musician, took a serious interest in Parry's progress.[5] Over the years Parry and Lady Maude became friends with such society musicians as Lady Muir Mackenzie, the Duchess of Leeds and the Countess of Radnor. But it was Eton and Oxford which provided the mainspring for Parry's social life; institutions that gave a Victorian gentleman membership of a formidable exclusive club.

Of the names that dominated Evans House, it was the relationship with the Lyttelton brothers which would prove most durable, of whom the Hon. Spenser Lyttelton (1847–1913), was the most musical and closest in age. These unconventional sons of the 4th Baron Lyttelton of Hagley Hall were 'bred in an atmosphere of fireside dialectics' and cricket matches in the Long Gallery, to the lasting detriment of its structure, and all eight brothers distinguished themselves in the Eton cricket team. Their sister Lavinia Lyttelton recalled boisterous meals, when Baron Lyttelton would indulge in pelting matches against his sons with balls of bread before the port was circulated, and 'the noise and merriment suddenly ending perhaps in a return to books or to a lot of part-singing, and to Spenser's beautiful voice singing song after song'.[6]

Spenser, a confirmed bachelor, lent support throughout Parry's life, often with Hamilton, Arthur Balfour (1848–1930) or his own cousin Mary Gladstone (1847–1928). They were present at Wilton and Highnam house parties, at the Gloucester performances of *Oh Lord Thou Hast Cast Us Out* and *Intermezzo Religioso*. Spenser was present at many Parry first performances; he sang in the 1879 concert in Balfour's house and attended the dinner party before Parry sailed to South America. He and Hamilton, a decade later, were guests at Highnam for the Parrys' Silver Wedding in 1898. He became a member of the Council of the Royal College of Music, which included friends such as Robin Benson, a fellow Eton footballer, next-door neighbour in Kensington Square and a fine-art connoisseur, and Lionel Benson, the conductor of the Magpie Madrigal Society for whom Parry wrote many part-songs.

Spenser's death in 1913 prompted a revealing self-reflection by Parry in a letter to Dorothea:

> I took it for granted he would outlast me and that some day when my work was not so exacting I should be able to enjoy the ancient friendship to the full. One never thinks of some things till too late; and I remember with pain how, when he would sometimes come into my room here when I was busy and sit down and talk, I used to get restive, when I ought to have been glad to get any opportunity to talk to him.[7]

Parry's overcrowded schedule after the 1880s often robbed intimate friendships of much potential richness.

The Pembrokes and the Lytteltons drew Parry into the heart of England's political life. Spenser's father, as a young man, had journeyed to Italy with William Ewart Gladstone (1809–98). There they fell in love with the sisters Mary and Catherine Glynne, and thus Lord Lyttelton and Gladstone became brothers-in-law. In time Parry knew all their nineteen children. He first met Gladstone in 1869 through his daughter Mary, who attended a Willis's Rooms concert (on 7 April) in which Frank Pownall sang one of Parry's *Anacreontic Odes*. The next day he was playing to Mrs Gladstone and Agnes Gladstone and 'spent such a morning as I shall never forget'. The Gladstones proved supportive to Parry's suit for Lady Maude, and Mary Gladstone's diaries testify to Parry's integration into the Gladstone–Lyttelton–Balfour social whirl.

On January 16th 1870, Mary Gladstone wrote: 'Hubert Parry's *Kyrie* successfully performed (at Hawarden Church) and highly approved of, which makes me as cocky as if I had been the inventor thereof.' In June she visited Oxford with Lady Adine Murray (Lady Maude's cousin) and, in the Hall of Exeter College, 'the very 1st person we set eyes on was the Archangel playing a duet with one called Powell – such fun seeing him again. It was a delicious concert.' This was no sublime vision, simply Parry's nickname; later that evening she 'went over to the Eton and Harrow ball for one dance with Hubert Parry, such a valse, quite mad.'[8] The heavenly accolades continue into 1871: 'Hubert Parry and Eddie (Hamilton) came to tea, the former played to us for an hour gem after gem' and a few weeks later at 'dinner with the Farquars; Hubert Parry there who played me into Paradise as usual.'[9]

These impromptu concerts were often elaborate affairs where celebrities such as Gounod had the habit of arriving unexpectedly and joining in. Parry sometimes resented the strain of being entertainer to the aristocracy, especially when he felt out of sympathy with the company. One visit to Wilton in 1873 prompted a severe invective about George's sporting friends: 'All aristocrats, specimens of the Upper Ten, Society's ornaments! It is enough to make one a bitter democrat to be long in the company of people brought up in luxury, utterly without aspirations of any kind.'[10]

Parry remained an ardent Gladstone supporter, although not uncritical, especially when the Prime Minister indulged in 'sophistries' as a dialectical gladiator. On Home Rule he persisted in accord with his policies; and we find him breakfasting with the old man when he was again Prime Minister in the 1880s. Gladstone lent active support to the founding of the Royal College of Music and spoke at the first meeting in St James's Palace in 1882, along with the Prince of Wales and the Archbishop of Canterbury, A.C. Tait (1811–82), a meeting which Parry attended.

In the 1870s Pembroke published two political tracts, *South Sea Bubbles* and *Roots: a Plea for Tolerance*. A lively correspondence ensued with Gladstone but over time Pembroke became more and more an ingrained Tory. So at Wilton, Parry soon found himself a political minority of one: 'The violence with which the family [Lord and Lady Pembroke and Sidney Herbert] talk about Gladstone is perfectly astounding. As Eddie said, it is quite indecent'; and some years later Parry was moved to declare that 'Toryism is a form of atrophy which is induced by centuries of over-eating.'[11]

These divergences were symptomatic of a fundamental shift in consciousness. Once Parry left Oxford, agnosticism replaced orthodoxy, liberal radicalism replaced Tory compliance, and criticism replaced allegiance to aristocratic values. Nonetheless the intermeshed Victorian political system ensured that Liberals and Tories belonged to one social club. There could never be a breach with Pembroke and Parry was the first to be distressed when the Earl turned down Lord Salisbury's invitation to accept the under-secretaryship of the Colonies in 1887. By that time Pembroke was already engaged in his losing battle with consumption. A few years later Parry describes Salisbury at an Academy dinner: 'I had been watching him at dinner and noticed that he looked as glum as could be and never spoke a word to his neighbour; but directly he began his speech his lumpy face quite changed and he kept the whole company in a roar of laughter.'[12]

In the 1870s, Parry found the opportunity to articulate his new-found philosophical expansion at 'The Essay and Discussion Club', which met at Hugh Montgomery's house. The artist Pepys Cockerell later recalled:

> We used to dine together and read and discuss short essays on various subjects – moral, philosophical or political. (Hubert and I were ardent students of Herbert Spencer). It brought about a good deal of intimacy . . . Hubert was well informed, impetuous, hardly calm enough to express himself with balance. The evenings ended with German songs by H.F.M. [Montgomery] and impromptus on the piano by Hubert.[13]

The Club consisted of Hamilton, Frank Pownall, Parry's friend from Oxford and later Registrar of the Royal College of Music, Robin Benson, Pembroke (occasionally) and Spenser Lyttelton. Later Parry became acquainted with Herbert Spencer and engaged in a fruitful correspondence on the music of primitive peoples.

Pepys Cockerell and Hugh de Fellenberg Montgomery continued to be part of Parry's and Lady Maude's intimate circle, and after Parry's death Cockerell wrote to Graves of his friend's physical magnetism, 'his regular features and flashing grey eyes. It was this which first attracted me to him, before I understood the man himself.' Parry recorded dinners with 'grand talks', congenial singing and playing and one particular 'evening fit for the Gods' when Cockerell and Robin Benson discussed Walt Whitman's poems. Cockerell 'derided their formless bathos' and preferred Shelley; Parry wrote afterwards that Whitman 'belongs to a totally different order, but I don't give up my sympathy for him all the same. Possibly it is the democratic tinge that fetches me in him and the way in which he faces our human problems and speaks ruggedly himself – and such a strange, wild, at the same time hopeful self.'

Cockerell delighted in Parry's enthusiasms from fungi – 'bringing home the most poisonous-looking specimens to be fried' – to motoring – when he 'always exceeded the speed limit' – to his inexhaustible delight in wild weather. In 1913 Parry invited Cockerell for a yachting trip, saying 'you know I shan't start unless there's a gale.'

Montgomery, a friend from Eton and Oxford, was a fine singer for whom Parry composed his *Four Shakespeare Sonnets* in 1874. When the Parrys moved to Kensington Square, Montgomery came round and 'we christened the Drawing Room with a Brahms song and my *Shakespeare Sonnets*'.

Spenser Lyttelton's youngest brother Alfred (1857–1913) also became an ardent supporter of Parry's music, including the *Ethical Cantatas*. By his middle twenties he was an established London lawyer, albeit with a 'leathery heart', as he confessed to Mary Gladstone. Then he met Laura Tennant (daughter of Sir Charles Tennant, the wealthy Liberal MP, who was soon bedazzled by Alfred's athletic prowess: 'How I love to watch his great strong figure clad in flannels and his mighty stroke that is meteor-like in its flight', she wrote ecstatically.[14]

Their marriage took place in May 1885, when Gladstone proposed the toast 'about the virtues of the wedded state', and on 13 June they attended the farewell dinner, given by Robin Benson in Kensington Square, the day before Parry departed for South America. The party included the Burne-Jones family, Spenser Lyttelton, Lady Maude and Lady Lonsdale – 'all very kind and friendly'.[15] The following year Laura Lyttelton died in childbrith, a sad reminder of why Parry had been so concerned for Lady Maude during her two pregnancies. The death of Laura had a profound effect on her friends. Parry noted: 'It does bewilder one to think of such wonderful vivacity and vigorous life being extinguished.'[16] Burne-Jones wrote: 'We shall all feel it, all of us, to the end of our days.'[17] He designed the memorial tablet for her and frequently, in subsequent paintings, would recapture her face.

During the mourning, her friends formed the concept of 'the Souls'. At its heart were about forty people though others, such as Parry and Lady Maude, were drawn in by family connections. Time enhanced Laura's mystique, but the process was nurtured by her vivacious sister, Margot. Parry would see much of Margot Tennant (1864–1945) over the decades as she became Margot Asquith, wife of Herbert Asquith, Liberal Prime Minister (1908–16).

The Souls had no official function or declared purpose; indeed they were curiously private, concerned about home entertainments, witty conversation, flirtations and frequent affairs. The latter were condoned but not allowed to rupture the outward fabric of marriage. At their centre was Parry's Eton contemporary, the Hon. Arthur Balfour, 'King Arthur', a multi-millionaire and nephew of Lord Salisbury. Outwardly devoid of sexual passion, Balfour contented himself with a platonic relationship with Lady Elcho, *née* Mary Wyndham. The brood of children she gave her husband Hugo Charteris, later Earl of Wemyss and March, included Lady Cynthia Asquith who befriended D.H. Lawrence, and a daughter by Wilfred Scawen Blunt.[18] Mary Elcho and Balfour attended the Parrys' warming party for Kensington Square in February 1887, in company with '3 B-J's' and Eddie Hamilton.

We sense the *joie de vivre* of such gatherings from Mary Gladstone's diaries, for example in 1882 'coming back from Wagner Concert. Came home 10 squashed in one compartment, including a smoking maukin. Everybody ate chocolate and talked at once. A.J. B[alfour], Maude Parry, Wortleys, Comptons and Mr. Baring.' Mary Gladstone was another vainly enamoured with Balfour until, at the age of 37, she married the attractive curate of Hawarden, eight years her junior, and produced a daughter at the age of 42, the irrepressible 'Dossie' immortalized in Burne-Jones's drawings.

Mary Elcho's sister Pamela married Edward Tennant, later Lord Glenconner, which formalized the connection between Wyndhams and Tennants. Their brother George shared their 'soulful' eyes, and in 1887 his looks won him Lady Sibell Grosvenor (1855–1929), the richest widow in England, and daughter-in-law to the Duke of Westminster. The Wyndham's parents, Percy and the bohemian Madeleine Wyndham, were also close friends of Lady Maude. Thus Wyndhams married Tennants, Tennants married Lytteltons, Ribblesdales and Asquiths. Another politician among the Souls was George Curzon (1859–1925), son of Baron Scarsdale and Conservative MP for Southport by 1886. Parry mentions a dinner party given by Lord Ribblesdale in 1890 where 'Arthur Balfour abused the humour of the *Meistersinger* and said he found it very heavy and Teutonic; George Curzon pleased me by sticking up for it.'[19]

The Souls frequently met at the residences of 'The Aunts', Ashridge in Hertfordshire (home of Adelaide, Lady Brownlow) and Wilton. Getey, Lady Pembroke, daughter of the Earl of Shrewsbury, was Lady Brownlow's sister. The sisters failed to bear any heirs and the amorous Harry Cust was doomed to wait in vain to inherit the Brownlow estate from his uncle, who eventually outlived him. In the meantime Cust edited the *Pall Mall Gazette* and helped launch H.G. Wells, who became another Souls intimate.

Getey's eccentricities confounded not only Lady Maude. In a letter to Mary Elcho, Balfour recounts his stay at Wilton in 1890:

> Our hostess's [Getey Pembroke] oddities, too amused me more and annoyed me less than usual – She was more than ever puzzled about the universe – had a brand new theory of evolution which she endeavoured (wholly without success) to explain to Hubert Parry, Alfred [Lyttelton] and me in turn: – considered that the (relatively) diminutive size of the Planet on which we have the misfortune to crawl for a few troubled years was a conclusive proof of the absurdity of xtianity [*sic*], and altogether was on her best form. With all this, thoroughly amicable and even delightful.[20]

Maude records that the aged Tennyson 'talked about Getey, said he was so devoted to her that he went about with her so much that people began to talk.'[21]

The Souls' political significance soon became apparent after the 1880s as the great ministries of Gladstone and Salisbury swept them into the political arena. Balfour, an MP from 1874, was groomed by Salisbury to become Conservative leader in the Commons, where he distinguished himself as an adept Chief Secretary for Ireland from 1887 to 1891. When Salisbury's health failed, Balfour – as the leading light amongst his relatives, nicknamed 'Hotel Cecil' – succeeded to the premiership (1902–5). Parry continued to remain a close friend: 'That was splendid fun coming up in Arthur Balfour's motor. I hope you weren't any the worse either from the rain. I enjoyed it all, including the rain!'[22] (Parry wrote to Willie Leigh in 1904.) Balfour was attacked for his 'unfortunate love of music' and he shared Parry's addiction to motors, while his medicinal use of cocaine curiously parallels Maude's dependency on veronal. His subsequent capacity for political survival was wittily compared by Winston Churchill to 'a powerful cat walking delicately and unsoiled across a rather muddy street.'[23]

In 1898 Curzon was appointed Viceroy of India and on his return to England in 1907 was elected Chancellor of Oxford University, when Parry was still Professor of Music. In these capacities the two men encountered Kaiser Wilhelm II at Windsor Castle, where

> the Kaiser came in, in uniform, with D.C.L. robes over it and stood facing us. Curzon made an admirable speech and the Kaiser responded. Then he shook hands with all us in very frank and pleasant fashion, saying a few words when he found opportunity. He completely fascinated one, and I quite fell in love with him.[24]

By then Asquith was Prime Minister, back in 1894 when Margot Tennant became his second wife he was already Gladstone's Home Secretary. His friend Spenser Lyttelton became private secretary to Gladstone (his uncle) during the 1880s and 1890s, as was Sir Edward Hamilton who rose to Under-Secretary of State at the Treasury. Alfred Lyttelton (a Liberal MP from 1895) was Colonial Secretary in Balfour's Government from 1903 to 1905, and George Wyndham (a Conservative MP from 1889) had acted as Balfour's Private Secretary during his time as Irish Secretary. In 1903 Balfour promoted him, disastrously, into the Cabinet as Chief

Secretary for Ireland, but drink and failing concentration contributed to his dismissal in 1905. Harry Cust found time away from love affairs to serve twice as Conservative MP and Willy Grenfell reflected the interchangeability of party allegiances by becoming a Liberal MP (1882–6) and later a Conservative MP (1900–5). His wife Ettie, infamous for her dislike of music, once observed to Parry: 'I hate music don't you?'[25] The question is likely to have been intentional and calculated to see its effect on Parry and the rest of the company. Since several composers have certainly hated music at different stages in their life, the comment may have been merely sympathetic. Whatever the real meaning she and Parry became good friends. As Lady Desborough, she arranged many notable concerts at Taplow Court; she claimed they allowed her the time for planning her next house party.

Political power gradually blurred any distinctions between the Souls and other Establishment groupings so that by 1900 they were the Establishment. During Victoria's final years, Sidney Pembroke was Master of the Queen's Household and Michael Pembroke held important diplomatic posts in Denmark, and then America. Their sisters Mary and Gladys had added further aristocratic connections through their marriages to the Catholic philosopher Freddie, Baron von Heugel and the Liberal Marquess of Ripon. The family's snobbish attitudes are wittily recounted by Lady Maude when she visited her aunt, Lady Ailesbury, after Thomas Gambier Parry's death in November 1888. Parry records that: 'The first thing her ladyship said was (in a most concerned way) "My dear, I hear you have not gained anything". Maude could not for the life of her think what she meant, but at length it came out she was afflicted because we had no increase in fortune so to speak of.'[26]

During Parry's directorship of the RCM, the Prince of Wales and his brother-in-law Prince Christian of Schleswig-Holstein were presidents. While Parry's relations with both men were cordial, he and Lady Maude were most fond of Queen Victoria's fourth daughter Princess Louise (1848–1939). A talented sculptor and painter, she infuriated her mother by falling in love with the sculptor Boehm and then refusing to have children by her 'arranged' marriage to the Marquess of Lorne. Parry had known Lord Lorne since student days when they would play fives. In the 1900s the Parrys were still part of the Princess's circle. In 1903, after a crowded day, 'the conductor of the Amsterdam Orchestra [Mengelberg] and his wife and the Russian composer Glazounov had to be shown over the college. To the Philharmonic concert for a while. Back early to pick up M. and take her to Princess Louise's, where we had music and supper that kept us till 1 in the morning.'[27] Graves makes the point that Parry was 'no courtier: he had no illusions as to the divinity of royal houses and . . . went so far as to recognize that Royalties might be "duffers of the first water"'[28] However, Princess Louise, always an exception, was duly forgiven when she arrived late for a college concert and totally disrupted it by insisting on sitting next to Parry.

The Souls prided themselves on their artistic discernment and set out to absorb leading painters, writers and actors into their orbit on equal terms. In consequence they became the nucleus for a cultural elite. Parry, early on, came into contact with Edward Burne-Jones (1833–98) and William Morris (1831–96). The studied aestheticism of Burne-Jones's paintings belies the fact that he and Morris, and their assistants in 'The Firm', were commercial craftsmen working in several media from stained glass to textiles, furniture, wallpapers and wood panelling. With the designer of ceramic tiles, William de Morgan, they brought a new regard for light, colour and textural refinement to Victorian decorative art. Burne-Jones's wistful, enigmatic women in soft, flowing dresses became exemplars for the Souls, who in turn became his models; thus Mary Elcho, Violet Granby and Laura Tennant influenced – and were influenced by – Burne-Jones's perspective. Parry's decision to incorporate The Firm's designs into Rustington was entirely consistent with the Souls' aesthetic.

Burne-Jones, his wife Georgiana and their two children, were neighbours, both in Kensington and at their country home in Rottingdean, not far from Rustington. Burne-Jones's nephews, the young Rudyard Kipling and Stanley Baldwin often visited, so it is likely Parry met them during this time. William de Morgan and his wife, the painter Evelyn Pickering, were already acquaintances before their marriage in the 1880s and in the same decade the Parrys were dining regularly with the Anglo-Dutch painter Lawrence Alma-Tadema.

Parry's acquaintance with G.F. Watts and Frederick Leighton went back to his youth and Leighton House is now the most famous testament to a time when the artist's house became an expression of his creative vision, a working studio, an opportunity for social concourse and a venue for contemporary music-making. Within this involuted artistic society Burne-Jones, particularly, was Parry's friend until his death but William Blake Richmond (1842–1921) was an even closer familiar. Today he is little more than a name but in his twenties he was court painter for Queen Victoria and later responsible for the decoration of St Paul's Cathedral. Parry considered his work unequal but the two men were an endless source of mutual encouragement. Parry taught Richmond composition, Richmond taught Parry painting. The Richmonds lived in Beaver Lodge, Hammersmith, but summers were spent at Littlehampton.

Richmond met Parry at Oxford in 1869, possibly at the home of Dean Liddell, Dean of Christ Church and subsequently Vice-Chancellor. Richmond had lived previously with the Liddells, when he produced a portrait of the Dean's daughters Ina, Alice and Edith. Parry was a constant inmate of the Deanery, and a great favourite with Mrs. Liddell and her striking daughters. They were all musical and Parry often performed at their festive parties. A typical diary entry mentions going to the Deanery, after an 'Adelphi' (club) dinner, where he had 'a most delightful evening playing and singing and bear fighting to any extent.' Today the Liddells are best known through the Head of Mathematics at Christ Church, the Revd Charles Dodgson, another familiar of Parry, who – as Lewis Carroll – published *Alice's Adventures in Wonderland* in 1867. *Through the Looking Glass (and what Alice found there)* followed in 1871; but 'Alice' was Alice Liddell and the stories were made up to entertain the Dean's daughters. Alice was a young woman by the time Parry knew her and the most 'conspicuous débutante' at a ball in Blenheim Palace in 1867, though Ina always appears to have been his favourite. Shortly before Dean Liddell retired at the age of 80, in 1891, Parry dropped in to the Deanery to revive old memories with Mrs. Liddell.

Richmond was an appealing eccentric, believing in ghosts, fond of practical jokes and a constant source of bemusement. Maude recounts one of her notorious train journeys in his company:

Up to town with Mr. Richmond. He was very funny in the train insisted upon shutting both the windows for fear we should spoil our beautiful eyes. Fortunately he went to sleep and we were able then to get a little air. When he woke up he said he felt sick, and rapidly became sicker and sicker. We implored him to sit next to the window. On reaching Woking he cheered up at the sight of the cemetery. Said what a terrible thing it would be if I got buried next to a bounder and then at the last day they would take me for Mrs. Bounder.[29]

Richmond had lost his first wife in the first year of their marriage and afterwards journeyed to Italy. There he too fell ill and was nursed by the beneficent Mrs Gladstone. One day while he was convalescing, Franz Liszt walked into his studio and with the remark, 'Shall I show you how to play Schumann?', seated himself at Richmond's hired piano and brought out of it sounds which his listener described as the greatest musical treat of his life.[30]

Richmond knew the Gladstone and the Lyttelton families from the 1860s, and dinner parties at the B-J's (as Parry called the Burne-Jones family) Parrys and Richmonds witnessed a dithyrambic interweaving of personalities that spawned memorable conversations. For example it was at the Richmonds' that Morris, according to Parry, 'indulged in a wonderful tirade against Americans: "I hate Americans – They're the idlest lot of scoundrels in the world. They never do anything. It's too much trouble for them to walk across the road. America's the most hideous country on the globe. – There is not a tree in it from one end to the other".' Parry notes that 'B.J. thought it a pity he [Morris] so diffused his powers in various lines and brought nothing to the highest perfection he might have been capable of with more concentration and patience. But we disagreed as to whether any other way of work would have been possible to him.'[31]

Parry's estimation of Burne-Jones increased with the years and we find him in 1890 going 'to see the two nearly finished pictures of the Sleeping Beauty series which really seem superb and quite snuff out the heaps of old things round them in the studio. The old King in his curiously rich bower of a green theme is magnificent, and the little sleeping maiden lovely in colour and design.'[32] It must have made a powerful impression to see a version of his own myth painted by a close friend. (Burne-Jones had also lost his mother at birth.) Like many of his friends, Parry had blinked at 'Ned' Jones's election to the Academy in 1886 and the prospect of his 'appearing among the Philistines and Prosers for the first time, and queer he will look.'[33]

Burne-Jones, the Garretts and the Richmonds were not the only friends to have local summer residences; Edward Dannreuther was also nearby at Hastings. These families made up an ideal holiday fraternity for Parry and Lady Maude who always preferred informal domestic entertaining to large gatherings – not that visits to Rustington were relaxing. Graves recounts how Parry initiated one guest into sailing:

She accepted readily, warning him that she knew nothing of boats and would probably be sick. Parry paid no attention to this warning; they started, and when Parry gave her the tiller while he went to look after the sails, she had to explain that she really could not understand his orders about 'keeping her in the wind'. Shortly afterwards he abruptly asked her, 'Can you swim in a skirt?' and when she said 'No', rejoined 'Then take it off, as we shall probably be in the water soon'. Happily the emergency did not arise.[34]

When such anecdotes are viewed in the context of Parry's infamous 'smack on the back', it is obvious he delighted in getting a rise out of people. One does not need Freud or Jung to know that this behaviour pattern is the common outcome of neglect in childhood and the 'smack on the back' remained an effective mechanism for attracting attention, particularly at the College.

Parry's diary records a host of artistic personalities, both famous and forgotten, who rubbed shoulders with the Souls. These include writers such as Matthew Arnold, Herbert Spencer, Pearl Craigie, Herbert Beerbohm Tree (who produced *Hypatia* in 1894 with Parry's incidental music and Alma-Tadema's set designs), Mrs Patrick Campbell (who performed *As You Like It* at Wilton) and Oscar Wilde, who annoyed Parry by taking on George Wyndham quite unsuccessfully. Other notabilities included Joseph Chamberlain, Henry James, and Thomas Hardy, whose novels Parry and Maude greatly admired; Parry dined next to him in 1914 at an Academy dinner, and described him as 'amiable and gentle'. Still preserved at Shulbrede is a charming note from Isadora Duncan thanking Parry for presenting her in performance at the New Gallery. The hint of scent still lingers on the pale violet paper.

Mrs Craigie reappears as a pianist, one time with Natalia Janotha (a pupil of Clara Schumann) and Lady Randolph Churchill in a charity performance of Bach's Triple Concerto conducted by Parry at St James Hall in 1898. 'The rehearsal on June 11 was made the occasion for photographing the performers, including Janotha's cat and icon, about which she was very anxious. The concerto went pretty fairly at the concert, 'Lady Randolph pounding along, Mrs Craigie gently helping in the background and Janotha looking like a war-horse.'[35]

By the time Parry had taken on the Directorship of the R.C.M. he had less patience for the Souls' artifice and they in turn were growing older, less original. On 8 February 1896 he: 'Dined with Lady Elcho, Burne-Jones and Lady B.J., Arthur Balfour, Asquith, and Horners, Evan Charteris, Haldane, Godfrey Webb etc. Conversation very artificial – a sort of business.'[36] Nonetheless friendships endured. In 1907 Alfred Lyttelton writes affectionately: 'My dear Hubert – I was 50 last week but felt 18 after hearing your beautiful and noble work. Were I a millionaire I should always have half an hour of, say, the "Sirens" before I made a speech. Then I should have the reputation of an orator, for your "musik" transfigures me.'[37]

Like the Lytteltons, the Garretts were members of the Liberal Party inner circle; and Millicent Garrett was married to Henry Fawcett (1833–84), the blind economist and Postmaster-General in Gladstone's Government. At Rustington, Parry mentions being struck by Fawcett's fearlessness when he walked and bathed in the sea. Mrs Fawcett was a leading educational reformer who helped found Newnham College, Cambridge, a novelist and a radical. It is likely the Parrys also knew her illustrious sister Elizabeth Garrett Anderson, the first qualified woman doctor in England.

Lady Maude had long sympathized with the Garretts and the Pankhursts in their fight for women's rights, rejection of fine clothes, dislike of class barriers and even pacifism. She writes in 1892 about one function where she 'met a lot of old fogies including Leslie Stephen who sympathised with me in my hatred of war' and twenty years later Parry notes that 'Maude went to a suffrage party at the Richmonds in the afternoon and made a speech and was much exhausted after'.

The death of Pembroke in 1895, closely followed by Leighton, Morris, Burne-Jones, Dannreuther, Michael Pembroke, Pearl Craigie and Getey Pembroke, fragmented the structure of Parry's social life and left him too dependent on dining out with acquaintances or over-working back at Kensington Square. But the years from 1895 to 1908 were when he was most absorbed in lecturing, writing and administration.

His main relaxation became his annual cruise, usually to Ireland, the Channel Islands or the West Coast of Scotland though he ventured as far afield as Hamburg, Copenhagen and Stockholm. Following the *Hoopoe*, his first yacht, cruises were in the *Latois*, a 21-ton yawl, and from 1901 taken in the *Humber* (renamed The *Wanderer*), until the outbreak of war. Longer trips were under Captain James Roach and the party, an all male affair, normally consisted of his brother Sidney, Frank Pownall, Dr Charles Hartford Lloyd (then organist of Christ Church), George Robertson Sinclair (organist of Hereford Cathedral), Hugh Allen (Parry's successor at the RCM), Sir Walter Raleigh (Professor of Literature at Oxford), and Logan Pearsall Smith, the American author and pioneer in semantics. These men were mostly younger and tended to reflect Parry's literary and musical interests, though Pearsall Smith recalled that: 'He spoke but little of his employments and the subject of music was hardly mentioned between us.' Nonetheless

> His genius could not be hid, it shone and flashed in his talk – that frank, delightful inexhaustible talk about the people he had known, the places he had been to, the books he had read, which made his company a perpetual delight.[38]

Pearsall Smith was a friend of Shaw, who spent a holiday in 1917 at Smith's Elizabethan mansion. Smith's friend, Arthur Ponsonby, was the only MP during the war to defend Shaw's pacifist stand and he too was a passionate admirer of Shaw's plays. One is bound to wonder whether Shaw and Parry did indeed meet long after the *Job* review. Shaw, through his Fabian connections was close to the Webbs and also Sir Harry Johnston. Johnston and Shaw were fellow lecturers at the Fabian Society and Johnston let his London house to Shaw's sister during the war.[39] Johnston in turn was a good friend of the Ponsonbys. Given these cross-connections it is puzzling why Shaw was so concerned to put down Parry's reputation in the 1920s. It all suggests a personal motivation that has never been discovered. All we know is that Shaw was extremely wary of Parry's charm.

Parry's enthusiasm left a lasting impression on another friend of Pearsall Smith, the young Compton Mackenzie, who played Pheidippides in *The Clouds*. Sixty years later he was still declaring that Parry's music was masterly and regretting, as editor of *Gramophone* magazine, that 'there are no records of Hubert Parry's magnificent choruses in "The Clouds".' He also recounts an unexpected visit from the composer in April 1905:

> Soon after three there was a terrific knock at the door and I saw Hubert Parry in motoring costume. He is a most delightful man. His conversation is discharged like a child firing off a toy-pistol, revelling in the noise. He was charmed with the house and the well. 'Pelléas and Mélisande, what, ah, devilish good, what? – grand – splendid.' Then I read a bit of a parody I had started of Princess Maleine which I called Princess

Migraine who was rescued by Prince Aspirin. Parry sat down at the piano and began to improvise a parody of Debussy. I don't know enough about Debussy to know how good it was but I chanted my Princess Migraine to his Debussy accompaniment.[40]

Parry often appears both fascinated and repulsed by Debussy which is surprising considering his ability to assimilate Stravinsky and over time Schoenberg. He followed Debussy's career with interest, attended performances armed with scores, and encouraged performances. However, several years after this encounter with Mackenzie, he admitted to Hugh Allen after attending *Pelléas et Mélisande* for the first time that he experienced 'difficulty in understanding what the composer was driving at. He could not feel convinced of the sincerity of Debussy, while recognizing his talent and charm.'[41] The difficulty may have centred on Debussy's musical personality: his ultimate Gallic temperament and emotional understatement were the antithesis of Parry's. Even here in MacKenzie's anecdote the bluff joviality, part Falstaff, part Captain Shotover, does not square comfortably with Parry's obvious musical erudition.

Of Parry the motorist, however, there are many lurid accounts: old women fainting, carsick chauffeurs, a collision with a flock of sheep, which Parry had to pull out from under the wheels, luckily unharmed, and Keystone Cops displays across the highways of England. As he ruefully explained to Plunkett Greene:

We were nearly finished off coming up to town in the Gladiator yesterday. The roads were just awful and we had no non-skids. She ran clean out of control four times; at Cheltenham clean off the road onto the side-walk between a couple of trees, and at Uxbridge she turned clean round on her axis and went backwards onto the side-walk. It's not pleasant, that sort of fun.[42]

Throughout his life Parry retained the priceless key to youth: it drew him to the children on the beach at Rustington, 'the Brownies' as he called them, and subsequently it infused all his relations with students at the College. In 1877 we find him taking 'the Brownies' to the circus, building sandcastles and playing 'very small cricket'. For 14 August there is a tender entry:

My little children friends' last day, so I spent it all with them. We went out in a boat in the morning, paddled and bathed, got a lot of seaweeds and had great fun together. In the afternoon we paid a last visit to the 'goody shop' and went down to the long pier and in the evening walked about on the sands, and said good-bye about 9 o'clock.[43]

Dannreuther's and Richmond's children were later 'Brownies' in whom Parry instilled a lasting love of the sea. One of Richmond's sons became an Admiral and in 1916 Captain Hubert Dannreuther was directing fire control in the *Invincible* at the Battle of Jutland up until the ship was blown up. One of only six survivors out of a company of 1,032, he was awarded the DSO. As Edward Dannreuther's brother Gustav affirmed, 'We all loved and adored him.' Indeed the affection Parry lavished on the young Helen Richmond was sufficient to make the younger Dorothea jealous.

Another important Rustington resident was Parry's dog Scamp who could upset his emotional equilibrium as much as Lady Maude:

September 20 [1890], – Scamp disappeared just at dinner time and couldn't be found anywhere. I sat up for him till midnight. Ultimately he arrived at 3 am. and barked vigorously outside. I let him in, but was in such a rage that I couldn't get to sleep again for several hours.[44]

Next day Parry bore no malice: 'After tea washed "Scamp" and slaughtered a number of fleas. Corrected band parts'. Magnanimity broke down a couple of days later when Scamp ran away again and was 'severely whacked,' to the anguish and wrath of the family. Parry and Lady Maude adored animals and visits to the zoo were always red-letter days.

The Great War drew away men from every aspect of Parry's life, such as his nephew Reginald Herbert, the young 15th Earl of Pembroke who succeeded his father Sidney in 1913 and was decorated for his services and Parry's brother-in-law Tynewell Cripps, whose family Parry looked after throughout the war. Nearly all the Souls lost sons in action, and overall fatalities among the aristocracy who fought were almost twenty per cent.[45] By the last year of the war few friends remained from the halcyon days when Parry and Lady Maude discovered Littlehampton. Sir William Richmond lived on – now old, ill and widowed – but Parry had not lost that 'kindling quality' as Herbert Howells called it. In 1920 Richmond recalled:

> Three years ago when I was ill, dangerously ill, his [Parry's] visits to me, which were frequent, seemed to bring into my sick-room a breeze from the sea. He knew my danger but never let me see it: when he left, so had he pulled me together that I sent for my books, my pencil and paper, and made an effort to work, and work saved my life.[46]

Once Parry had become director of the College new associates rarely replaced the old friendships with Grove, Dannreuther, Fuller Maitland and Plunkett Greene. After Dannreuther's death, Parry wrote in 1909 enigmatically to Gustav Dannreuther of his brother's musical legacy: 'I believe it will grow into quite a legend – a tradition of a mysterious personality which pervaded the life of the college.' Was Dannreuther also 'mysterious' to Parry or merely to his students? Parry visited Dannreuther 'every Sunday – and often other days – when they were both in London', until his death. Yet Dannreuther's later career failed to fulfil the early promise. After he gave up the Orme Square Concerts in 1893 and became Professor of Pianoforte at the RCM, his impact on the wider musical world was apparently over. Perhaps this had an inhibiting effect on Parry's creativity, as the inducement to produce new chamber music weakened. It also argues that Dannreuther became less fitted to be Parry's compositional adviser. But this may be a premature judgement and until a well researched study of this important figure is undertaken, any opinions must be provisional.

But musicians of every type crossed Parry's life. In his twenties he became acquainted with the rising composers of his own generation: John Stainer at Oxford, who remained on close terms until his death in 1900, Charles Villiers Stanford (1852–1924) and Alexander Mackenzie (1847–1935). Parry held a great affection for Mackenzie but a dim opinion of his music while his relationship with Stanford was stormy, a reflection more on the Irishman than on Parry. Despite Stanford's early championship of Parry's music their friendship deteriorated once Parry became Director. For Stanford, who was conductor of the Bach Choir and the Leeds Festival, it cannot have been easy to accept Parry's often autocratic leadership. In addition Stanford's international reputation was higher, for his operas were performed in Germany and, ultimately, Mahler took up his Irish Symphony. While Stanford's presence greatly benefited the Royal College it was a self-destructive decision to stay on after 1895.[47]

By contrast Parry maintained an easy cordiality with Arthur Sullivan, stepping in to cover for him as conductor at the Leeds where Sullivan was always supportive of Parry's music. Parry's professional career brought him into regular contact with a wealth of half-forgotten musicians such as Frederick Cowen, Frederick Corder, W.S. Hannam at Leeds, Sir Walter Parratt, Sir Henry Hadow, Sir Frederick Bridge, Dr Henry Coward, conductor of the Sheffield Musical Union, and Barclay Squire, later librarian of the R.C.M., who assisted Parry in much research.

In contrast it is striking that Parry could number no close friends among foreign composers. Unfortunately he remained too unknown internationally to act as a magnet, but social connections ensured that he met Liszt, Wagner, Joachim, Clara Schumann and Gounod, while his academic positions brought him in touch with Grieg, D'Albert, Saint-Saëns and Dvořák. Richard Strauss conducted at the College and entertained Parry with stories about the Kaiser. Glazunov and Rachmaninov also visited, but it is unfortunate that – to my knowledge – Parry never met Brahms, Bruckner, Tchaikovsky, Debussy, Verdi or Puccini (though he admired *La Bohème*). While he may not have met Debussy, he arranged a performance of Debussy's *String Quartet* at the College, which Debussy gratefully acknowledged by letter. Parry's interest in recent music, very different from Debussy's own, partially explains the significance of Parry's influence as a teacher on younger British composers, although he gave no private lessons after he became Director of the RCM.

Of course even a gifted pupil does not really know their teacher – unless a social friendship ensues. They fall under the spell of a persona, however sincere a reflection that may be. Parry ran into trouble when Hamish MacCunn wanted to assume a social intimacy. MacCunn resigned his College scholarship in 1887 over differences with his tutors. He wrote an impassioned letter to Parry exempting him from his criticisms but, while thanking him for many acts of kindness, berating him for not offering personal friendship.[48] It is one more sad reflection on the human condition that an exceptionally kind, generous man is often taken to task for not being selfless. Perhaps that is why there are fewer and fewer of them.

Nonetheless, no criticisms have been handed down of Parry the teacher and lecturer. Gustav Holst gave his impression of attending Parry's lectures on music history: on one occasion Parry 'looked up from his notes and said "I suppose you all know what was going on in Europe at that time?" He then stood up, and while walking about, he gave us, so it seemed to me, a vision rather than a lecture.' Ralph Vaughan Williams wrote about his time as a private composition pupil: 'You could not hear the sound of his voice or feel the touch of his hand without knowing that "virtue had gone out of him".'[49]

Sometimes his gift for teaching was combined with a personal philanthropic interest. Dr Herbert Howells described in the memorial issue of the RCM magazine how Parry, quite unbeknown, replaced his broken glasses:

He had changed his plans for the week-end, had gone down to Gloucester, had called on the optician who possessed the prescription, and by threat or entreaty had prevailed on the good man to have the new glasses ready by Monday morning. He had collected them and brought them up to London. All this to save time and to spare an obscure student a few extra hours' discomfort.[50]

Herbert Howells, despite his usual modesty, was not an 'obscure student' and his magnificent *Missa Sabrinensis* (Mass of the Severn), by way of tribute, includes subtle near-quotes from Elgar and Vaughan Williams but also from Parry. At the end of the Kyrie he writes a descending phrase for solo bass clarinet which in mood and place (as the penultimate phrase at the end of the movement) parallels the final bars of Parry's *Ode on the Nativity*.

There is considerable evidence that Parry related to the College as an extended family, a feeling particularly marked when associates performed his own compositions. Sir Walford Davies (1869–1941) was sympathetic to Parry's ethical preoccupations and took up *Voces Clamantium* and the *Ode on the Nativity* with organ accompaniment at The Temple Church. 'The Performance of the "Nativity" was astonishingly good', Parry wrote in 1916. Davies claimed later that 'I loved him too dearly and feel him still so near me as to make it hard to appraise him as a man.'[51] Davies's work at the Temple Church was taken up by two organists from the RCM, George Thalban-Ball and Harold Darke. The latter worked with Parry on his late organ pieces, as Parry recorded in May 1915: 'to St. James's, Paddington, to hear Darke play some of my Chorale Preludes which he did finely. Interrupted by a wedding and went back to the College where Darke played some more.'

Another pupil, Adrian Boult, conducted the off-stage Chorus in *The Frogs* (1909) and shared *The Archanians* in 1913 with Hugh Allan. Sir Adrian makes it clear that Parry attended the Henry Wood performance of the Schoenberg *Five Orchestral Pieces*, in September 1912 (Parry's diary is blank for that week):

I had a gangway seat and was astonished to feel a thump on my shoulder immediately the work was finished, and, looking up, saw a radiant smile from a total stranger and heard 'Bless my soul, that's funny stuff, don't you think so? I must say I rather like it when they do it loud, like Strauss, but when it's quiet all the time like this, it seems a bit obscene, doesn't it?'[52]

Sir Eugene Goossens always avowed that *Prometheus Unbound* was the 'most remarkable work produced by an English composer in the eighties'[53] and Leopold Stokowski, in the 1960s, was still recommending young composers to 'study Parry.'

After his daughters married, singers such as Agnes Nicholls (later Lady Harty), Muriel Foster and Gladys Honey became his 'god-daughters'. Their relationship was the more potent because they gave expression in performance to the 'fem insperatus' in the long series of soprano arias which distinguish his cantatas. It is unlikely Parry ever had a sexual relationship with these singers, though Graves' assertion that no scandal was ever attached to his name still leaves the case open. Gladys Honey worked with him on 'Armida's Garden' (from the *English Lyrics*, set IX): 'Many times I went with him to his downstairs room to try bits for him which didn't quite please him, and which he gave me to read in a very much blotted and erased manuscript.[54] Agnes Nicholls arranged all the flowers in his room at the college, for Parry adored flowers: they were 'his friends and his constant joy'.

Nonetheless it was usually composers who elicited his particular concern. In 1912 he writes to W.S. Hannam: 'What has become of Butterworth? We didn't keep him so long as I hoped. I hope his worthy father is all right. I liked him so much when we were with you together last festival.'[55] George Butterworth's father, Sir Alexander Butterworth, was a leading Army Officer and Parry later referred bitterly to 'this indiscriminate carnage' when he wrote to Sir Alexander after the death of his son in August 1916.

At the College, Parry wrote all his letters by hand and kept in touch with numerous ex-pupils. The letters of Ivor Gurney[56] are an indication of the old man's concern for a younger generation fast disappearing around him. In 1915 Gurney wrote to Marion Scott: 'I send you a song which you have not yet seen. When you have finished, please send it and the letter to Sir Hubert, for whom it is meant.' A year later he speaks of 'Sir C.H.H.P.' writing 'a cheery letter a few days ago in which he expressed his surprise that the love of music has survived in his young men.' Gurney's estimation of the older composer remained high and, in a letter to Marion Scott of 25 October 1916, he wrote: 'Did Sir CHHP really say my song was the most tragic thing he knew? If so, what an enormous praise!'

Gurney sensed Parry's vulnerability, which escaped other observers, commenting to Miss Scott: 'I am sorry to hear of the accident to Sir Hubert, which is bad news, since he is so little able to stand shocks.' Gurney was referring to 8 October when Parry was driving to Shulbrede with Maude and 'we got along well till past Fernhurst when suddenly on a greasy bit of road she skidded and whirling from side to side rushed headlong into the hedgebank. The glass of the body cracked and when I turned around Maude was heaped insensible with her face streaming with blood.' Parry fortunately was unhurt and Maude by the next day 'seemed surprisingly better – had even got up and laid on the sofa.'

As the College became denuded by the War, Parry depended greatly on Hugh Allen for support and, through the Bach Choir, for performances of his final compositions. With regard to composition itself, it was his erstwhile pupil and ex-principal of Holloway College, Dr Emily Daymond who became his assistant at the College and at Rustington, where she would irritate Maude. The satirical comment circulated at the College that Emily Daymond dotted Parry's crotchets. It is questionable whether she was a wholly beneficial influence; however, she offered valued support once George Schlichenmeyer, Parry's factotum, had been interned.

Parry continued to maintain close ties with Oxford, especially with Dr Thomas Strong, Dean of Christ Church and (like Dean Liddell) later Vice-Chancellor. It was Strong who subsequently confirmed Parry's intense interest in Schoenberg's music; Parry insisted Strong should include it on the syllabuses. This had repercussions for William Walton, a chorister in the Christ Church Choir for six years from 1911. Lady Walton[57] tells how his 'first introduction to modern music had come early when Dean Strong had asked the boys to come to him for confirmation classes after the service on Sunday morning and had played Schoenberg's six little piano pieces to them lasting half a minute each'. Walton was not particularly impressed. On one occasion when Parry was staying with Dean Strong – as the

Dean later wrote to Hubert Foss – 'It so happened that the examinations for music degrees were going on just then and Parry was staying with me. He picked up W[alton]'s mss. and was interested. I remember him saying, "There's a lot in this chap. You must keep your eye on him".' Later Parry asked Strong to arrange a meeting. Walton recounted: 'I went to see Sir Hubert Parry on last Sunday afternoon and had quite a long talk with him.'[58] Parry's devotion to teaching was matched by an eye for talent.

However, his most assiduous student never studied with him, yet Edward Elgar absorbed Parry's style more successfully than any other English composer and transformed it into a personal, multi-faceted medium of expression. Parry was consistently helpful to Elgar and their relationship always remained cordial, but there is no evidence that the two men were close. Elgar, at the height of his fame, still championed compositions by the older composer: *The Lotos-Eaters*, *Ode to Music*, and *The Vision of Life*. In 1907 Elgar wrote to Jaeger: 'I say! That "vision" of Parry's is fine stuff and the poem is literature: you must hear it some day.'[59]

What of Parry's negative characteristics? From Graves's account it is clear that, at the R.C.M., Parry could be an enlightened despot, occasionally an autocrat, and resistant to change if it was for the sake of falling into line with other establishments, even if the idea was innately sound. Today it is more difficult to arrive at an assessment since a later Director, Sir George Dyson, himself a former RCM pupil, destroyed all the Committee and Council Minutes from when Parry was Director.

By 1900 Parry had become a master of political survival; his positions at the RCM and Oxford were unassailable and his hold over the Leeds Festival and the Three Choirs was considerable. For example, the Leeds Committee in 1900 asked Parry's advice regarding a successor to Sullivan as conductor. Parry recommended Stanford, and Stanford in turn then ensured that Parry's works were well represented.

His presence on committees and his political connections made him a formidable proposition for 'radical' composers such as Bax, Wallace and Delius. Free from the aegis of the College they were less beguiled by Parry's bluff persona. His Establishment connections sometimes required him to take a non-committal stand on innovative musical issues. A case in point is his initial refusal to support the Music League. When Delius heard from Bantock that Parry had subsequently sent a conciliatory letter, he remarked: 'The old fox'.[60] No doubt Parry's change of stance was prompted by Elgar's acceptance of the Presidency. Though Parry admired Delius's music, 'good and special in its way' as he said in 1909 Delius preferred to avoid contact with the man who, he feared, would set the whole Bible to music.

In 'Farewell, My Youth', Arnold Bax dismissed Parry as old-bufferish, arguing that 'I cannot divine any possibility in him of the "Chaos at heart which gives birth to a dancing star".'[61] (Obviously Bax never heard Parry's *Ode on the Nativity*.) William Wallace, a vociferous Parry critic and secretary of the Philharmonic Society, nicknamed Parry, Stanford and Mackenzie 'the three Mandarins', which soon returned to roost. Parry's diary suggests, however, that in his presence Bax and Wallace could be more susceptible than they wished. In 1912 Parry noted: 'Went to Balfour Gardner's concert. Quite an exhilarating affair, lots of good things. His own and also Grainger's folk tune music. Grainger's conducting very extravagant and jolly. Sat next to Bax who was most communicative.' Two years earlier, his diary recorded, of a Philharmonic concert: 'Sat with Walford Davies and Wallace!!! actually shook hands with the latter!!' Even Bax had to admit that Parry had taken the trouble to attend an early song cycle of his, Parry's opinion being that 'Young Bax's stuff sounds like a bevy of little devils'. Nonetheless, Bax's reminiscences prove irrefutably that Bax did not really know Parry – there, however, he was in good company.

On the evidence I have seen few people could claim to know him: the obvious exceptions are Lady Maude and George Grove, the only people who achieved the requisite level of affectionate understanding to know when he needed criticism or advice, the only people who honestly came to terms with his shortcomings. Witness Grove's 1894 observation: 'He is the best, but oh my dear in so many things he will be very poor – no backbone, no power of saying no, or of resisting those whom he likes.'[62] Of his peers only George Pembroke stood up to him; others either fell into uncritical acceptance or preferred to remain at a critical distance – such as his half-brother Ernest.

Parry undoubtedly showed the negative attributes of his personality, and further research may unearth more instances of individuals bearing the brunt of his character. Certainly Parry would have been horrified at the quasi-saint like image given him later by RCM pupils. However, it would take a mass of unknown criticism to alter my opinion that Sir Hubert Parry was one of the finest men of his time and the seminal creator of the English Musical Renaissance.

9 The Last Journey to *Jerusalem*

My way is near its end at last. Light shall be my step across the threshold. Like trees we must part with our fruit, and even the leaves of age will have to fall, as autumn turns to winter.

(Hindemith, Mathis der Maler)

Throughout 1907 Parry's health deteriorated. He endured a long operation in April and severe heart irregularities in October. Even his summer cruise on The *Wanderer* was spoiled by adverse weather. Doctors' advice to 'pull up' were, as usual, ignored and he remained on the verge of collapse, 'Just keeping my head above water'. His negative response to the performance of *The Vision of Life* at Cardiff did not help his mood and he struggled to complete his book on Bach by February 1908. Later in the month his heart problems intensified, producing other complications. Dr Dawson took a dim view of his illustrious but now elderly patient and pronounced he was also suffering from an enlarged liver and dropsy in both legs. Dr Dawson's demands were strict: he ordered him to resign the Oxford Professorship and take three months' rest. That 'rest' was reduced by a month but in addition he relinquished the Presidency of the Mendelssohn Scholarship and on the last day of February the tired composer started out for Sicily to join the Ponsonbys in Taormina. After his return his health remained poor: 'I'm going through a spell of the most outrageous despair I have ever lived through', he complained to Plunkett Greene;[1] and it remained touch and go whether he would manage to complete *Beyond These Voices There is Peace* for the Worcester Festival.

For a composer by then generally regarded, among contemporary musical opinion, as a 'back number', the portents were anything but propitious; and to make matters worse, friends, contemporaries and pupils were dying around him. In 1906 he came to the financial assistance of Hurlstone's family on the untimely death of the composer at the age of 30, and he paid for the ailing Jaeger to have an operation in Switzerland. Getey Pembroke passed away after years of suffering and Sir August Manns died, severing a major link with himself as a young composer. The year 1907 saw the death of Edvard Grieg, whom Parry had presented to convocation at Oxford for an honorary doctorate of music in the previous year and Jaeger died in 1909. It was fitting that Parry's ninth set of *English Lyrics* were all settings of the contemporary poet, Mary Coleridge, who died suddenly at 45 in 1907.[2]

Parry's breakdown in health should have heralded a premature end, but his physical woes were in part the result of over- not under-activity and his body was still the body of an erstwhile athlete. At 60, the ex-Keeper of the Field was still capable of taking the helm of The *Wanderer* in the roughest of weather and swimming daily in the ocean.

With hindsight there were positive signs of creative development, of which the most crucial were musical. In 1908 he heard Sibelius's *Finlandia* and Third Symphony – 'ingenious and curious'[3] – and in October 1909 Rachmaninov visited the College to perform the British première of the Second Piano Concerto and conduct his 'singularly unmoscovite'[4] Second Symphony. This magnificent symphonic essay in E minor was not wasted on a composer about to revise his own Fourth Symphony written in the same key. The revision displays a new elaboration in the string writing, in particular divided strings with the resultant harmonic enrichment, increased use of brass, especially the horns, and most obviously the glorious new coda for the first movement, with its reiteration of a melodic pattern reminiscent of both Rachmaninov and Sibelius. In the new scherzo there is a pizzicato passage towards the end which recalls Sibelius's Third Symphony, as does the woodwind writing throughout the movement.

Sibelius's First Symphony (also in E minor) was the child of Tchaikovsky's Fifth and Brahms' Fourth, but Parry's E minor symphony had been the first offspring. These E minor analogies from two composers of the next generation may have given him a stimulus. In December 1908, he attended the first performance of Elgar's First Symphony: 'Place packed. Work received with enthusiasm. Very interesting, personal, new, magnetic. A lofty standard'[5], he wrote; and later he concluded that the Violin Concerto was 'of the very finest quality'.[6]

He remained receptive to other new ideas. In Taormina, 'after dinner we had a performance of two guitars and two mandolins playing with great artistic feeling and wonderful gradations of light and shade.'[7] We find him re-reading *Also Sprach Zarathustra* on his Irish cruise in 1909, partially in response to Beecham's performance of Delius's *A Mass of Life*, of which he wrote 'sensation uncanny' but 'worth going through again', which he did later.[8] At other times, musical inquisitiveness sent him in a going-through-again mood to the Opera where he attended repeat performances of both Charpentier's *Louise* and Debussy's *Pelléas et Mélisande*, to which (in May 1909) he took a score for studying in the interval: 'To Debussy's Pelléas and Mélisande in the evening. Curious sensation. A sort of subtle undercurrent of ticklings of the sensations. I was interested. I suppose especially by the strangeness of the play. Lots of young enthusiasts, college and others.'[9] The following year, he wrote: 'To Charpentier's Louise – Fantastic, but the final scene justifies the strange mixture of fooling and passion of the rest and makes it into a real tragedy'.[10]

His own recent compositions failed to achieve any impact with the public but musicians continued in their admiration. Elgar's enthusiasm for *The Vision of Life* remained undimmed and, though he failed to secure a second performance with the Leeds Festival in 1913, his faith meant much to the older composer. It 'will be the most permanent of consolations', Parry had written to him in 1909.[11] 'It's really strong bracing stuff and like your odes, some of us love it and love you for giving us these things', Elgar wrote from Italy in May 1909.[12] The work has never received a second performance.

1   Thomas Gambier-Parry

2   Isabella Fynes-Clinton, Mrs Gambier-Parry

3   Lucy Parry

4   Charles Clinton Parry

5   Parry aged 17 – Eton Group

6   Hubert Parry

7 Highnam Court

8   George, Earl of Pembroke

9   Lady Maude Herbert

10 Hubert Parry

11   Parry on board the *Wanderer*

12   Sir Hubert and Lady Maude

13   Sir Hubert and Lady Maude at Rustington

14   Lady Maude in action leading a suffragette march

15   Four generations

16   Parry, 1893

17 Lady Maude

18   Parry at Shulbrede with grandchildren

19 Sir Hubert and Lady Maude motoring

20   Eddie Hamilton and Parry at Oxford

21   Henry Hugo Pierson

22   Arthur Balfour and Spenser Lyttleton

23 Mary Gladstone

25 George Grove

26 Edward Dannreuther. His *carte-de-visite*

27   William Morris and Edward Burne-Jones

28 Philip Burne-Jones

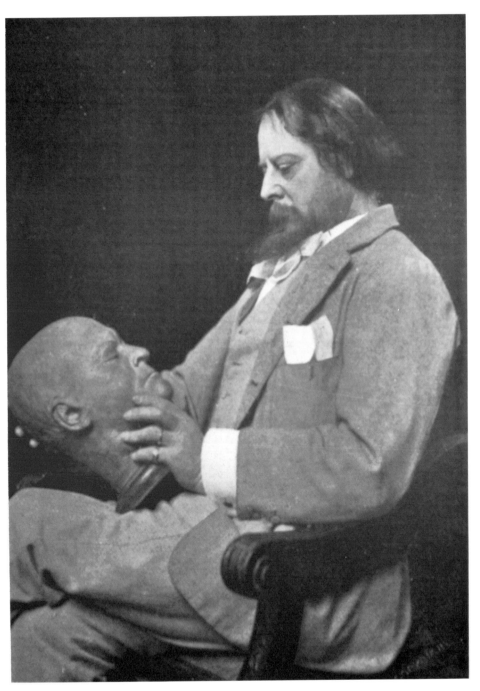

29   William Blake Richmond with a life mask of William Blake

30   Harry Johnston in later years

31   Robert Bridges

32   Ralph Vaughan Williams

Though no one could have realized it in 1909, the stage was set for what I termed, several years ago, Parry's Indian Summer. This late creative flowering came into being for several reasons, the most significant being that he had more time to compose. That it was necessary for his health to collapse in order to cut down on other activities was typical of his hyperactive personality. Breakdowns had happened many times before; but this time, because it was more severe, and he was over 60, he reacted in a more mature, more creative way. I think there were other reasons as well. His eclipse by Elgar was now history, but Elgar's constant loyalty and genuine enthusiasm for the *Ethical Cantatas* meant a great deal to him.

In contrast, Parry was never entirely happy with Vaughan Williams's *A Sea Symphony* (1910), as his diaries show. He considered at one performance the scoring was too blatant and after a Bach Choir concert that revived *The Glories of Our Blood and State* he wrote: 'They did The Glories fairly well and fairly revelled in Stanford's 2nd series of Sea Songs and gave a very good performance indeed of Vaughan Williams's Sea Symphony. Big stuff, but full of impertinences as well as noble moments.'[13] He may have felt he had something important to contribute again; after all he was the master who most understood how to set great English verse, and like the Frankfurt group of composers, all much younger than himself, he was concerned directly with the latest developments in German music. Jung claimed that clairvoyants can tell the future because it is long prepared for in the past. Certainly it can be claimed that the seeds of creative renewal were germinating in Parry's unconscious long before they emerged in the works of the Indian Summer.

The *Eton Memorial Ode*, written in 1908 to a poem by Robert Bridges, shows a new directness of expression, and a new more subtle kind of lyricism with some atmospheric scoring for side drum and glockenspiel. The performance given at the school in front of King Edward VII and Queen Alexandra was 'vigorously sung and went well without any hitches'; 'Boys delightful I loved them'.[14] Nonetheless, the continuous flow of large-scale choral works had ceased and he contented himself with revisions and re-scorings of earlier compositions as they came up for performance: *The Glories of Our Blood and State*, *The Frogs* for the 1909 Oxford revival and *L'Allegro* for Southport. With this attitude he tackled the Fourth Symphony in the final months of 1909. The successful revision for the 1910 Philharmonic Society performance, displays an increased sense of fancy (in the scherzo) and new lyrical flowerings (in the first movement coda): it was another signpost. Two months later he conducted it again – successfully – in Birmingham, and the following year in Bournemouth.

In September 1910 The Gloucester Festival revived *Beyond These Voices* for which he made minor revisions to the scoring. It was by all accounts, including his own, an excellent performance and did much to sustain Parry's new found creative self-confidence: 'performance of *Beyond These Voices* very good indeed. Chorus completely in hand. Heard Elgar Symphony (No. 1) in the Choir. The Cathedral associations did not suit it. Lunched at Dean's. People very sympathetic about *Beyond These Voices*'.[15] On the following day *The Times* gave it a perceptive review:

It is a reflective work of the kind which no modern composer can handle as Sir Hubert Parry can. Indeed it is possible to count on the fingers of one hand the number of composers who have succeeded in dealing with such introspective subject matter without denigrating into a morbid-type expression. Bach of course is the greatest of them, Brahms in the *Requiem* and in the *Rhapsody*.

In the evening the Festival successfully revived the *Ode to Music*, which *The Times* called a work of 'dignity and fine feeling'.

It is likely he took his doctor's warnings literally and concluded his time was short; his output was in effect completed. These revisions to earlier compositions really amount to putting his affairs in order. The death of Edward VII in May 1910 heightened his sense that an era was ending as a new king, a generation younger than himself, ascended the throne. At his college address in September, Parry spoke from personal experience when he said: 'The King, who was the inventor and Founder of the College in days before most of you were born, was so true and liberal and large-hearted in his goodwill to the college that our circumstances can never be quite the same now he is gone from us'.[16]

The coronation itself necessitated yet another revision: *I was Glad* was included with the enthusiastic approval of George V and required an expanded introduction. It also brought a commission for the coronation *Te Deum*. The event was not without diversions: 'We watched the general rehearsal with amusement. The peers in their coronets looked extremely foolish and muddled hopelessly.' The performance of *I was Glad* was satisfactory, the *Te Deum* less so: Parry was happier with the Worcester Festival performance in September.

It is a curious postscript that the culminating scene of the Lawrence Olivier film of Rattigan's *The Prince and the Showgirl* (1957) features an ecstatic Marilyn Monroe gazing at that procession of coronets in the 1911 Coronation while *I was Glad* is ringing out, not in Parry's 1911 orchestration, but anachronistically in the Gordon Jacob rescoring.

A month later Lady Herbert died at 89, after two strokes. Although Parry travelled from Highnam by car and Maude by train, they failed to reach Herbert House, London in time. Mary Herbert, 'very done up and distressed', took Parry 'up to see poor Mama's body. Very distressing. Marble look of the face: very peaceful and horribly pathetic. Sisters praying disturbed me'.[17] For the next few days he and Maude were caught up in the elaborate Catholic funeral arrangements culminating in a Requiem Mass at Westminster Cathedral: 'Processions of priests and acolytes, genuflections, manoeuvres. Long sing[ing] some of it very bad'. At the luncheon afterwards in Portman Square Parry had an 'Unfortunate dispute with Gladys, who thought the singing the loveliest she had ever heard!' This was followed by the service at Mill Hill, 'Very long and very tiring business. Finished at 3.15. Said good-bye and came away with Maude. Maude dreadfully done up in evening'.

He continued to avoid ambitious projects and contented himself with a set of Chorale Preludes for Organ promised as a gift for C.H. Lloyd. Lloyd's enthusiasm encouraged him to produce a number of late organ works that continue to be played. But no one at the end of 1911 could have predicted the unprecedented five-year burst of creativity that concluded with *Jerusalem* in 1916.

The new year began auspiciously with a powerful setting (for organ and bass voice) of the soliloquy 'I believe it' from Browning's *Saul*, written for the Browning Centenary. Did Parry's feelings reflect David's explanation to Saul of the divine spark in himself as the future king from whose seed the Christ would come? Browning's lines inspired Parry to write a dark, but consoling meditation which sets the stage for the entire Indian Summer *œuvre*. Perhaps Parry had a spiritual experience, a vision or a dream; maybe the more contemporary transcendental view of the biblical story, as found in Browning's poem, led him to rethink – and partially surrender to – the idea of the Messiah's appearance on Earth to lead man back to the source of creativity and light. The word 'surrender' is a key word in almost all spiritual experiences that result in a conversion or a reaffirmation of religious belief. This is a feminine attribute, not in the gender sense, but in the polarity of masculine and feminine which is present in the psyche of all human beings. It was the increase of this aspect in Parry's personality which was the pivotal factor in the new-found radiance of the works from this late period.

Parry cuts straight into the most ecstatic part of David's vision:

> I believe it! Tis thou, God that givest, 'tis I who receive.
> In the first is the last, in thy will is my power to believe.

He then connects this declaration to the final lines, ending on David's remarkable affirmation: 'See the Christ Stand'. Parry holds the 'see' for two and a half bars on high D flat, before rising, by a chordal shift on C sharp, to D natural for the word 'Christ'. There is no equivalent to this explicit Christian declaration in any of the *Ethical Cantatas*; 'God is a spirit', the climactic setting of Christ's words in *The Soul's Ransom*, is the closest. To choose these lines from the vast range of Browning's verse suggests a distinct shift of attitude which would be confirmed by the subject matter chosen for succeeding compositions.[18] The sheer fiery magnificence of the *Ode on the Nativity* and the exultant earnestness of *Jerusalem* point to this idea as a possibility. These works continued the theme expounded in David's vision of Christ. There are further pointers: in 1913 Parry chose David's troubled but affirmative Psalm 46, *God is Our Hope*, to set for the Festival of the Sons of Clergy and the valedictory *Songs of Farewell* are further meditations on transcendent visions of states beyond death.

Graves emphasizes that Parry went on learning and adapting to the very end. In these final years he betrayed a metaphysical dimension not apparent in his earlier writings.

> The average mind which understands very little feels that the things which it knows are too common and obvious to have any inspiring qualities. There is no mystery about them. But it is different with more developed minds. The more men know, the less they need the fascination of the unknown to lift them into the higher plane of that ecstasy which belongs to Religion.[19]

Parry added, in a notebook from this period, that 'Art is a form of devotion. Everything that endeavours to beautify and make loveable the surroundings and the ideas of man is part of devotional religion.[20]

In May he took time away from other commitments to produce the charming one-scene ballet *Proserpine* staged at the Haymarket Theatre for the Keats–Shelley Festival. The ballet is structured in three orchestral sections: Prelude, Intermezzo and Conclusion linked by a setting of Shelley's 'Song of Proserpine' for unaccompanied female chorus. The music is lighter, more feminine, and strangely translucent – a step forward.

His health continued uncertain with several operations for cysts. In July his old friend Alma-Tadema died: Parry attended the St Paul's funeral on 5 July aware that Sir William Richmond was the last survivor from the entire group of artists who had enriched his middle years. Fortunately his four-week cruise to Ireland, his last to those waters, with Pearsall Smith and Sir Walter Raleigh, revived his health, so that despite his doctor's threats he attended the last pre-war Hereford Festival with renewed enthusiasm. It was propitious, for the major part of the year 1912 had been taken up with the creation of what I have always regarded as Parry's masterpiece, his setting of William Dunbar's *Ode on Christ's Nativity* for soprano solo, chorus and orchestra.[21]

The *Ode on the Nativity* was premiered on 12 September 1912 during an afternoon concert in the Hereford Three Choirs Festival. A few years later *The Times* said it 'has such overflowing freshness and charm that many who cared little for his earlier cantatas were among its most enthusiastic admirers'.[22] His own subsequent references to it assure us he was very proud of the work. Parry chose Dunbar because he felt Milton's verse in this instance lacked the requisite variety for a successful musical setting. (Parry, however, omits the fourth verse of Dunbar's poem, which cites the praises of the clergy!) Another reason may have been that John Blackwood McEwen's major work for chorus and orchestra was a setting of the Milton (1906). McEwen, later director of the Royal Academy of Music and a fine composer, was on good terms with his older colleague. The score of his splendid border ballad *Grey Galloway* in the Royal College is a presentation copy to Parry.

Certainly Dunbar's great poem, which is filled with the most brilliant late Mediaeval Christian imagery, opened Parry's imaginative faculties to their utmost. He obviously considered Dunbar's poem to be a kind of Magnificat – hence the soprano solo is again The Virgin Mother praising the Creator. Here, however, she is praising on behalf of all human kind. The Nativity motive is, of course, a central part of Everyman's myth. By some mysterious process Dunbar's poem, celebrating the birth of the Saviour, for a moment in time filled the lifelong void in Parry's psyche. The poem contains all the birth and renewal (resurrection) symbols of the Christian faith, which ties it in with the visionary preoccupations in Browning's *Saul*. One of Parry's favourite paintings was *The Coming of the Magi to the Infant Christ*, by an early Italian master. The painting was acquired by Parry's parents and Gambier Parry placed it in Highnam Church, which of course was dedicated to the memory of Parry's mother. H.C. Colles wrote in 1916: 'Whenever I hear *Ode on the Nativity*, Sir Hubert's music brings that picture before my mind.'[23]

What do we really know about the processes which bring about artistic creation? The different graduations of talent and genius remain mysterious in their origins and even in their functioning. Certainly introversion and solitude are often necessary to set the various creative mechanisms into motion. As stated earlier,

Parry did not usually adhere to these prerequisites, unlike Brahms who jealously guarded them, even risking his financial security to protect them. Parry only occasionally crossed the threshold from the various levels of talent into genius.[24]

He did so, entirely, in this luminous setting of Dunbar's *Nativity* poem. All the consummate craft gathered from a lifetime of composing for chorus and orchestra is displayed without ostentation. Parry serves Dunbar's text and its meaning with the same inspired craft – rather than a display of ego – that we find in the Juggler of Notre Dame legend, when the impoverished juggler performs in front of the statue of the Virgin.[25] The superb overall structure suggested embryonically by the poem itself is related variously to the 'Gloria' of the *Missa Solemnis*, the early tone-poems of Strauss, and to the late massive adagio spans of Bruckner. It is questionable how much of Bruckner's music Parry knew, or what he thought of it.[26] But the combination of sonata form elements with single and double variation techniques strongly suggests this idea.

The work's splendid dancing melodic ideas (one thinks of Charpentier, Schütz and Bach) similar to, but subtly different from, each other are welded together with a sureness of touch and an ingenuity, which rival the finest Elgar. Programmatic strokes are kept to a minimum, but when used they support and flower on the structure rather than detract from the overall plan. The rich but often delicate orchestration is still derived from Mendelssohn and Brahms, but there is something French about it. The concert public is so used to thinking that 'French' means Debussy and Ravel, that it is often forgotten that Gounod, Saint-Saëns and Franck were strongly indebted to Bach, Mendelssohn and Schumann. As with *The Lotos-Eaters* and the *Invocation to Music*, the principal precursors to this ode, it is important to remember Parry's Huguenot ancestry.

The *Ode on the Nativity* is all the more extraordinary for being completely free of Victorian sentimentality and late romantic *angst*. To have the unique musical richness of those interlocking periods without their questionable attributes further enhances its artistic value. The influence from Liszt and Wagner is less overt than in several other late Parry scores but it is still there, especially in the use of the lower orchestral colours and sonorities, and in the constantly shifting tonal scheme. But like all works of real genius every influence, every precursor, is forgotten when playing or listening to it.

The 48-bar orchestral introduction creates the tonal landscape for the entire work. The score's pivot key of B flat major is reached only after the composition's principal harmonic–melodic cell has been reiterated four times on the tonic chord of the key a major third above (D major) and a major enharmonic third below (F sharp), finally reaching the tonic through the enharmonic dominant F sharp (D flat) and F the home key's dominant 7th. These tertial relationships Parry learned from his study of late Beethoven, especially the *Missa Solemnis*. The principal cell oscillates between the tonic and the 1st inversion of the supertonic giving a modal inflection to the harmony – late Beethoven again. Parry remains in the pivot key for only eight bars before developing the cell through a further 20 bars of finely chosen secondary dominants which I can only describe as spiritualized *nobilmente*. He then returns to B flat for ten bars before the entrance of the solo soprano followed by the chorus.

ODE ON THE NATIVITY.

William Dunbar.   C. Hubert H. Parry.

Ex. 20   opening from *Ode on the Nativity* piano reduction

The score is filled with ingenious developments and variations of these harmonic prototypes which, like every constituent of this score, are both complex and subtle. One example should be dwelt on, the music created around the words 'sing heaven imperial'. After five bars in F major (dominant of the pivot key), Parry – in four splendid ascending bars – modulates to the chord of G flat with the tenors

Ex. 21   'sing, heaven imperial' from *Ode on the Nativity*

entering on 'sing heaven imperial'. When the basses enter on E flat in the next bar we remain in mid-flight, being carried along on another series of secondary dominants heading toward the pivot key (B flat) reached eight bars later. But even the arrival of the pivot key is not a complete resolution – like a quick change of plane on a continuing journey. Only after another 35 bars and three further modulations does Parry come to a climactic resolution on the words 'heaven, earth, sea, man, bird, and beast', in a series of big dominant and tonic chords in D major leading tertially into a calm F major. The effect is an oral equivalent of the late Renaissance paintings of angels flying symmetrically in the upper firmament (El Greco for instance). The passage is the high point in Parry's large *œuvre* for solo chorus and orchestra, and it ranks with the most inspired and beautifully crafted moments in Western music.

Parry handles the soprano solo in a manner suggesting a concerto. It weaves in and out of the structure, often floating on top of the chorus. It is the most elaborate and integrated use of a solo voice in all his works. Here at last is the voice of the anima, soaring freely, unfettered by the overly masculine, extrovert side of his nature. Parry who, until the end, missed the relationship with the mother he never knew, the sister who died, the daughters who had left him to marry, here at last found the feminine aspect of the creative principle within himself.

In the week before the Hereford première of the *Ode*, he began work on what is arguably his most personal symphony, No. 5 in four linked movements – a symphony in beige and brown as I have described it in Chapter 6. Perhaps, more than any of his mature works, it was not written for a dear friend, or to fulfil a Philharmonic Society commission, but simply for himself.

A remarkable indication of his new-found artistic maturity is that, with Lady Maude in the grip of veronal, problems at the college with Stanford whose Seventh Symphony he disliked (referring to it as 'mild conventional Mendelssohnic – but not so interesting as Mendelssohn'[27]), and the deaths of Coleridge Taylor and Dr Kitchen, his inspiration to compose was not dampened.

Soon after the Fifth Symphony and the *Ode on the Nativity*, Parry produced a setting of Psalm 46, *God is Our Hope*, for double choir, bass solo and orchestra, including organ concertante, for the 259th Anniversary of the Festival of the Sons of Clergy. It was premièred at the service in St Paul's on 24 April 1913. Parry commented that the large choir 'sounded rather fluffy' in the cathedral's wayward acoustic. There is no evidence that the work, comparable in length to *Blest Pair of Sirens*, was repeated in its orchestral version; though Sir George Thalban-Ball (Temple Church) revived the piece in the 1970s with organ accompaniment. The orchestral reduction of the vocal score is the worst ever inflicted on Parry. It should be ignored in arriving at a critical judgement of the work. This was confirmed by Thalban-Ball who decided to go back to the full score to construct an effective organ accompaniment.

In this late psalm, Parry returns to a stylistic preoccupation which had its roots in *Concertstück*, namely the Liszt–Wagner element which found its fullest expression in *A Song of Darkness and Light*. But it is also present in *Prometheus*, *De Profundis* and the Second Symphony; and arguably it is most perfectly blended with other style aspects in *The Soul's Ransom* and the *Elegy for Brahms*. The closest parallel to the setting of Psalm 46 is the later tone poem *From Death to Life*. In common with the first movement of that score, the colouring here is unusually dark even for Parry. Note the opening phrase: and there are the same abrupt changes of texture between phrases, which give the paragraphs that evolve from them a feeling of experimentation. The work's weakness, some conventional rhythmic patterns, does not alter the fact that Parry was seeking a new musical syntax. Through the same process of osmosis by which Parry always grew as a composer, Réger and Schoenberg were being added to the fibre of his musical thought.

Parry is not borne away on the words as he had been by Dunbar's 'Ode on the Nativity', and would be again by Donne's 'At the Round Earth's Imagined Corner', nor is the musical argument as inspired as that of the Fifth Symphony. Here Parry is meditating on the psalm's meaning – a philosophic, musical investigation of the ancient text. The spirits of Liszt and Nietzsche hover around the music, particularly in their role as Mephisto: their attempt to undermine the nineteenth century concept of Christian good and evil. It is a genuinely interesting work, the last in this direction, the Faustian direction, which Jung, in reference to Nietzsche, described as 'unpopular, ambiguous, and dangerous, it is a voyage of discovery to the other pole of the world'.[28]

In March 1913 Sidney, Lord Pembroke, the last of Maude's brothers, died suddenly in Rome and Parry wrote an 'Elegy' for the service. By May his own health had collapsed again and he suffered recurrent heart trouble from overwork. During the summer he sailed up the Irish Sea to the Western Isles of Scotland, including Mull and Iona – his last major trip in the The *Wanderer*. After the Gloucester Festival performance of his 1900 *Te Deum*, recast for the English text, he was under the surgeon's knife for a throat operation which left him in a shaky condition. Death continued to follow him: in July Alfred Lyttelton was fatally injured by a stray cricket ball during an amateur match, and only five months later his elder brother Spenser died unexpectedly; 'a most terrible loss', Parry lamented.

Throughout these surface disturbances, his creative equilibrium remained intact. By the end of 1913 he had completed a 300-page score for Aristophanes' *The Archanians*, his valedictory essay in the genre of allusion and satire. This time he embraced Strauss (a Waltz from *Der Rosenkavalier*), Schumann, Elgar, Debussy and a medley of popular songs. Aristophanes' preoccupations with the threats of war accorded well with Parry's belief that the scaremongers were wrong and that peace would be maintained, which adds a curious poignancy to this last of the Oxford 'Parrystophanes' scores, premièred only a few months before the outbreak of World War One in February 1914. Its wide frame of musical reference parallels the richness of the London concert scene in those last years of pre-war England. Parry's diary reactions are just as pointed and critical as they were when he confronted Brahms and Dvořák for the first time thirty years before.

Parry was always keenly interested in the latest sounds but it took him a long time to digest them and make them his own. In this respect his reactions to Mahler and Schoenberg are no different to his early diary entries on his contemporaries. For example, his diary entry of 18 January 1913: 'Mahler's Symphony No. 7 bothered me. Such aggressive noisy stuff. A very unpleasant personality and sometimes crude in scoring, though most of the scoring is ingenious. I met several people who liked it as little as I did – including young Schuster.' I find Parry's reaction hardly surprising: the Seventh, with the exception of its magnificent opening theme complex and a few later melodic ideas, is not one of Mahler's finest creations. If Parry had been introduced to Mahler's music by way of the Third and Fourth Symphonies or by *Das Lied von der Erde*, his reaction probably would have been very different. In fact Mahler's Fourth shares some of Parry's own stylistic preoccupations and, as I mentioned in Chapter 5, Parry was quite happy to use a Mahlerian ländler for the central section of the scherzo in his own Fifth Symphony.

Scriabin's Piano Concerto and *Prometheus* also elicited his curiosity and he arrived at the Queen's Hall armed with a full score of the latter. The performances in 1913, given with Scriabin as soloist, were not first rate and he was disappointed that *Prometheus* did not have a bigger sound.

Schoenberg's *Five Orchestral Pieces* had been the *cause célèbre* in 1912 when Wood performed it and we know from Adrian Boult that Parry was there. He also attended the 1914 performance conducted by Schoenberg himself. The full diary entries read: 'Very much amused . . . elaboration of noises which reminded me of the Nursery when children play with toy instruments. But I noticed the band applauded and it surprised me. There was much applause at the end. Mackenzie very angry'.[29] Several days later he was still picking up comments: 'Much discussion of Schoenberg at luncheon. Sam who led the orchestra said Schoenberg lost his place altogether in the last movement and the orchestra went all to pieces. – But he admitted it "didn't make much difference".'[30] Parry would continue to champion Schoenberg's music in the college and at Oxford, as we know from Dr Strong.

One of the high points of those years was Beecham's Russian series. Parry responded with enthusiasm to the operas *Ivan the Terrible*, *Le Coq d'Or*, *Boris Godunov*, *Khovanshchina* and *Prince Igor* and fairly revelled in Stravinsky's *Le Rossignol* and *Petrushka* of which he wrote: 'It really is a marvellous piece from every point of view. Stravinsky's wild fancy, the story, the dancing – all wonderful'.[31] The performance of *Boris Godounov* (the Rimsky-Korsakov version) on 10 June 1914 particularly intrigued him: 'A confused piece as far as the play goes, but most enjoyable – warm, ingenious: a glimpse from a new region altogether. I enjoyed it thoroughly throughout. Music mostly barbaric with its constant reiteration of short figures – wonderfully effective.'[32]

These were halcyon days when he and Maude regularly went on to Romanoff's restaurant, often after the opera or the theatre, when no doubt the grand-daughter of the Countess Woronzoff enjoyed protracting the Russian mood. In contrast, on evenings at home in Kensington Square, Parry's normal diary entry is 'read to Maude' and then 'to bed'. The first London performances of *Parsifal* allowed him to revisit old impressions: 'Took Maude to Parsifal. Found the dialogue much too long but the Grail scene impressed me as of old. It was finely put on. The dialogue in the later parts again tiresome and the last scene seemed to me this time an anticlimax; the emotional situation not sufficient to make up for the much less impressive finale than that of the 1st Act'.[33]

The growing popularity of Vaughan Williams' music, threatening to rival that of Elgar, gave his old teacher opportunities for continued assessment. In addition to *A Sea Symphony*, Parry heard the first performances of the *Tallis Fantasia*, 'Vaughan Williams' queer fantasia for strings', the *Suite from the Wasps*, which he felt was too short and *A London Symphony*: 'Vaughan Williams' London City, full of interest and thought, with fine effects of scoring which Bob Schuster told me were not all his own, as some other young musicians had helped in that a great deal'.[34]

Graves tactfully left off Schuster's comment in his biography; however, taken *en masse*, Parry's comments do suggest an element of jealousy towards the pupil whose musical talent surpassed that of his teacher. Haydn displayed the same response to the younger Beethoven, although it is difficult to determine whether he was in any way conscious of this. Parry's assessment of Elgar's later work is more objective but no less critical. *The Music Makers* and *The Spirit of England* disappointed him; the Second Symphony was the last major work Parry wholeheartedly admired.

As Europe edged towards war Parry was planning an extensive trip to Norway and Sweden, and decided to have a motor fitted to The *Wanderer* for negotiating the fjords. On 3 August 1914 he set out with Pearsall Smith and Raleigh from Littlehampton through the Solent. They were busy dodging 'strange looking buoys when a navy launch came at us full tilt and told us we were going over mined ground and should be fired into if we didn't turn back.' The next day, the fateful 4 August, an attempt to sail out of the Solent was frustrated when three shots were fired across their bows. After further delays permission was granted to go to Dartmouth, but by 7 September Parry was back at Rustington.

He was soon preoccupied over the internment of his German servant of twenty years, George Schlichenmeyer; but attempts to secure naturalization (a direct appeal to the Home Secretary) fell on deaf ears and George was soon interned. The college was fast depleted as members joined up, including Butterworth, Bliss, Dyson, Farrar, Moeran and Vaughan Williams. Parry firmly believed exceptional individuals should be protected from the war as he stated in many letters. For instance in January 1915, of one musician – 'A' – he wrote to Vaughan Williams:

> My dear old V.W.,
>   I am not altogether surprised, but I am thoroughly bothered. A's a most awkward situation! I have written to Major Darwin and hope to see him tomorrow and discuss the matter further.
>   As to you enlisting, I can't express myself in any way that is likely to be serviceable.
>   There are certain individuals who are capable of serving their country in certain exceptional and very valuable ways, and they are not on the same footing as ordinary folks, who if they are exterminated are just one individual gone and no more. You have already served your country in many notable and exceptional ways and are likely to do so again; and such folks should be shielded from risk rather than exposed to it. We may admit the generosity of the impulse, and feel – I will not say what.
>   Yours affectionately,
>   C. Hubert H. Parry'[35]

In the autumn of 1914 Parry still hoped the war would be over by Christmas and the decision to persist with the Brighton Festival in November gave him the opportunity to write his final orchestral score, *From Death to Life*, discussed in Chapter 4. By 1915 Parry was actively engaged with 'Music in Wartime' and other related committees. Sir Homewood Crawford's letter to *The Times*, written in October 1918 after Parry's death, testifies to the dedication Parry brought to this charitable work:

> Committees were at once set up and Sir Hubert Parry readily accepted the chairmanship of the Music-in-Wartime Committee. For upwards of four years Sir Hubert Parry gave the committee the benefit of his valuable services presiding over all committee meetings

and personally investigating and supervising every detail of the work entrusted to the Committee.'

Soon death touched the college. On 18 March 1915, the date of *From Death to Life*'s second performance, he saw Claude Aveling's nephew leave for the front. By 3 May the young recruit had died of severe wounds: 'It depressed me so much that I could hardly get through the [college] address without breaking down'. In the same week Frank Pownall's only son died at Gallipoli.

Against the background of an ever darkening world, Parry's ideas for *Instinct and Character* started to synthesize. Although the manuscript of Parry's last book had not reached its final form when he died in October 1918, he had worked on it since 1915 and hoped it would eventually be published in some form. On 30 May 1918, he wrote to Macmillan, for whom he had prepared a version for their consideration:

> It is [a] sort of apologia which I could not resist the craving to make, in connection with my having devoted my life mostly to art which so many people think to be merely self-indulgence. Indirectly the book has a close connection with music, as one of the main objects is to deal with the spiritual and material influences in life, which in these times have become so urgent. If I was not at least egotistical enough to feel that the subjects it deals with are so peculiarly urgent I would be content to let it remain unprinted, as an attempt to clarify my own mind by thinking out the things which have presented themselves in my particular sphere of work – But the line that has presented itself to me is rather different from what I am accustomed to hear around me and I believe very much in the usefulness of having many points of view, so I dare to think it may be useful. It works out to something like the same conclusion as Kidd's Social Evolution, but by a very different road – and the matter of the road seems to me to affect the conclusions and what will follow from them.[36]

In early June he met Macmillan for lunch to discuss the matter but came away pessimistic. On 14 June, Macmillan wrote, declining publication.

In this letter of 30 May, Parry set out his reasons for writing the book, and why he would like it published. He never realized that, in attempting a philosophical treatise, he had entered a field where he was only an enthusiastic amateur. Though Parry's prose retains its usual vigorous straightforward clarity, the style is perfunctory, and impersonal. Perhaps this is due to the violent change of subject matter. The version which is available for reading was prepared by Arthur Ponsonby, after Parry's death. There is an enormous imbalance between the all embracing subject matter and the paucity of inventive thinking and factual material which makes up the text. It reads like a crammed outline for a treatise in twenty volumes. There are occasionally some interesting, even powerful thoughts, but they dissipate quickly into disjunct commentaries on other subjects, or generalizations without any acquired empirical data. Parry discusses 'the instincts' sequentially and fails to achieve meaningful cross-analysis. The result is a rather exhausting over-extended list of observations, which do not cohere.

If Parry's intention was to uphold his idealist concept of man's progress, then as a whole the book gives the opposite impression. By the middle of the war I think Parry was disillusioned both with common humanity and the aristocratic politicians who decided its fate. His feelings of desperation at the young composers going to the front are not surprising. Ponsonby, in his lengthy introduction, says that Parry was planning to rewrite the work in a more concise form. He had begun this revised version in the summer of 1918 and hoped it would find favour with a publisher.

The book suffers in comparison with the great nineteenth-century philosophers, just as the oratorios, and those cantatas which attempt the profoundly tragic, suffer in comparison with the dramatic masterpieces of Berlioz, Verdi and Wagner. The opening evocation on the universal forces of energy and motion is as flat and second-hand as the prelude and opening arioso in *Job*. 'Parrystophanes' could be clever and amusing, 'Parrystotle' and 'Parrymedes' are not.

Much of the book's morally didactic tone is unpleasant to read. His views on sexual matters are puritanical, full of attitudes but devoid of insights. They could hardly appeal to anyone looking for enlightenment on the subject. His lack of insight in this area is truly astounding. Parry did not realize that, in the opinion of many psychologists, such as Alfred Adler and Wilhelm Reich, Victorian sexual repression was one of the principal causes of the world-destroying war (1914–18) which horrified him and darkened his final years. However, he would not have been the first old man to react in this way, once sexual desire had become a dim memory. Perhaps the tragedy of Clinton's dissipated collapse and the appalling legacies of syphilis strengthened his negative attitudes. This is not the only area of the human experience in which Parry has little insight. When writing on the religious instinct and the arts, the tone is flat, uninspired. His clever turns of phrase, which abound in his other books, are lacking here.

The unself-reflecting arrogance which led him to compose *Job* and *The Pied Piper* led him astray again in old age. He deluded himself that he was a genuine historian–philosopher, with equally disastrous results. I believe it was fortunate for Parry that the manuscript was never published, although later Parry scholars may feel differently. Happily the ageing composer was inspired to continue his remarkable Indian Summer, despite the horrors of the First World War. The *Songs of Farewell* are one of the high points in his life's work.

The *Songs of Farewell* consist of six a cappella motets whose origins date back to 1906, when Parry produced a setting of Lockhart's 'There is an Old Belief' at Parratt's request for a memorial service held at the Royal Mausoleum, Frogmore in January 1907. It is surely not a coincidence that this original version was written soon after *The Soul's Ransom*, nor that he decided to revise it in 1913 following his *Ode on the Nativity* and *God is Our Hope*, with their renewed interest in varied choral textures. In addition to the six-part 'There is an Old Belief', Parry made first drafts of 'My Soul There is a Country' and 'I Know My Soul Hath Power to Know All Things (both in four parts), and of a five-part setting of 'Never Weather Beaten Sail'. He continued to work on them through 1914 and 1915 when the *Songs of Farewell* reached their final form with the composition of the seven-part setting of Donne's 'At the Round Earth's Imagined Corner' and Psalm 39, 'Lord Let Me Know Mine End', which like *God is Our Hope* is once again for double choir. The first four were tried over at the RCM and Oxford under Hugh Allen, who gave the official première of the first five motets with the Bach Choir at the Royal College on 22 May 1916. 'Lord Let Me Know Mine End' was given by Allen a year later on 17 June 1917 with the Oxford Bach Choir at New College, Oxford.

These songs are intimate secular pieces on sacred subjects. They possess great strength, but the strength is a quiet, inward strength. Often music and words are so perfectly united that the listener has the feeling they existed together from the beginning. Parry – who so often crowded out the essential quiet core of his music, by hyperactivity during his everyday life – here preserves his inner peace intact. One can almost see the old composer quietly humming the opening phrases of these pieces before notating them. To say the flavour of these choral songs, and the atmosphere they create, is singular would be an understatement. If they remind me of anything it is Charles Ives' Psalm settings and in No. 5, 'At the Round Earth's Imagined Corner', the later motets of Anton Bruckner. Like the Ives settings they belong to a twentieth century which never came into being: a peaceful golden age devoted to creativity and philosophic speculation. Then 1914 intervened and plunged Western man into a holocaust from which he has never recovered. But these songs offer consolation for the inward man.

Ex. 22   from 'At the Round Earth's Imagined Corner'

They must have been a consolation for Parry too, witness his own account of the Bach Choir concert held on 22 May 1916 at the College, when they sang the new motets: 'I never felt anything so sympathetic. They encored the 6-part one and the Choir paid a singular compliment to the 7-part 'At the Round Earth's Imagined Corner', as they all stayed while the audience went out and then sang it again, even better than the first time.'[37] Performers of these motets should know they were written for fairly large choirs like the Bach Choir. The Anglican tradition of using boys' voices to replace sopranos and altos is deadly for these songs. All too often, the white, expressionless, slightly flat, strained sound of boy trebles robs this music of its glowing warmth.

The first half of 1914 had been taken up revising *The Vision of Life* for Norwich, but the Festival was cancelled at the onset of war. Parry also spent time on composing some movements for strings, later entitled *An English Suite*. This was left unfinished at his death. The ubiquitous Emily Daymond chose the order of the eight movements and named two of them 'Caprice' and 'Frolic'. The work doesn't cohere: it remains a collection of movements, some dating back to the *The Lady Radnor Suite* (1894). Nevertheless no lover of Parry's music would be without it, especially the particularly charming minuet – Falstaff sauntering through his garden in a mellow mood. At the end of the year he produced an intriguing addendum to the *Songs of Farewell*: an intricate five-part setting of Keats's 'La Belle Dame sans Merci' performed by the Bristol Madrigal Society.

The war stopped all Parry's sailing activity and motoring was restricted for lack of petrol; his efforts to obtain war work were dismissed out of hand. Against this background it is curious that he determined in 1915 to take an extended trip to North America with Hugh Allen, seventeen days at sea in the American ship *The Corsican* and eighteen on land. Considering the fate of the *Lusitania*, which Parry had seen in 1912 off Ireland, the trip was not without danger. The two men travelled to Quebec, Montreal and Toronto, where they visited the musical conservatory, before going on to New York, Boston and finally Harvard, to inspect the Observatory with E.C. Pickering, Professor of Astronomy.

Such a risky trip taken with no specific purpose raises the question whether Parry and Allen were possibly engaged in government work, perhaps as high class messengers. The *Lusitania* had been torpedoed only three months before on 8 May, and on their return journey the *St Paul* projected additional lights onto its American flags. Parry's diary is curiously reticent about the whole trip. In his first letter to Lady Maude on 7 August, he states: 'I shall be thankful when the expedition is over and I am back again. There is not the least likelihood of my enjoying it.' In both the First and Second World Wars it was common for the rich and famous to take on such work under the convenient cover of their position.

Later that year Lady Richmond was killed by a motor car at Hammersmith; 'Willie behaved with marvellous self command and dignity at the funeral which Maude, Dolly and Freddie [von Hugel] attended'.[38] At another funeral in 1916 Parry sat with Mackenzie and Sir Frederick Bridge in front, close to the big aperture in the pavement through which the coffin was lowered; 'I noticed how the representative musicians were all ageing together'. In January Frank Pownall died, a release from years of illness, a few months later George Butterworth was killed in action and Hamish MacCunn died at only 48, after a long illness.

'Here's a tune for you old chap. Do what you like with it.' With these words Parry handed Walford Davies the music for *Jerusalem*, his immortal setting of William Blake's verses beginning 'And did those feet in ancient time'. It was the poet Robert Bridges who had suggested Parry should write 'suitable simple music for Blake's stanzas, music that an audience could take up and join in'.[39] The occasion was a meeting in 1916 of the Fight for Right propaganda movement in the Queen's Hall, to which Parry gave a guarded allegiance. Two years later he included the setting in the Albert Hall concert to celebrate the Votes for Women campaign of which he was an avid supporter. His old friend Mrs Fawcett wrote afterwards to thank him for organizing the music. 'The council passed a special vote of thanks to you, The Bach Choir and the orchestra yesterday, but this is a little personal line. Your *Jerusalem* ought to be made the women voters' Hymn'.[40]

On this occasion Parry's unison song was performed in his own arrangement for standard orchestra (the original was for organ accompaniment) and it was frequently given in this version. It is unfortunate that Parry's most famous work is now generally known only in the Elgar orchestration which was designed to give the Leeds Festival of 1922 a version for a very large orchestra, and not to replace for all time Parry's original orchestration. It would be a serious mistake, however, to view Elgar's orchestration as anything but a labour of love. It is also forgotten that Parry intended the first stanza of *Jerusalem* to be sung by a solo female voice, the massed voices joining in only for the second. No one wrote a more fitting epitaph to *Jerusalem* than Harry Plunkett Greene: 'It is said that the greatest benefactor of a country is the man who writes its tunes; if he had left us nothing but *Jerusalem* we could never repay him for what we owe him'.[41]

The Battle of Jutland in June 1916 prompted Hugh Allen to request a commemorative work from Bridges and Parry for the Bach Choir. Parry wrote the elegiac five-part setting of *The Chivalry of the Sea* at Rustington in September and dedicated it to the memory of Charles Fisher, Adeline Vaughan Williams' brother, who died in the battle. *The Chivalry of the Sea* – his last Cantata and last collaboration with Robert Bridges – and the unison song *England* were written after the *Songs of Farewell* and *Jerusalem*. Unfortunately they have a tired backward-looking quality. For Parry the war had gone on too long; failing health and constant depression show only too clearly in these last creative embers and after a splendid five-year flowering it would be unfair to dwell on them.

Films of the horrors at the front shocked Parry deeply – 'Dreadfully vivid' – and by the end of 1917 he had the bitterness of seeing the woods of Highnam decimated for the war effort, including 'Magog', the smaller of the two elms. People noticed he was ageing and becoming taciturn because of the war. Christmas was spent ill in bed but he was back in harness for the new term. In the same month as his 70th birthday he was 'infuriated by the way people forced themselves in out of their turn'[43] as he waited in the food queues at Barkers at the top of Kensington Square.

He maintained his full working schedule throughout 1918. At the end of the summer term he paid his last visit to Highnam and visited George Schlichenmeyer at the stone quarry where he worked, met the Manager and 'spoke to lots of the men'.[44] After a brief return to London, where he told George's wife of his visit, the final weeks of his life were spent in Rustington. He was out of sorts and felt 'worn out' on arrival. Once more he endeavoured to obtain war work. An official from the London Board of Agriculture 'proposed rather feebly some visiting with inspectors of agriculture but evidently without conviction so being unwilling to trespass on his time I left.'[45]

At Rustington he spent much time condensing *Instinct and Character*, interspersed with visits to Littlehampton for supplies and cycle rides with Emily

Daymond. One such ride with the over energetic Emily on 6 September left him exhausted. 'At dinner I chafed her about it and she took violent offence and sulked all dinner and went to bed immediately afterwards.'[46]

By the morning there was a large swelling in his groin, probably caused by a rupture and the doctor ordered him to bed. Given his long history of cysts and his weakened condition he was unable to fight off the onset of blood poisoning and over the next six weeks steadily declined. Vaccines, from cultures of his blood, failed to revive him and for five days he remained unconscious, dying in the evening of 7 October, a month before the war ended. Arthur Ponsonby wrote in his diary of the last moments:

> Lifeless staring eyes – not yet – a little October sunshine the sun setting through the poplars, the wind dropping – come up, you had better come up – breathing slower – would there be another, yes, yes and still another on again for a little – slower, slower – the last one silence – what a tremendous silence. And then the chirping song of a bird at the window – a bird who had followed him when he moved to another room and had sung to him in the morning.[47]

The funeral in St Paul's was conducted by the Archbishop of Canterbury, the Very Revd R.T. Davidson, and all the leading members of the musical profession attended: Elgar, Stanford, Mackenzie, Cowen, Bridge, Lloyd and Parrot. The coffin was carried by nine Etonians, led appropriately by the Keeper of the Field. In a memorial lecture given at the RCM fifty years later, Dr Herbert Howells began by saying:

> On the last day of February in 1918, away in the Yorkshire Wolds, I received a letter – the only one to reach me on that morning, in the blissful pre-5d. epoch. It had been written on the previous day, the 27th. Opening it, I found a first sentence that shook me: 'I have come to the last milestone; and looking back I am troubled to realise how little I have been able to do.' Of all people it was Hubert Parry who wrote those words – on his 70th birthday. With his endearing courtesy he was writing to thank an obscure ex-student of the College who had sent him a birthday greeting.[48]

In a telephone conversation with Dr Howells, two years before his death in 1983, I asked him, at this stage in his life, what he thought of Sir Hubert Parry. There was a short silence and then: 'Mr Benoliel, I can't tell you what Ralph Vaughan Williams meant to me both as a composer and as a man, and in my long life I have met many great and interesting men; but Hubert Parry was the greatest man I have ever known.'

Parry was indeed a great man, but more than that he was also a highly complex man and a genuinely great composer. The value and integrity of Parry's finest writing on music will ensure its place in music history for the scholar, but in itself it will not ensure his survival in the minds of the general public. In fact his books and articles become infinitely more interesting if the reader already accepts the premise that they are written by an important composer. It is because of his compositions that he will not end up as a mere byway in histories of nineteenth-century England. In his most successful works for orchestra, and chorus and orchestra, Parry's music approaches the longed-for music of the spheres. Such music will continue to live and to influence because it is loved and because it is needed.

II Selected Published Writings of Hubert Parry

An Introduction to the Writings of Hubert Parry

Parry's books and articles display a high degree of general intelligence, and an exhaustive knowledge of music history. His prose style is exemplary for its clarity of expression and freedom from Victorian mannerisms. He was one of the first authors on music to relate musical history to the wider framework of Western civilization in general.

Parry's books have all long been out of print. Occasionally a library specializing in books on music may have a copy of one or two of them, but they are very scarce. Hence this selection of excerpts, which makes up the second half of this book. Obviously the choice has had to be a personal one and for reasons of space it is not always possible to edit the texts without some abrupt elisions. For this I am entirely to blame, as one of Parry's great strengths as a writer is the logical flow of his discourse.

Parry learned his trade, and indeed established his reputation as a music historian, working for Sir George Grove. From 1875 he was Sub-Editor of Grove's *Dictionary of Music and Musicians* and became a major contributor to the first edition. Most of Parry's own articles had been written by the time Grove invited him to become Professor of the Department of Musical History at the Royal College of Music in 1883, and over the next 30 years Parry published six books:

Studies of Great Composers (1887)

The Art of Music (1893, revised 1896 as *The Evolution of the Art of Music*)

Summary of Music History (1893)

The Music of the Seventeenth Century (1902)

Johann Sebastian Bach (1909)

Style in Musical Art (1911)

In addition a number of lectures were published as articles and after his death H.C. Colles edited his *College Addresses* which Macmillan published in 1920. I have not included any selections from his *Summary of Music History*. It is a school primer, that offers no subject matter Parry has not covered with greater insight elsewhere. Finally there is Parry's last and still unpublished book *Instinct and Character*. After considerable deliberation on its contents I have decided not to include any material from this manuscript. My reasons for this decision are contained in Chapter 9, 'The Last Journey to *Jerusalem*'.

When it came to choosing a selection of Parry's writings, there were four categories of writing I felt were most important:

- passages which reflect most clearly Parry's own personality, that relate to Parry the composer, or that reflect the workings of his mind as historian and analyst

- writing which shifted contemporary attitudes and had the greatest sway with his colleagues, pupils and the general musical readership

- those passages of greatest historical importance, writings where Parry's own research, presentation of his material and conclusions influenced the musicology of the future

- the writings which should provide the most informative and enjoyable reading for lovers of music today, especially within the English-speaking world

The reader should be aware that this selection is a small fraction of Parry's complete published writings.

10 Contributions to Grove's *A Dictionary of Music and Musicians:* Symphony

Introduction

George Grove was working for Macmillan as Editor of *Macmillan's Magazine* when he announced the prospectus for *A Dictionary of Music and Musicians* in January 1874. The enormous concept was finally published in book form by Macmillan in 1890 in four volumes.

Grove had known Parry since Sullivan introduced them at the Gloucester Festival of 1868 and in 1875 he published Parry's set of poems *A Sequence of Analogies*. Two months later, in a letter dated 14 July 1875, Grove invited the 27-year-old Hubert Parry to become a contributor to the new dictionary: 'I am quite determined that you shall have something to do with it, and now that I have got a lovely subject for you, you must consent – you must be "beautiful Paris" and not "evil hearted Paris." The subject that you are to write about is "Arrangement" . . . Oh very dear Paris, it's a jolly subject.'[1] Parry took up the invitation with enthusiasm and completed the article during September.

Grove soon needed an editorial assistant as contributions poured in from Prout, Stanford, Sullivan, Dannreuther and Davison among others. In November Grove appointed Parry as Sub-Editor – 'A grand opportunity for me to work and to learn', Parry commented in his diary. When the first edition appeared he had contributed 123 entries, all on the technical aspects of the art. They range from brief paragraphs to full-scale articles of more than 25,000 words on 'Sonata' and 'Symphony', which Grove commissioned in July 1879 saying 'the author of "form" should treat the two great vehicles of it.'

Edward Elgar said in 1904, when commenting on Grove's *Dictionary*: 'but the articles which have since helped me the most are those of Hubert Parry'.[2] It is not so much that Parry offers his readers new insights – which the *Dictionary* was not designed to do in any case – but he presents his ideas with remarkable clarity so that even someone barely acquainted with the fundamentals of musical terminology can readily understand the meaning of his discourse. In his extensive 'Symphony' article the language is genial but precise and Parry's enthusiasm for his subject shines throughout. He is not too erudite to include a joking reference in the paragraph on the Pastoral Symphony to the 'land question' which bedevilled agricultural policy in the 1880s. It should be added that many of his ideas on Beethoven's compositional innovations, such as his very expanded symphonic finales and the emotional impetus behind them, now seem very commonplace although they were new at the time. Indeed these articles set the standard and the tone which later musicologists, critics and commentators adopted as common practice.

Symphony

[Beethoven]

The greatest of all masters of the Symphony followed so close upon Haydn, that there is less of a gap between the last of Haydn's Symphonies and his first than there was later between some of his own. Haydn's last was probably written in 1795. When Beethoven wrote his first cannot be ascertained; sketches for the Finale are found as early as the year last mentioned; but it was not actually produced in public till April 2, 1800. Like Schumann and Brahms in later days, he did not turn his attention to this branch of composition till comparatively late. The opus-number of his first symphony is 21. It is preceded by eleven pianoforte sonatas, several works for pianoforte combined with other instruments, the well-known Septuor in E flat, and several chamber compositions for strings. So that by the time he came to attacking Symphony he had had considerable practice in dealing with structural matters. The only works in which he had tried his strength with the orchestra were the two concertos—the B flat, op. 19, which was written in or about 1795, and the C major, op. 15, which was written about 1796.

He showed himself at once a master of the orchestra; but it is evident that at first he stepped cautiously in expressing himself with such resources. The 1st Symphony is less free and rich in expression, and has more elements of formality, than several works on a smaller scale which preceded it. This is explicable on the general ground that the orchestra, especially in those days, was not a fit exponent of the same kind of things which could be expressed by solo violins, or the pianoforte. The scale must necessarily be larger and broader; the intricate development and delicate or subtle sentiment which is quite appropriate and intelligible in the intimacy of a domestic circle, is out of place in the more public conditions of orchestral performance. This Beethoven must have instinctively felt, and he appears not to have found the style for full expression of his personality in either of the first symphonies. The second is even more curious in that respect than the first, as it comes after one of the richest and most interesting, and another of the most perfectly charming and original of the works of his early period, namely the Sonatas in D minor and E flat of op. 31.

However, even in these two symphonies there is a massiveness and breadth and seriousness of purpose, which mark them as products of a different and more powerfully constituted nature than anything of the kind produced before. At the time when the 1st Symphony appeared, the opening with the chord of the minor 7th of C, when the key of the piece was C major, was looked upon as extremely daring; and the narrow-minded pedants of the day felt their sensitive delicacy so outraged that some of them are said never to have forgiven it. The case is very similar to the famous introduction to Mozart's C major String Quartet, about which the pedants were little less than insulting. Beethoven had to fight for his right to express what he felt to be true; and he did it without flinching; sometimes with an apparent relish But at the same time, in these early orchestral works he seems to have experimented with caution, and was content to follow his predecessors in a great deal that he put down.

There are characteristic things in both symphonies; for instance, in the 1st the transitional passage which begins at the 65th bar of the Allegro, passing from G to G minor and then to B flat and back again, and the corresponding passage in the second half of the movement. The working out of the Andante cantabile and the persistent drum rhythm are also striking points. In the 2nd Symphony the dimensions of the Introduction are unusual, and the character of all the latter part and the freedom of the transitions in it are decisive marks of his tendencies. The Slow movement has also a warmth and sense of genuine sympathy which is new; the Scherzo, though as yet short, has a totally new character about it, and the abrupt sforzandos and short striking figures and still more the coda, of the Finale, are quite his own. In the orchestra it is worth noting that he adopted clarinets from the first, apparently as a matter of course; in the first two symphonies he continued to use only the one pair of horns, as his predecessors had done; in the third he expanded the group to three. In the 4th he went back to two, and did not use four till the 9th. The disposition of his forces even in the first two is more independent and varied than his predecessors. The treatment of the several groups of instruments tends to be more distinct and appropriate, and at the same time more perfectly assimilated in the total effect of the music.

The step to the 3rd Symphony is however immense, and at last shows this branch of composition on a level with his other works of the same period. It is surrounded on both sides by some of his noblest achievements. Opus 47 was the Sonata in A for violin and pianoforte, known as the 'Kreutzer'. Opus 53 is the Sonata in C major, dedicated to Count Waldstein. Opus 54 is the admirable little Sonata in F major. Opus 55 is the Symphony and opus 57 the Sonata known as the 'Appassionata'. It appears that Beethoven had the idea of writing this symphony as early as 1798, but the actual work was probably done in the summer and autumn of 1803. There seems to be no doubt that it was written under the influence of his admiration for Napoleon. His own title page had on it 'Sinfonia grande, Napoleon Bonaparte', and, as is well known, the name 'Eroica' was not added till Napoleon became Emperor; after which event Beethoven's feelings about him naturally underwent a change. To call a great work by the name of a great man was quite a different thing from calling it by the name of a crowned ruler. However, the point remains the same, that the work was written with a definite purpose and under the inspiration of a special subject, and one upon which Beethoven himself assuredly had a very decided opinion.

The result was the richest and noblest and by far the biggest symphony that had ever yet appeared in the world. It is very possible that Beethoven meant it to be so; but the fact does not make the step from the previous symphonies any the less remarkable. The scoring throughout is most freely distributed. In the first movement especially there is hardly any one of the numerous subjects and characteristic figures which has not properties demanding different departments of the orchestra to express them. They are obviously conceived with reference to the whole forces at command, not to a predominant central force and appendages. The strings must necessarily have the greater part of the work to do, but the symphony is not written for them with wind as a species of afterthought. But it is still to be noticed that the balance is obtained chiefly by definite propositions and answers between one group and another, and though the effect is delightful, the principle is rendered a little obvious from the regularity of its occurrence.

The second movement is specially noticeable as reaching the strongest pitch of sentiment as yet shown in an orchestral slow movement. In the earliest symphonies these movements were nearly always remarkably short, and scored for fewer instruments than the first and last Frequently they were little better than 'intermezzi', attached on both sides to the more important allegros. Even Mozart's and Haydn's latest examples had more grace and sweetness than deep feeling, and frequently showed a tendency to formalism in the expression of the ideas and in the ways in which the ornamental *fiorituri* were introduced. In the Eroica the name 'Marcia funebre' at once defines the object; and though the form of a march is to a certain extent maintained, it is obvious that it is of secondary importance, since the attention is more drawn to the rich and noble expression of the finest feelings of humanity over the poetically imagined death of one of the world's heroes, than to the traditional march form. The music seems in fact to take almost the definiteness of speech of the highest order; or rather, to express the emotions which belong to the imagined situation with more fulness and comprehensiveness, but with scarcely less definiteness, than speech could achieve.

In the third movement appears the first of Beethoven's large orchestral scherzos. Any connection between it and the typical Minuet and Trio it is hard to see. The time is quicker and more bustling; and the character utterly distinct from the suave grace and somewhat measured paces of most of the previous third movements. The main points of connection with them are firstly the general outlines of form (that is, the principal portion of the Scherzo corresponding to the Minuet comes first and last, and the Trio in the middle) and secondly the humorous element. In this latter particular there is very great difference between the *naïf* and spontaneous fun of Haydn and the grim humour of Beethoven, sometimes verging upon irony, and sometimes, with evident purpose, upon the grotesque. The scherzo of the Eroica is not alloyed with as much grimness as some later ones, but it has traits of melancholy and seriousness here and there. The effect in its place is chiefly that of portraying the fickle crowd who soon forget their hero, and chatter and bustle cheerfully about their business or pleasure as before; has had its humorous or at least laughter-making ironical side to any one large-minded enough to avoid thinking of all such traits of humanity with reprobation and disgust.

The last movement is on a scale more than equal to that of all the others, and, like them, strikes an almost entirely new note in symphonic finales. The light and simple character of Haydn's final rondos is familiar to every one; and he was consistent in aiming at gaiety for conclusion. Mozart in most cases did the same; but in the G minor Symphony there is a touch of rather vehement regretfulness, and in the C major of strength and seriousness. But the Finale of the Eroica first introduces qualities of massiveness and broad earnest dignity to that position in the symphony. The object is evidently to crown the work in a totally different sense from the light cheerful endings of most previous symphonies, and to appeal to fine feelings in the audience instead of aiming at putting them in a cheerful humour. It is all the difference between an audience before the revolutionary epoch and after. The starting point of the movement is the same theme from the Prometheus music as that of the pianoforte variations in E flat (op. 35). The basis of the whole movement is mainly the variation-form, interspersed with fugal episodes; and a remarkable feature is the long Andante variation immediately before the final Presto—a somewhat unusual feature in such a position, though Haydn introduced a long passage of Adagio in the middle of the last movement of a symphony in F written about 1777; but of course in a very different spirit. The Finale of the Eroica as a whole is so unusual in form, that it is not wonderful that opinions have varied much concerning it. As a piece of art it is neither so perfect nor so convincing as the other movements; but it has very noble and wonderful traits, and, as a grand experiment in an almost totally new direction, has a decided historical importance.

It is not necessary to go through the whole series of Beethoven's Symphonies in detail, for one reason because they are so generally familiar to musicians and are likely to become more and more so; and for another because they have been so fully discussed from different points of view in this Dictionary. Some short simple particulars about each may however be useful and interesting. The order of composition of the works which succeeded the Eroica Symphony is almost impossible to unravel. By opus-number the 4th Symphony, in B flat, comes very soon, being op. 60; but the sketches for the last movement are in the same sketch book as parts of Fidelio, which is op. 72, and the Concerto in G, which is op. 58, was begun after Fidelio was finished. It can only be seen clearly that his works were crowded close together in this part of his life, and interest attaches to the fact that they represent the warmest and most popular group of all. Close to the B flat Symphony come the Overture to 'Coriolan', the three String Quartets, op. 59, the Violin Concerto, the PF. ditto in G major, the Symphony in C minor, and the 'Sinfonia Pastorale'. The B flat is on a smaller scale than its predecessor, and of lighter and gayer cast. The opening bars of the Introduction are almost the only part which has a trace of sadness in it; and this is probably meant to throw the brightness of the rest of the work into stronger relief. Even the Slow Movement contains more serenity than deep emotion. The Scherzo is peculiar for having the Trio repeated—altogether a new point in symphony-writing, and one which was not left unrepeated or unimitated. What the Symphony was meant to express cannot be known, but it certainly is as complete and consistent as any.

The C minor which followed has been said to be the first in which Beethoven expressed himself freely and absolutely, and threw away all traces of formalism in expression or development to give vent to the perfect utterance of his musical feeling. It certainly is so far the most forcible, and most remote from conventionalism of every kind. It was probably written very nearly about the same time as the B flat. Nottebohm says the first two movements were written in 1805; and, if this is the fact, his work on the B flat and on the C minor must have overlapped. Nothing however could be much stronger than the contrast between the two. The C minor is, in the first and most striking movement, rugged, terrible in force; a sort of struggle with fate, one of the most thoroughly characteristic of Beethoven's productions. The second is a contrast, peaceful, though strong and earnest. The Scherzo again is one of his most original movements; in its musical spirit as utterly unlike anything that had been produced before as possible. Full of fancy, fun, and humour, and, notwithstanding the pauses and changes of time, wonderful in swing; and containing some devices of orchestration quite magical in their clearness, and their fitness to the ideas. The last movement, which follows without break after the Scherzo, is triumphant; seeming to express the mastery in the wrestling and striving of the first movement. It is historically interesting as the first appearance of trombones and contrafagotto in modern symphony; and the most powerful in sound up to that time. The next symphony, which is also the next opus-number, is the popular 'Pastoral', probably written in 1808, the second of Beethoven's which has a definitely stated idea as the basis of its inspiration, and the first in which a programme is suggested for each individual movement; though Beethoven is careful to explain that it is 'mehr Empfindung als Malerei'. Any account of this happy inspiration is clearly superfluous. The situations and scenes which it brings to the mind are familiar, and not likely to be less beloved as the world grows older. The style is again in great contrast to that of the C minor, being characterised rather by serenity and contentment; which, as Beethoven had not heard of all the troubles of the land question, might naturally be his feelings about country life. He used two trombones in the last two movements, but otherwise contented himself with the same group of instruments as in his earliest symphonies

After this there was a pause for some years, during which time appeared many noble and delightful works on other lines, including the pianoforte trios in D and E flat, the Mass in C major, op. 86, the music to Egmont, op. 84, and several sonatas. Then in one year, 1812, two symphonies appeared. The first of the two, in A major, numbered op. 92, is looked upon by many as the most romantic of all of them, and certainly has qualities which increase in attractiveness the better it is known and understood.* Among specially noticeable points are the unusual proportions and great interest of the Introduction (*poco sostenuto*); the singular and fascinating wilfulness of the first movement, which is enhanced by some very characteristic orchestration; the noble calm of the slow movement; the merry humour of the scherzo, which has again the same peculiarity as the 4th Symphony, that the trio is repeated (for which the world has every reason to be thankful, as it is one of the most completely enjoyable things in all symphonic literature); and finally the wild headlong abandonment of the last movement, which might be an

---

* Beethoven's own view may be read just below.

idealised national or rather barbaric dance movement, and which sets the crown fitly upon one of the most characteristic of Beethoven's works.

The Symphony in F, which follows immediately as op. 93, is again of a totally different character. It is of specially small proportions, and has rather the character of a return to the old conditions of the Symphony, with all the advantages of Beethoven's mature powers both in the development and choice of ideas, and in the treatment of the orchestra. Beethoven himself, in a letter to Salomon, described it as 'eine kleine Symphonie in F', as distinguished from the previous one, which he called 'Grosse Symphonie in A, eine meiner vorzüglichsten'. It has more fun and light-heartedness in it than any of the others, but no other specially distinctive external characteristics, except the substitution of the graceful and humorous 'Allegretto scherzando' in the place of the slow movement, and a return to the Tempo di Menuetto for the scherzo.

After this came again a long pause, as the greatest of all symphonies did not make its appearance till 1824. During that time however, it is probable that symphonic work was not out of his mind, for it is certain that the preparations for putting this symphony down on paper spread over several years. Of the introduction of voices into this form of composition, which is its strongest external characteristic, Beethoven had made a previous experiment in the Choral Fantasia; and he himself spoke of the symphony as 'in the style of the Choral Fantasia, but on a far larger scale'. The scale is indeed immensely larger, not only in length but in style, and the increase in this respect applies to it equally in comparison with all the symphonies that went before.

The first movement is throughout the most concentrated example of the qualities which distinguish Beethoven and the new phase upon which music entered with him, from all the composers of the previous half century. The other movements are not less characteristic of him in their particular ways. The second is the largest example of the typical scherzo which first made its appearance for the orchestra in the Eroica; and the supreme slow movement (the Theme with variations) is the finest orchestral example of that special type of slow movement; though in other departments of art he had previously illustrated it in a manner little less noble and deeply expressive in the slow movements of the B flat Trio and the B flat Sonata (op. 106).

These movements all have reference, more or less intelligible according to the organisation and sympathies of the hearer, to the Finale of the Symphony, which consists of a setting of Schiller's ode 'An die Freude'. Its development into such enormous proportions is of a piece with the tendency shown in Beethoven's previous symphonies, and in some of his sonatas also, to supplant the conventional type of gay last movement by something which shall be a logical or poetical outcome of the preceding movements, and shall in some way clench them, or crown them with its weight and power. The introduction of words moreover gives a new force to the definite interpretation of the whole as a single organism, developed as a poem might be in relation to definite and coherent ideas.

The dramatic and human elements which Beethoven introduced into his instrumental music to a degree before undreamed of, find here their fullest expression; and most of the forms of music are called in to convey his ideas. The first movement of the symphony is in binary form; the second in scherzo, or idealised minuet and trio form; the third in the form of theme and variations. Then follows the curious passage of instrumental recitative, of which so many people guessed the meaning even before it was defined by the publication of the extracts from the MS. sketchbooks in the Berlin Library; then the entry of the noble tune, the theme of the entire Finale, introduced contrapuntally in a manner which has a clear analogy to fugal treatment; and followed by the choral part, which treats the theme in the form of variations apportioned to the several verses of the poem, and carries the sentiment to the extremest pitch of exultation expressible by the human voice. The instrumental forces employed are the fullest; including, with the usual complement, four horns, three trombones in the scherzo and finale, and contrafagotto, triangle, cymbals, and big drum in the finale. The choral forces include four solo voices and full chorus, and the sentiment expressed is proportionate to the forces employed.

[Schubert]

Another composer's symphonies did not have much immediate influence, chiefly because they were not performed; what they will have in the future remains to be seen.* In delightfulness, Schubert's two best works in this department stand almost alone; and their qualities are unique. In his earlier works of the kind there is an analogy to Beethoven's early works. Writing for the orchestra seemed to paralyse his particular individuality; and for some time after he had written some of his finest and most original songs, he continued to write symphonies, which were chiefly a mild reflex of Haydn and Mozart, or at most of the early style of Beethoven. His first attempt was made in 1813, the last page being dated 28th October of that year, when he was yet only sixteen years old—one year after Beethoven's Symphonies in A and F, and more than ten years before the great D minor. In the five following years he wrote five more, the best of which is No. 4, the Tragic, in C minor, the Andante especially being very fine and interesting, and containing many characteristic traits of the master.

But none of the early works approach in interest or original beauty to the unfinished one in B minor, and the very long and vigorous one in C major; the first composed in 1822, before Beethoven's No. 9, and the second in 1828, after it. In these two he seems to have struck out a real independent symphony-style for himself, thoroughly individual in every respect, both of idea, form, and orchestration. They show singularly little of the influence of Beethoven, or Mozart, or Haydn, or any of the composers he must have been familiar with in his early days at the Konvict; but the same spirit as is met with in his songs and pianoforte pieces, and the best specimens of his chamber music. The first movement of the B minor is entirely unlike any other symphonic first movement that ever was composed before. It seems to come direct from the heart, and to have the personality of the composer in it to a most unusual degree.

---

* As we write, the announcement appears of a complete edition of Schubert's works, published works and manuscripts, by Breitkopf & Härtel.

The orchestral forces used are the usual ones, but in the management of them there are numbers of effects which are perfectly new in this department of art, indicating the tendency of the time towards direct consideration of what is called 'colour' in orchestral combinations, and its employment with the view of enhancing the degree of actual sensuous enjoyment of a refined kind, to some extent independent of the subjects and figures. Schubert's mature orchestral works are however too few to give any strong indication of this in his own person; and what is commonly felt is the supreme attractiveness of the ideas and general style. As classical models of form none of Schubert's instrumental works take the highest rank; and it follows that no compositions by any writer which have taken such hold upon the musicians of the present time, depend so much upon their intrinsic musical qualities as his do. They are therefore in a sense the extremest examples that can be given of the degree in which the status of such music altered in about thirty years.

In the epoch of Mozart and Haydn, the formal elements absolutely predominated in importance. This was the case in 1795. The balance was so completely altered in the course of Beethoven's lifetime, that by 1824 the phenomenon is presented of works in the highest line of musical composition depending on the predominating element of the actual musical sentiment. It must be confessed that Schubert's position in art is unique; but at the same time no man of mark can be quite unrepresentative of his time, and Schubert in this way represents the extraordinary degree in which the attention of musical people and the intention of composers in the early years of the present century was directed to the actual material of music in its expressive sense, as distinguished from the external or structural aspect.

The relation of the dates at which more or less well-known symphonies made their appearance about this time is curious and not uninstructive. Mendelssohn's Reformation Symphony was produced only two years after Schubert's great Symphony in C, namely in 1830. His Italian Symphony followed in the next year, and Sterndale Bennett's in G minor, in 1834.

11 *Studies of Great Composers*: Robert Schumann

Introduction

In 1884 Parry was asked to write a number of articles on the great composers for Miss Leith's *Every Girl's Magazine*. These were published in book form by Routledge & Kegan Paul in 1887 with a new introduction by Parry.

The book consists of eleven chapters devoted to the following composers: Palestrina, Handel, Bach, Haydn, Mozart, Beethoven, Weber, Schubert, Mendelssohn, Schumann and Wagner. (Perhaps this is where Neville Cardus got the idea for *Composers XI.*) The final chapter, entitled 'Conclusion', includes the music of only one living composer, Brahms: 'The list of the greatest composers closes with him and though his work may be little more than half done, his position is quite clearly defined.' Of equal interest is the group of composers Parry surveys in the final pages where wisely he argues that 'composers' names who are almost unknown to the public at large are sometimes worthy of the highest honour', and mentions Lulli, Scarlatti, Corelli, Purcell, C.P.E. Bach, Gluck, Cherubini, Berlioz, Chopin and Spohr.

His natural sympathy for young people and his enthusiasm for teaching combined to excellent effect in this the most popular of his books; my own copy, undated, is the 25th Edition. There is no sense of writing down to his young audience. The language is straightforward adult prose, enhanced by Parry's sense of intimacy with his subject and his young readers: that charm again. Even Shaw could not resist him in this once-removed form, forgiving Parry for writing *Judith* on condition that he wrote some more essays on the great composers. In their time they appealed to the broad musical public as well as to the young. Today, because of the enormous advance in biographical research during the last fifty years they have become somewhat outdated in their factual material, though a modern illustrated edition with a minimal amount of additional information would still be welcome.

I think, for today's reader the essay on Schumann is the finest of the series. Parry was an acquaintance of Madame Clara Schumann and her daughters, who obviously related much information first hand. Arguably Schumann is the composer whose inward life and musical imagination Parry was to mirror most closely. This is not mitigated by the principal difference that Parry's own finest inspirations are found in his works for chorus and orchestra.

Robert Schumann

In the early part of the history of modern music, the aims of the greatest composers seem easily intelligible to those who come after. The roads to great achievements were open in all directions, and after preliminary difficulties had been overcome by men whose names have for the most part passed out of remembrance, the great heroes of the art came upon the scene, and with strenuous vigour made sure of one new province of art after another, till by the second quarter of the present century there hardly seemed any new lands left to conquer. The great provinces of oratorio, opera, symphony, and song, were taken complete possession of, and the artistic principles upon which they needed to be worked out seemed theoretically to be so thoroughly well settled and decided, that it is not easy to see what was left for great composers to do. The matter of merely improving upon an established form of art is not nearly so enticing as the perfecting of one which is not mature, and does not seem to offer such opportunities for individual distinction. In art, just as in the circumstances of outward life, it is always more inspiriting to adventure into new lands and open them up for the first time, than it is to cultivate and improve them when some one else has discovered and conquered them.

When great material resources are at the command of many people, there are plentiful opportunities for average men to make themselves useful, but less for individual men to tower into rare eminence above their fellows. The sum of work done may on the whole be greater than what was done in earlier stages of history, but it is more diffused, and more hands have a share in it. Individual greatness may show itself still, but its signs and tokens seem less clearly marked out, and to depend on subtler conditions, and to have less of monumental and isolated conspicuousness about them. Men have to use what has been used before, and do what has been done before, and their individual prominence depends chiefly upon the way in which they can adapt themselves to phases of mind and action in their time, or the manner in which they use established forms so as to illustrate the taste and characteristic modes of feeling of their generation. They may rise to eminence as illustrators, as many painters do; or they may revive and combine different branches of art; or they may become great critics, and by appreciating thoroughly what has been done in the past, find out also where there is something which has not been done, or at least not done in the sense which appeals most powerfully and naturally to the people of their own time. The mere copying of other people's ways of expressing themselves can never be of much use to the world. People who only write blameless symphonies and sonatas after the accepted models, with nothing of their own to mark them by, might just as well let composing alone. They are only taking up time which would be better employed in attending to the original masterpieces. The only chance for the composer who has no new point to make is for him to have a genuine spur in himself arising from some phase of contemporary life which appeals strongly to him, or a deep and unusual feeling for poetry and romance and colour, which makes him produce spontaneous effects as the result of his exceptional organisation, and can be achieved by him alone.

The immense accumulation of material which had been organised sufficiently for musicians to work upon by the end of the first quarter of the nineteenth century, produced a very great number of fair composers, who ministered to the average wants of the day. The works of the great masters supplied them with the outlines of ideas, and the principle of arranging them in an orderly manner; and they sometimes attained to a point of real usefulness without breaking new ground. Some obtained a place of mark in history by doing exceptional work of a special kind; as by enlarging the resources of the pianoforte, or improving the management of orchestras, or by introducing national elements of a striking character into the domain of art. But the power of thought and character which is wanted to make a really memorable composer, becomes no commoner with the increase of fields to work in. Reputations are more plentiful than master minds; for nearness of time always makes it difficult to escape from misleading influences in judging who are really first-rate and who are only made-up successes. Men who fifty years ago were universally regarded as among the great composers of all time, and were hailed at every appearance with wild enthusiasm, are beginning to drop so entirely into neglect, that the younger scions of the living generation know of them as little more than empty names. But as these lesser lights die out and sink into obscurity, some few names stand out all the clearer, and with more steady brightness, for being free of the crowd of ephemeral stars; and at least one among them, after being looked at rather suspiciously by professors of classical views in art, and fiercely opposed by critics, even till some time after his death, has been of late years becoming gradually more and more established in the affections of all people of large musical sympathies; and not only wins appreciation for what is lovable in his work among those who only care for what pleases them, but also a place in musical history as a foremost and most characteristic champion of the progressive tendencies of musical art.

Robert Schumann was the first composer who illustrated several thoroughly modern traits of character in his life and work. He was the first composer of dignified instrumental music in whom certain romantic and mystic influences came to a head; the first who combined singular gifts of appreciative criticism and a capacity for analysing the inner meaning and purport of music with a power of original musical production; and the first of great mark in whom the modern tendency to luxuriate in warm and rich colouring in every department of art became decidedly pronounced. The circumstances of his parentage and education were peculiar for a musician, and though favourable in some ways, evidently unfavourable in others. His father, August Schumann, was a publisher and bookseller in Zwickau, in Saxony, who had decided literary tastes and gained some distinction by translating Byron's *Childe Harold* and *Beppo*, as well as some things of Scott's, into German, and by writing some original treatises. His wife was the daughter of a surgeon of some repute in another town of Saxony, and she is recorded to have been extremely practical, and at the same time inclined to sentimentality, but to have shown no traits which could account for the direction taken by her son's genius; for she certainly had no kind of sympathy with it. Four children preceded Robert into the world, where he made his first appearance on 8 June, 1810.

The bent of his nature towards music seems to have asserted itself early, and it must have done so without encouragement. He was sent to school when he was six, and received some musical teaching, probably of no very high order, from an excellent man called Kuntsch; who, though not capable of grounding him very securely in music, nevertheless inspired him with affection and esteem. At school he is recorded to have shown a peculiar ability for taking off the characters of his schoolfellows in extemporary pieces which he played on the pianoforte, before he was ten years old. From school he advanced to the Zwickau Academy, where again he showed his musical inclinations by making special friends with any boys who had any liking for the art; and he even succeeded in organising a few of them into a little band, consisting of two violins, two flutes, a clarionet, and two horns, and with his accompaniment on the pianoforte they managed to perform works of solid artistic merit, and also some things which Schumann himself wrote for them. To these performances the father was not at all averse, and indeed seemed ready to fall in with his son's tastes; for he even went so far as to make overtures to Carl Maria von Weber to take him as a pupil.

But unfortunately, in 1825, when the boy was yet only fifteen years old, the good father died; and the mother, always averse to the son's musical inclinations, insisted on his preparing himself to become a lawyer. His education was carried on with this view for some years, and when he was eighteen he was sent to Leipzig University, where he was entered as a student of law. But wherever he went his inclination for music asserted itself; he always sought out friends who could sympathise with him, and spent his time in the enjoyment of making music with them and practising, and occasionally trying his hand at composition. The only taste which vied with music was that for poetry and literature of a sentimental and imaginative kind. He was chiefly taken possession of by the writer Jean Paul Richter, familiarly known to the world as Jean Paul, whose peculiar fancy and style of thought coloured his ways of looking at things for the greater part of his life. He took to writing poetry of his own and setting it to music, and otherwise showed the state of his mind by breaking into effusions which were inspired by the influence of his favourite writer, and were by him called Jean-Pauliads.

The most important friendship he made at Leipzig was that of a very able teacher of music and the pianoforte, called Friedrich Wieck, under whom he studied. This master had a daughter called Clara, who was an astonishing musical prodigy and though at that time only nine years old had made her appearance in public as a pianist with great success. He became more and more determined to adopt music as his profession, but was obliged by force of circumstances to keep up the appearance of studying law; and with that view, after a year at Leipzig, he passed on to Heidelberg to complete his education, where he was placed under the direction of a famous professor of law by name Thibaut, who happened also to be musical. The professor seeing in course of time the decided disinclination of his pupil for legal studies and his equally decided musical gifts, was inclined to encourage him in the latter.

At Heidelberg he went on practising with more ardour than ever, and began to gain a reputation as a pianist; while at the same time he also made experiments in composition, some of which had sufficiently solid qualities in them to be kept among the works which he recognised as worthy of his ideals in later years. At last he made an appeal to his mother and his guardian to release him from the drudgery of the legal studies to which he had never really succeeded in accommodating himself; and when his master Wieck backed his appeal by expressing his belief in the boy's powers, they yielded to the inevitable, and he was allowed to prepare for the career of a musician unchecked.

But it was as a pianist that he intended to come before the world; and with the view of making himself fit for the career of a performer he returned to Leipzig and took up his abode with his master Wieck, with whom he remained for two years. But the rather amateurish way in which he had been forced to work at the piano till this time caused him to be somewhat behindhand for his age in matters of technical mastery, which are very necessary for a pianist in modern times; and though he worked very hard, he did not get on fast enough to satisfy himself. His impatience at last drove him to try and discover some means of making his fingers more pliant without such prolonged drudgery, and he invented a machine which he supposed would enable him to arrive at complete facility at once. He applied it to his right hand first, and instead of curing his deficiencies, maimed it completely from that time forward. At first he hoped it would come right, and went on practising with his left hand for some time, but though everything was tried which could be thought of, it was without avail, and the chances of his becoming a public pianist were entirely put an end to.

This naturally made him turn his attention more fully to composition, and the work he had gone through in practising was not by any means wasted, as it served him in very good stead in writing for the pianoforte, and in songs. But he had a good deal of lost time to make up, and though he felt he had something in him which was worth putting down he found it hard to express it at first. He was of course obliged to give up working at the pianoforte with Wieck; but he still lived in his house, and worked at composition and the departments of musical art which go with it, under a man called Dorn, who held the position of conductor in the opera at Leipzig. With him he began almost at the very elements, and worked his way through the drudgery which most aspirants to the fame of a composer complete almost in boyhood. But his spirits were high, and he never seems to have been particularly cast down by the necessity of having to give up all hopes of being a great pianist. Composition supplied him with a thoroughly congenial alternative, and he did not know how hard and trying the fight would have to be to win a hearing for his works.

He tried various lines of composition at this time, and works both of large and small calibre. A symphony was completed, and the first movement of it was played at his native town Zwickau, at a concert where Clara Wieck, then a girl of thirteen, also made her appearance as a pianist, and fired the quiet people of the place with musical enthusiasm for the first time in their lives. He also wrote a concerto, which with the symphony was ultimately consigned to oblivion. The larger works of this time were all afterwards laid aside by him, and only the lesser works for pianoforte have survived; and in reality he expressed himself most naturally in the latter line at first; partly owing to the lack of education in the principles of composition, and partly to his sympathy with the instrument to which he had lately given so much attention. This sympathy was still all-powerful, and made him think most of his music from the point of view of a pianist—a condition which he never altogether freed himself from, though it grew less prominent as years went on. But in this line his poetical and susceptible disposition served him in good stead, and in the early years of his work as a composer he produced many of his happiest and most successful compositions in the form of highly imaginative pianoforte music. The line he chose was one in which few composers of the highest rank had hitherto done much; but it was thoroughly in consonance with the spirit of the age. His bent was towards short vivid pieces, in which he expressed some definite idea. They belonged to the same order as Mendelssohn's "Songs without Words", but were far more characteristic and original, and more poetical and romantic. Even when he went to work to make large works and long movements, he constructed them by knitting a series of such little pieces together in a style more like mosaic than the continuous development of the sonatas by earlier great masters. But the standard of his ideas was so high, and his treatment of the instrument so rich in colour, that he raised this branch of art to a point which it had never attained before, and left a mass of genuine lyrics which are the most enduring and enjoyable of all the thousands of such works which have come into existence in the present century.

The circumstances of his life, and even the apparent defects of his education, seemed in this way to make him a high representative of the tendencies of his time, and enabled him to treat forms of art which have too often been of very slight value and of very flimsy construction, so as to give them a standing among works of real artistic importance. He also tried his hand in the line of sonatas; but he could not bring himself to the proper standpoint of a sonata writer of the conventional type, and rather experimented than wrote with deliberate and conscious judgment as to what was possible and worth doing in that form of art. For either his poetical impulses dominated him, or else he had to sacrifice something in the constraint of confining himself to accepted regulations. It is natural to suppose that this was partly caused by want of discipline in his earlier years; but it is certain, that if his nature had been regulated by much of the work necessary to make a composer of the old-fashioned classical pattern, he would never have produced the kind of pianoforte music which is so characteristic of himself, and also of the time when he lived.

In the early years of his musical career, after the necessary abandonment of the project of becoming a great pianist, he was drawn into another line besides that of composition, which is equally characteristic of his position in relation to his art. Many of the young and enthusiastic musical friends he had made in the course of his time at universities used to meet together in a restaurant, and their talk turned chiefly upon music. They discussed the lowness of the taste of the public, and the badness of musical criticism, and came to the conclusion that they might do something themselves to remedy it. Schumann himself had tried his hand at criticism, and made his first appearance in that capacity with a warmly appreciative article on an early work of Chopin in one of the principal newspapers of the time. They now determined on a definite and decisive plan of action, and founded a regular musical newspaper, in which the friends were to write criticisms and discuss important subjects connected with music. Among the helpers Schumann had in the work was a friend called Schunke, his pianoforte master Friedrich Wieck, and an able writer called Knorr.

The first number of this paper, which was called *Die Neue Zeitschrift für Musik*, came out in April, 1834. Schumann himself, in after years, wrote a preface to the series of his own articles which appeared in it, and gave an account of the conditions under which the newspaper was started, and the objects of its enthusiastic promoters. In it he said, "The musical situation was not then very encouraging in Germany. On the stage Rossini reigned, at the pianoforte nothing was heard but Herz and Hunten; and yet but a few years had passed since Beethoven, Weber, and Schubert had lived amongst us. One day the thought awakened in a wild heart, 'Let us not look on idly, let us also lend our aid to progress, let us bring again the poetry of art to honour among men'. From such ideas our most unique newspaper began. But the original band could not long hold together. Schunke died; others were drawn away from Leipzig by the necessities of their lives, and it nearly came to an end."

Schumann then goes on to describe himself, and his words clearly define his position in relation to art at that time. "One of the party—the musical visionary of the society—who had dreamed away his life until then rather over the pianoforte than among books, decided to take the editorship of the paper into his own hands, and carried out his decision for ten years until 1844." Hence began a series of articles, and sketches on music and musical subjects, which are without parallel in the literature connected with the art. The style is fanciful, but singularly telling and attractive, and deals with all subjects in the genuinely appreciative spirit which is so extremely rare among writers upon music. His is not the spirit which speaks well and in words of well-regulated enthusiasm of an established great work, or pats a dull composer on the back because he had written respectably and according to rule; but the spirit which searches out what is really and substantially good, in the by-ways as well as the high-ways of art; and endeavours to show the public where the point lies, and how and wherein the power and value of a new work may be felt. It really was a splendid mission to undertake, and no man in the world was more fit for the office. His position as a genuine composer himself gave him insight into many ways and virtues of his brother composers, which it takes a long time for the public or even a good critic to grasp; while his generous sympathies and his poetical disposition, and even the way in which the work of Jean Paul had influenced him in earlier years, gave him a tone and style which were peculiarly happy, in dealing with a subject which really is a difficult one to manage, so as to avoid coldness on the one hand and frothy exuberance on the other.

In this way he was able to play a most honourable part, for nearly all the rising musicians of the day were at one time or another liberally helped by the generous words he wrote about their works. Of Chopin he had written already before the paper was regularly started, and further criticisms upon his works followed later on. In its pages he also wrote of Mendelssohn, Gade, Sterndale Bennett, Franz,

Henselt, Stephen Heller, Berlioz, Liszt, Thalberg, Hiller, Ernst, Vieuxtemps, Moscheles, and Johannes Brahms, and always in a way which showed marvellous perception of their good points, and touched their faults lightly and generously. It was the mission he had undertaken to further good and sound art; and he did it rather by extolling freely what was worthy of such treatment in the works of his contemporaries than in the more easy but less lovely way of pulling rubbish and impotence to pieces.

His position was a really singular one, for most of the men he praised were immeasurably inferior to him in the very department of art about which he was writing, and yet he never put himself forward or showed any bitterness at the absence of encouragement and sympathy for his own work which he so liberally gave to others; and it is not less remarkable that several of the men he praised and helped so generously were utterly incapable to the end of their days of showing any appreciation of the work of the man who had been their public champion. His position in these respects is altogether a most noble one, and the familiar truth that it is harder to see real beauties than blemishes, enhances it; for he always aimed at hearty praise, even of things which were absolutely new to the world, and when dealing with works which an ordinary critic would either have written an involved account of, so as to prevent any one knowing whether he meant to praise or to blame, or else have endeavoured to amuse the public by extravagantly abusing.

Schumann's insight in such respects was a quarter of a century ahead of his contemporaries. The most signal instance of this fact was the enthusiastic article he wrote about Johannes Brahms, who as a young man was sent to him by Joachim, the famous violinist. Schumann saw into him directly, and recognised in possibility what he has come to be in the world's estimation in ultimate reality; and he no sooner saw it than he proclaimed it, in no measured terms. It so happened that the musical public did not accept his judgment at the time, and Brahms had a very long fight of it to win his way to the front; but this only enhances the acuteness of Schumann's insight, especially when it is remembered that Schumann himself was by that time getting on towards the end of his musical career, when most people are less open to fresh impressions than they are in young and expansible times.

The newspaper was not, of course, solely devoted to praising and expressing sympathy for brother composers, but also contained articles and discussions about great masters of the past and their works. And not a little of this was carried on in a most peculiar way, which serves to connect Schumann's music with his literary work. He invented a fanciful name for the group of friends who joined with him in carrying on the newspaper. They were the Davidsbündler or Davidites, whose mission was to wage war against musical Philistinism and obstruction—that is, against narrowness, pedantry, commonplace, and vulgarity, and all the many other forces and perversities which mislead or bewilder the well-intentioned public. This Davidsbund comprised many names, which partly represented types of thought and feeling, and partly real persons, so far as the persons could be identified with the types. Schumann himself was represented by several names, which personified the various qualities which he felt to exist within himself "Florestan" represented his impulsive and ardently imaginative side; "Eusebius" the more thoughtful and critical side; "Meister Raro" stood between the two and interposed in their discussions. Other names were now and then used to express the different moods in which different articles were written. Mendelssohn was Felix Meritis, Clara Wieck was sometimes "Chiarina," sometimes "Cecilia," and numbers of other less-known persons had characteristic titles. By using the names representing different types of mind dialogues were carried on upon matters of musical interest from different points of view; or a string of aphorisms with the names of the personified types appended gave similarly effective impressions.

An instance will give the best explanation of this curious device. Florestan, the impulsive Schumann, says, "Where is the use of dressing a hair-brained youth in his grandfather's furred dressing-gown, and putting a pipe in his mouth to make him regular and orderly? Let him keep his flowing locks and easy attire. I love not the men whose lives are not in unison with their works". Meister Raro—the moderating Schumann—follows with another aphorism: "Warn the youth who composes. Fruit that ripens too early falls before its time. The young mind must often unlearn theory before it can be put in practice". Eusebius, the reflecting, meditative Schumann, follows with yet another: "It is not enough that I know something, unless I can make use of what I have learned in the conduct of my life". There is obviously no dialogue here, but each character taking the same thought in mind supplies something from his point of view towards a complete judgment in the matter. Another ingenious plan is for two or more articles upon the same subject to be given side by side In this way one of Chopin's concertos is discussed by both Florestan and Eusebius; and on such a question as a proposed monument to Beethoven no less than four personified abstractions write independent articles. Sometimes Florestan and Eusebius discuss things adversely, as happens over Hummel's Studies, on which occasion "Meister Raro" steps in at the end and disagrees with both of them. The idea is clearly a new one in musical criticism, and it is singularly happy and entertaining; but it could only be possible with young and fresh minds, and can hardly be imitated successfully by any one.

This literary device was also carried on in connection with Schumann's own music, which was in some cases attributed to different personalities. The largest of his sonatas, that in F sharp minor, was attributed at first to both Florestan and Eusebius. Another work with many different pieces in it is called *Davidsbündlertänze*: in the "Carnival" he returned to the practice which was attributed to him as a boy at school, and gave fancy musical portraits of several members of the ideal confraternity, including Chopin, himself in different moods, Clara Wieck, and Ernestine von Fricken, a person by whom he was at one time considerably attracted; and the whole ends up with "a march of the Davidites against the Philistines". In such ways the curious fancy of the "Davidsbund" coloured all the first period of Schumann's musical life, and represents his ardour for advancing the art by both teaching and example, and infusing it with poetical fancy. As he advanced in years the names were dropped, and he lived more in practical realities. They ceased to appear in connection with his musical works early, and the last is said to have appeared in his literary works in 1842.

Editing a newspaper is hard work at any time, but when a man has a cause at heart, and throws himself into it with all his soul, it is most exacting. Schumann had to supply something for his readers constantly, and would never do it without getting something genuine out of himself. He had facility in writing, but it is not to be wondered at that in the earlier years of his editorial work he did very little in the way of composition; but what he did do was of a very high order; and at least one of his most successful large compositions for the pianoforte, the *Études Symphoniques*, was written in the first year that he was busy as the representative Davidite. But this absorption in literary work can hardly be regarded as a misfortune. The world is a gainer by what he wrote, and the cause of first-rate music was a gainer. Besides, it is probable that he also profited greatly by his drudgery. He himself said that in earlier years he was inclined to dream his time away at the pianoforte; and the necessities of the editorial work were bracing to his mind, and forced him to get something definite done. As he got more into the habit of doing his literary work systematically his impulse to compose returned, and after a year or two a flood of works for the pianoforte came forth, many of them among his finest works; such as the great Fantasia in C, the *Fantasiestücke, Humoreske, Novelletten*, and many others. In these years, and as long as he only seemed to represent the branch of pianoforte writing, the reception of his works by critics was decidedly encouraging, and he had good reason to hope well of his prospects; but the representatives of classical respectability soon showed signs of being suspicious of him, and their feeling became more pronounced as he began to attack branches of composition which were considered to have more importance, and to entail greater responsibilities.

Among the circumstances which are said to have exercised influence upon Schumann's career must be mentioned the arrival of Mendelssohn in Leipzig as conductor to the Gewandhaus Concerts. Mendelssohn acted without actual intention or invitation as a very able coadjutor in the cause of the Davidites; for his presence seemed to have an electric power to stir people up and make them energetic about performing and hearing good music. Schumann was roused to a pitch of very high enthusiasm about him. He admired the mastery of art which he showed, and the balance and clearness of his works; and may have been impelled to admit a little more of consideration for classical form, together with the poetical impulse, after contact with the better regulated master. Mendelssohn, on the other hand, seems scarcely to have thought of Schumann as a composer at all, but only as a literary man and art critic, and consequently there must always have been a sense of antagonism lurking in his mind, such as is natural between the producer and the appraiser. But they were a good deal together, chiefly owing to Schumann's admiration, and they discussed musical matters as freely as Schumann's singular taciturnity admitted of.

Another most important influence which began to exert itself about this time was the love which developed in him for Clara Wieck. He had been a great deal with her in the days when he was living in her father's house, but she was too young then to inspire him with any great passion. He admired her powers enthusiastically, but personally she had not sufficient influence upon him to prevent his susceptible disposition from being captivated by Ernestine von Fricken, and other sympathetic ladies. But as Clara Wieck developed into womanhood a far more powerful feeling took possession of him than any he had before experienced, and her feelings responded to his. When they both found out the state of their affections, Schumann applied to the father to allow them to marry, but the father, on considering his prospects, saw little that was promising in them, and refused. From a worldly and practical point of view he seemed right, and Schumann for the time acquiesced. He set about at once to find a sphere of action which might give him a better chance of winning the father's consent, and struck upon Vienna as a likely place for getting something to do, and, with Clara Wieck's consent, went there to see if anything could be achieved.

His idea was to bring out a newspaper like the one he had worked upon in Leipzig, and get enough support in a place which had such reputation for being musical as Vienna had, to bring him both position and funds. But he was cruelly disappointed. The Viennese people no longer cared for really great and good things, but were altogether under the dominion of Rossini, and light dance writers, and virtuosi of the pianoforte who delighted their frivolous minds by spinning endless tinkling variations and fantasias on familiar tunes.

He stayed there for half a year, and the greatest fruit that came of the visit was the routing up of Schubert's manuscript compositions He had always been an enthusiastic admirer of Schubert, and being now in Schubert's own native town he naturally sought out traces of him. He went to see Beethoven's and Schubert's graves, which were close together in the Währing cemetery; and it is illustrative of his character that he took possession of a steel pen which he found lying on Beethoven's tomb and kept it, as if it had some mystical sanctity, to use on special occasions, one of which was the writing of his own B-flat Symphony. But a more tangible result came from his visiting Schubert's brother Ferdinand, who still kept many of Schubert's manuscript compositions. While he was turning these over he came across the score of the great Symphony in C, Schubert's last, written but a short while before his death. He was so struck with it that he asked to have it sent to Mendelssohn for performance at the Gewandhaus concerts. Mendelssohn duly brought it out in March 1839, and it interested people so much that it had soon to be played again, and from that time began by slow and sure degrees to win a prominent place among the most successful great works for orchestra in existence; and the impression it made at the time also began to draw people's attention more to other works of the same master besides his songs.

When Schumann returned to Leipzig he could no longer refrain from pressing his suit for Clara Wieck. He had a little money of his own, and his newspaper also brought him in a tolerable profit, and he felt confident that his compositions would help further to augment the sum total. But the father did not take the same view, and in the end Schumann took his case into the law-courts—for in Germany a man who refuses to let his daughter marry can be forced to explain the reason of his refusal in a court of justice. It must have been an unpleasant operation to go through, and cannot have conduced to a happy frame of mind as long as the contest lasted; but fortunately the courts decided in Schumann's favour, and after about a year of anxiety the marriage took place in 1840.

His marriage was the beginning of a new life for Schumann in more ways than one. One of the happiest results was that he burst into song for the first time. The winning of the object of his love seemed suddenly to open the flood-gates of a stream which till then had been pent up and unknown in him; and in the one year that succeeded his marriage he poured out in rapid succession all his finest songs, to the number of over 130. In them he showed powers with which no one till then would have credited him. There was no laborious process of developing his style in the particular branch of art; he no sooner faced it than his mastery seemed complete. In this respect he resembled Schubert, who had written many of his finest songs in the earliest years of his mature productive period. Schumann adopted much the same method of dealing with his poems that Schubert did. He did not aim at making tunes with accompaniment and fitting the words to them, but he looked to the poet's conception to guide his own inspiration. Everything available was made to minister to the purpose of intensifying the design, thought, and metre of the poet by the music. The pianoforte part and voice part had well-balanced functions. The voice did all that was possible in the way of melodious declamation, and the accompaniment supplied colour, character, rhythm, and all that must necessarily fall to its share, in the most perfect manner possible. Moreover, Schumann, by nature a poet himself, seized the purpose and spirit of the poems he set with an astonishingly powerful grip, and conveyed infinite shades and varieties of meaning in forms which are almost always perfect works of art in detail and in entirety. He expressed with equal success, pathos, passion, bitterness, humour, joy, exultation, and even gaiety and sarcasm. It was probably the happiest period in his life when he did this work, and the work itself represents him in his best and clearest phase.

When the year was ended he himself thought he had done all he could of the best kind in song writing, and to some one who expressed hopes of further achievements in that line answered, "I cannot venture to promise that I shall produce anything further in the way of songs, and I am satisfied with what I have done". The way in which he grappled at once with this branch of art, and worked it out to the full limits of his powers to the exclusion of other work, became characteristic of him in his best time. He had written all his best pianoforte music before his marriage; in the year following it he wrote all his best songs; and in the years that succeeded he worked in similar manner at one province at a time, taking up new ones in succession, and achieving a great quantity of work in each before passing on to another province. Immediately after the long bout of song-writing he went to work at symphonies, and in one year produced three of his most important works in that line. The first one was in B-flat, which was performed in the spring of the year 1841 at Leipzig under Mendelssohn's direction; and this being regular and clear in form and expression was received with favour. Two more were performed at the end of the year, and these, possibly owing to their containing some rather experimental features, were not so well received.

In the following year Schumann took up yet another province in the shape of chamber music, and in this again he was surprisingly successful. His earliest essays were string quartetts, one of the most difficult branches of art for a composer of high aims to succeed in. His work interested people very much, and even surprised men who had not up to that time recognised his abilities; but he himself seems to have felt that they were not the best that he ought to do. He followed these with the famous quintett for pianoforte and strings, and the quartett for similar combination, which have gained him most popularity in Europe by their thoroughly modern qualities of rich colour, volume of sound, romantic style, extraordinary attractiveness of melody and rhythmic figures, and genuine go. They stand by all the qualities which appeal to sympathetic imagination and feeling, and not by the old ordinances of classical form, and in this sense they mark Schumann again as a thorough representative of his time.

In the next year he took up yet another new line, and attacked choral composition for the first time. The work with which he presented himself before the public was a setting of a cantata adapted from Moore's *Lalla Rookh*, called *Paradise and the Peri*; and this was received with such evident delight, that he forthwith proceeded to another attempt in the same line but on a grander scale; and in the course of 1844, he began to set scenes from Goethe's *Faust*. But after writing four numbers, his work was interrupted by a serious break-down in health.

Since his marriage he had lived very quietly, devoting himself chiefly to composition. But he had found other work to do which tasked his strength. He had managed to reduce his work upon the musical paper by degrees, but in its place he had taken up the labours of a professor in the new Conservatoire founded at Leipzig through Mendelssohn's exertions, which was probably less congenial to him than literary work. It is recorded that he had no great aptitude for teaching, and this of itself must have been trying to him. But he found it also trying to be obliged to hear so much music, and he became oppressed with exhaustion and weariness. He began to be troubled with loss of musical memory, sleeplessness, and strange and uncanny fancies; showing a decided disorganisation of some kind, either of nerves or brain. For the sake of rest and quiet he determined on leaving Leipzig, and going to Dresden, where he soon found some relief. He wrote to Ferdinand David, "Here one can get back the old lost longing for music, there is so little to hear! It just suits my condition, for I suffer still very much from my nerves, and everything affects and exhausts me". This state of things was better for him than the turmoil of Leipzig, but it was long before he had a return of really satisfactory health, and little work could be done. He lived very much alone, and the habits of silence and abstraction which had always been characteristic of him began to grow more and more marked. It was not till 1846 that he showed signs of being more himself again, and then he began at once to turn his attention to composition with his former ardour.

It is curious that he became at this period more eager about clearness of part-writing in his music. He had always been a most ardent worshipper of J. S. Bach, but had loved his works rather for what they express and the general power of intellect and emotion which they display than for their technical merits. But now, late in the day, he began working more decidedly at counterpoint, Bach's own special field of technical triumphs; and the results of this study were a number of works such as canons for pedal pianoforte, pianoforte fugues, and a set of very fine fugues for the organ on the notes representing the letters of Bach's name. Other great works were also brought forward soon after his reappearance in the world, such as his most important Symphony in C, and the famous concerto for pianoforte. These works must have been partly written during the period when he was more or less withdrawn from society, but it must be confessed they show little sign of obscurity of mind or failing of nerve. The Symphony is full of vigorous thoughts, and is clearly expressed and well worked out; and the concerto has won its popularity by a profusion of most attractive ideas and beautiful melodies, which often have a certain pensive sadness in them, but no traces of morbid melancholy. Early in the year 1847, he and his wife paid a visit to Zwickau, where they were most cordially welcomed, and these two new works were both performed with success.

Schumann now had his mind set on trying an opera. He had long had desires in that direction, and thought German composers had not done enough in that field. In 1842 he had written in his newspaper, "it is high time German composers should give the lie to the reproach that has long lain on them of having been so craven as to leave the field in possession of the Italians and the French. But under this head there is a word to be said to the German poets also". It might be reasonably answered that one of the reasons why German composers had done so little in real German opera in comparison with other nations was, that they took a more serious and thorough view of art; and unless very considerable compromises are admitted and a very light view taken of the requirements of reason and criticism, an opera is a most difficult thing to arrive at. Schumann himself was brought face to face with these difficulties just as Beethoven had been. He first of all found it very difficult to settle on a story which satisfied his high ideas, on the score of being suitable and worthy of setting to music. Many were the subjects which came sufficiently near to satisfying him to be mentioned—such as *Faust*, *The Veiled Prophet*, *The Wartburg Tournament of Song*, but for one cause or another they were all dropped. At last he fixed on the story of *St. Geneviève*, which had been already put into a poetic and dramatic form by two German poets. But when he had settled upon his subject he met a new difficulty. The literary form in which the story stood in the works of Hebbel and Tieck was not fit for musical setting; and it was no easy matter to find any one to recast it. Hebbel himself refused to reconstruct his work, another poet called Reinick tried, but failed to satisfy Schumann; and in the end the composer was driven to try his own poetical powers and make up the opera book for himself. That and the work of composition necessarily took time, and it was not till 1848 that the opera, under the name of *Genoveva*, was ready for performance. Then it was the sensitive Schumann's turn to realise the usual miserable and repulsive preliminaries of such theatrical performances. He tried to get it done at Leipzig, where he knew he had many friends; and his hopes were raised by a promise to bring it out in the spring of 1849. But when the time came, first his own circumstances stood in the way and then other people's, so that with evasions and postponements, the whole year passed without a sign of performance. Schumann naturally grew irritated, and when a promise by the director on his honour that the work should be performed in February 1850, was likewise broken, it was as much as his friends could do to prevent Schumann making the director's apparent dishonour public, and taking his case into a law court.

In the end the opera was performed in June of that year, and Schumann himself superintended. The result was not altogether satisfactory, and Schumann attributed it to the unsuitable season of the year for bringing out a new work. "Who goes to a theatre in May or June, and not rather into the woods?" But nevertheless he had many friends and admirers to support him with their presence, and they were delighted with much of the music, which is indeed in parts superbly beautiful and appropriate; but they were not convinced that opera was one of Schumann's special provinces, nor were they roused to any great enthusiasm. Schumann was disappointed and distressed by the want of sympathy which he felt, and by the tone of the criticisms which appeared in print. The cold impression left by the work is probably owing partly to the way in which the plot is worked out. For the characters do not all explain themselves spontaneously to an audience as they should do, and there is a want of clearness and balance in the form of the drama. This Schumann was inclined to lose sight of through feeling that the music satisfied his sense of the requirements of the situations; and the coldness of the public and the strictures of critics only struck him as galling stupidity.

Another work which employs similar resources to opera was the setting of scenes from the second part of Goethe's *Faust*, which he carried to a condition fit to be performed by the time the opera was brought out. This work was received with much more favour than the opera in Leipzig, and was soon repeated at other musical centres, and its fame spread widely. The choruses at the end of the work have generally been considered to be among his finest conceptions, while the music of some earlier scenes expressed so well the poet's intention that people said things were brought home to them in the poem which they had never understood before. In later years Schumann added considerably to the work, and wrote an overture and scenes from the first Part, but these bear traces of his failing powers more than any others of his great works, and hamper its fitness for general performance.

Schumann's stay at Dresden came to an end when political disturbances broke out there in 1849. He was unfitted by his reserved and retiring disposition to take any part in such public manifestations, and he retired first to a village called Kreischa, where he went on working quietly at his compositions even within a few miles of the exciting scenes of the insurrection. This first move was soon followed by a more decided one. While in Dresden he had first had a little experience of systematic conducting. A men's choral society had been prospering there under the direction of Schumann's friend Hiller, and when he left to take another post in Düsseldorf, Schumann went on with the work. But Schumann was not really fitted for the ways of a German singing club, and the chief advantage of the experiment was that it led to his getting the command of a larger choral society with mixed voices, where he had better opportunities and a more congenial atmosphere. This roused him a good deal in many ways, and afforded him opportunities of trying the effect of choruses in the setting of *Faust*, and doing practical work which took him a little out of himself The experience so gained led to a hope that he might get some definite post as a conductor, and when Ferdinand Hiller moved on from Düsseldorf to Cologne, Schumann obtained the appointment of Capellmeister there.

At first this new line of work seemed a success. The people of Düsseldorf welcomed gladly such an acquisition to their musical forces as he and Madame Schumann represented; and his enthusiasm for his art, and his reputation, gave a decided impulse to music in the place. But Schumann appears to have been no more really fitted for conducting than for teaching. The natural impulse in him to look inwards rather than outwards, and his reserve and habits of silence, were all against it. He had a singular disinclination for asserting himself, and this prevented his beat from being as decisive as it ought to be: and when the band made mistakes it also prevented him from calling their attention to the fact; and all he did in such cases was to make them play the passage over again, and if the mistake happened again he only got angry, and yet could not bring himself to explain. His want of fitness for such work increased as time went on, and the signs of a return of mental troubles such as he had had before when he left Leipzig first for Dresden, began to make ominous appearance. But the work of composition still went on steadily, and as yet the material produced was of admirable quality; one of the greatest works of his time at Düsseldorf being the important one known as the *Rhenish Symphony*, which is full of vigour, colour, and character.

The failing of his mind showed itself much in the concerns of outward life, but most seriously in his conducting. Among the stories that are told of its effects are, that he fancied music was taken too fast, and slackened the pace of things that were performed under his direction in an unintelligible manner. He is reported to have gone on beating time after the band had stopped; and when such infallible signs were added to the fact that he was unfitted by nature and disposition for the business of conducting, it became obvious to the directors that someone must be found to take his place. They tried all they could to spare Schumann's feelings, but it was impossible to get through such a difficult operation with a man whose mind was in an unhealthy condition without disaster. Schumann could not be persuaded to meet the directors half way and ease the rupture, and in the end the parting was effected in a manner which left a painful impression upon the composer's mind

When he left Düsseldorf he went with his wife for a concert tour in Holland, which seemed to enliven him, and the sympathy they met with in that country soon raised his spirits; but his health was gone too far in a serious direction for return to the happiness and clearness of spirit and work of earlier days. Hallucinations of a strange kind began to present themselves, and nervous disorder and depression became more frequent and irresistible. The working of the disease was intermittent, and in the intervals he still continued to work and to carry on his relations with people as usual. He himself felt so unsafe from the effect of these visitations that he even wished to be taken to an asylum—though for many years past he had had a morbid horror of such places. At last the crisis came, and in the afternoon of 27 February, 1854, in one of his fits of acute depression he tried to put an end to his life by throwing himself from a bridge into the Rhine. His life was saved by some boatmen, and he was taken to a private asylum near Bonn, where he remained for the rest of his life. He was still able in his happier and clearer moments to carry on correspondence and see friends and relations, but no more composition of importance was undertaken, and after two mournful years he died on 29 July 1856, in the arms of his noble and loving wife.

The nature of the disease which brought his life so sadly and prematurely to an end is said to have been the formation of bony masses in the brain. Schumann appears to have inherited this disorder from his mother, who also was subject to violent headaches and depression; and the earlier stages of the development of the evil began to exert influence upon his character and habits long before a serious crisis came about. It seems that even before his marriage he was subject to fits of excessive depression and gloomy forebodings, and he had a singular dread and horror of lunatic asylums. His extreme irritability may also have had some connection with the disease, and that presented itself to a noticeable degree even as early as his twenty-fourth year. The most curious feature of his character was his silence in company. In his most familiar circle and at home with his family he was bright and talkative, but outside, with acquaintances and strangers, it was difficult to get him to utter a word. The natural bent of his disposition seemed to be to look inwards, and not to act or initiate. He listened to others and took in what they said, responding sometimes to anything that he sympathised with especially by a peculiarly bright and expressive look. But words became constantly rarer as he grew older. When he was in Dresden he used to go often of an evening to a particular restaurant, where he drank beer; but he did not join friends or enter into conversation, but used to sit at a particular table alone, with his back to the rest of the people and his face to the wall, either working out musical ideas—which he sometimes whistled softly to himself—or meditating about things which interested him. Even with friends that he was very fond of he liked to maintain silence if he could, without intending to show any want of appreciation of their company. A story was told by a great friend of his in comparatively early years, called Henriette Voigt, how after she and Schumann had been enjoying music together one lovely evening in summer, they went out in a boat together. And there they sat side by side for over an hour without either speaking a word. When they parted, Schumann said, with a pressure of the hand that expressed his feelings, "To-day we have perfectly understood one another".

These silent habits certainly stood in the way of his exchanging and discussing views with other musicians, or doing much in any practical line, such as organising or conducting; but on the other hand they served to intensify his originality and allowed his views of art to develop undisturbed by doubts and hesitations. Fortunately he was always inclined to be extremely liberal, and isolation never made his judgment narrow or pedantic. He had too powerful a sense of the meaning of music to be led into the common trap of taking details for essentials, and expending his force upon technical matters. This is illustrated by the style of his writings on music, in which he showed that most rare gift of going to the heart of his subject and carrying the reader along with him, and convincing him without any of the affectation of learning which is commonly used as a cloak for total barrenness. His principle rested upon the broad foundation of apprehension of the historical progress of music, and the feeling that art cannot stand still, but must either advance or deteriorate.

He felt as much as most men similarly placed, that it is always hard to tell what direction the new paths are to take; but he was ready to welcome any endeavour that seemed to be made in an earnest spirit. This was one of the spurs which drove him to write about art, and he expressed his hopes and views in many places, both in the newspapers and in letters to his friends: "Consciously or unconsciously, a new and a yet undeveloped school is being founded upon the basis of the Beethoven-Schubert romanticism, a school which we may venture to expect will make a special epoch in the history of art. Its destiny seems to be to enter into a period which will nevertheless have many links to connect it with the past century". The last sentence clearly implies that he felt that the work of the past must be the basis of the progress of the future, and this conviction may be seen also in his own work.

He knew that art could not make a totally new start or ignore the principles which had been discovered in the course of centuries of musical development. He knew the difference between clap-trap or tall talk and genuine performance, and did not seek to find new principles, but to understand better the principles of the past, and apply them to liberal uses in that spirit of poetry and romance which was the increasing tendency and feature of the music of modern times, and his own most notable characteristic. He also knew and understood the doctrines of most revolutionary men, such as Berlioz, and as far as he found them earnest and clear-sighted, and gifted with qualities which would really further good art instead of misleading the public, he cordially expressed his sympathy with them; but he never had any patience with people who showed great gifts and put them to sordid and ignoble uses, or truckled to low public tastes for the sake of success.

He was yet another example among Germans of that type of the musician so entirely possessed by the love of his art that any other view than that of improving it and spending all his energies to master higher and higher ground seemed inconceivable. His aims were always of the noblest, and the style of his musical expression corresponded with them. His habits of introspection made him critical of himself even more than he was of others; and as long as his health lasted, he was always trying to improve and enlarge his powers. But the growth of the disease against which it was impossible to contend, made it inevitable that all the most attractive part of his work should be done in his earlier years; when youthful power and enthusiasm were yet vigorous in him, and he was able to shake off the obscuring influence of the fits of melancholy. It is true he kept his art wonderfully free from traces of morbidity long after the disease had laid its remorseless hand on him, and long after his relations with people in every-day life had become strange and uncertain. But the average of really successful works became smaller as the years rolled by, after the first brilliantly productive time directly after his marriage; and most of the works of the latter part of his life contain but an uncertain reflex of the vigorous breadth and imaginative power and freshness of his earlier years.

It was natural that the works of a man having such liberal and advanced views about art should be slow to make their way. His position as editor of a successful musical newspaper certainly helped him in early years. He himself knew it, and expressed it in the words, "If the publisher were not afraid of the editor, the world would hear nothing of me". To the average critic his works were a sealed book. They could find little that they understood, and much that altogether revolted their conventional notions of propriety; and the result was, that even till long after his death, when the public were becoming universally captivated by his works, they were condemned by the journalists in the most reckless and unrestrained terms. But he left his message to the world in the very best possible hands. His wife having won a position as a pianist almost unrivalled in Europe, and having perfect knowledge of the meaning of his works and the way he wished them to be expressed, could carry on the most grateful task of making his music known to all the world by her playing; and so triumphantly has she maintained the cause that he became one of the best-loved composers of the generation after his death, and to many people, whose hearts and sympathies are warm, the composer who most truly represents the tendency of modern art since the days of Schubert and Beethoven.

The success which was won first by his pianoforte works and songs, and chamber music, was ultimately won also by such large works as overtures and symphonies; and though other men have attained greater popularity in the last branch of art, his works stand at the highest level of nobility and vigour of style and variety of interest between Beethoven's time and our own. His influence has naturally been very great upon later composers, and some have gained even re-markable popularity by doing little more than reproducing his style and methods. His influence upon the musical world in general has also been great and of the very best quality. His style of criticism first awakened people to more generous and self-respecting views of art, and his music in its turn roused them to feel what is really beautiful and nobly emotional, rather than to rest content with a cold and me-chanical emptiness which too often succeeds in passing itself off as classical art because it does not violate conventional proprieties.

The spirit which lived in Bach and Beethoven lived also in him; and in spite of the deficiencies of his education and the troubles of his later life, gave him finally a secure place among the immortals.

12 *The Evolution of the Art of Music*

Introduction

In his preface Parry informs the reader that the 'Evolution of Musical Art' was written at the request of Mr Kegan Paul during 1884. It was not surprising that the steady increase in information available on the music of primitive cultures, folk and medieval music delayed the book's completion, and publication was not until 1893. The original title was *The Art of Music*; it was republished in a revised form with the new title *The Evolution of the Art of Music* in 1896, when it appeared as volume LXXX of Kegan Paul's *International Scientific Series*. Parry felt the Darwinian allusion suggested 'the intention more effectually'.

Shaw reviewed the book in *The World* on 4 April 1894. He did not miss the opportunity for reviving his printed opinions on *Judith* and *Job* and pointing out Parry's considerable number of academic titles, and he disagreed with some of Parry's musical and historical conclusions. What really caused a Shavian tirade was Parry's equation of some motivic tonal procedures with Beethoven's genius, because Beethoven often used them. Shaw found this fallacious. He pointed out that most mediocre composers used many of the same procedures. He also did not forget to mention that he thought Parry was not capable of writing genuinely tragic music. He closed however by thanking Parry for giving him much information he did not know.

The first five chapters of the book are now so outdated as to be obsolete; for example, the performance and influence of oriental music – especially from the Indian sub-continent and the South Pacific – was increasing to an enormous degree. First with composers and musicologists, especially in France, and then with the informed public, oriental music became a part of Western culture. Parry was having a hard time, understandably, in keeping abreast of these developments. This also applied to primitive music and Western music of the medieval period.

However, beginning with Chapter 6, 'The Rise of Secular Music', Parry sets out in the remaining nine chapters a well informed, finely written, easy-to-follow discussion on the history of music from Bach to Wagner. Some of his opinions, such as his comparisons of Bach and Handel, became standard for nearly 75 years.

The Perfect Balance of Expression and Design

The tendency to use the art for expression naturally led Beethoven to identify his work occasionally with some definite idea or subject. As in the Eroica Symphony, which was intended for his ideal of Napoleon (so soon shattered); the Pastoral Symphony, which embodied his feelings about the fields, and brooks, and woods, and birds he loved so well; the "Lebewohl" Sonata, which embodied his ideal musical sense of friends parting, of absence, and of the joyous coming together again. But with him, for almost the first time, the true principle of programme music is found, and he indicates it with absolute insight into the situation in his remark on the Pastoral Symphony. That it was "mehr Ausdruck der Empfindung, als Malerei"—"More the expression of inner feeling than picturing". The most common failing of minds less keen than Beethoven's is to try to make people see with their ears. Beethoven goes to the root of the matter. For, as pointed out in the first chapter, it is not the business of music to depict the external, but to convey the inner impressions which are the result of the external. And music is true in spiritual design only when it is consistent in the use of the resources of expression with the possible workings of the mind in special moods or under the influence of special external impressions. With Beethoven and Bach the consistency of the harmonic, melodic, and rhythmic elements of expression is so perfect, that with all the infinity of change, and the variety that is necessary for design's sake, the possible working of a mind affected by some special exciting cause is consistently represented by the kind of treatment that is used. That people often can feel this for themselves is shown by the general adoption of such a name as "the Appassionata", which was not given by Beethoven, but which is eminently justified in every particular by the contents of that wonderful sonata.

Beethoven's opportunity lay in the comprehensive development of the resources of art, and in the fact that the principles of a singularly malleable type of design were ready to his hand when he came upon the scene. His imagination and his powers of concentration were equal to his responsibilities. The resources of effect were as yet not so great as to tempt him to extravagance. Indeed he himself had to collect and develop and systematise much of them, and he enlarged them more than any other man except Bach. The sonata form, moreover, was new enough to afford him scope without forcing him either to risk common-place, or to resort to hyper-intellectual devices to hide its familiarities. In his hands alone the forces of design and of expression were completely controlled. Self-dependent instrumental art on the grandest and broadest lines found its first perfect revelation in his hands, not in a formal sense alone, but in the highest phase of true and noble characteristic expression.

Modern Tendencies

Beethoven stands just at the turning point of the ways of modern art, and combines the sum of past human effort in the direction of musical design with the first ripe utterance of the modern impulse—made possible by the great accumulation of artistic resources—in the direction of human expression. After him the course of things naturally changed. In the art of the century before him formality was prominent and expression very restrained; in the times after him the conditions were reversed, and the instinct of man was impelled to resent the conventions of form which seemed to fetter his imagination, and began his wanderings and experiments anew in the irrepressible conviction that every road must lead somewhere. A new artistic crisis had been passed, similar to the crisis of Palestrina and Bach, but implying a still greater organisation and a richer accumulation of actual resources than was available for either of the earlier masters. All three crises represent a relatively perfect formulation of human feeling. Palastrina without emotion embodies the most perfect presentation of contemplative religious devotion. Bach, more touched by the secular spirit, and fully capable of strong emotion, formulates a more comprehensive and energetic type of religious sentiment, and foreshadows, by his new combination of rhythm and polyphony, the musical expression of every kind of human feeling. Beethoven expresses the complete emancipation of human emotion and mind, and attempts to give expression to every kind of mood and of inner sensibility which is capable and worthy of being brought into the circuit of an artistic scheme of design

But only at particular moments in the history of art are such crises possible. For it needs not only the grandeur of a man's nature to think of things worthy of being grandly said, but it requires a condition of mankind which shall be as appreciative of artistic considerations as of expression. There may be nobility, truth, and greatness in art at all times; but the perfect adjustment of things which is necessary to make a grand scheme of art, and to render possible examples of it which are nearly perfect from every point of view, is only to be found at rare moments in the history of human effort. The love of art for art's sake is generally a mere love of orderliness in things which require a great deal of ingenuity to get them into order; at best it is a love of beauty for itself At one stage in art's history an excessive delight in design and abstract beauty of form is inevitable, but humanity as it grows older instinctively feels that the adoration of mere beauty is sometimes childish and sometimes thoroughly unwholesome; and then men are liable to doubt whether human energies are not sapped by art instead of being fostered by it.

After a period in which men have gone through experiences such as these, a condition of art naturally follows in which the worshippers of abstract beauty and the worshippers of expression both find satisfaction; but inasmuch as the momentum generated is in a direction away from things purely artistic, a period is liable to follow in which things tend to leave the grand lines which imply a steadfast reverence for the highest phase of abstract beauty, and men seek a new field wherein to develop effects of strong characterisation. Art comes down from its lofty region and becomes the handmaid of everyday life. It seems to be so in most of the arts; for they each have their time of special glory, and are then turned to the more practical purposes of illustration. The greater portion of the arts of painting and drawing in modern times is devoted to illustration of the most definite kind; and even the pictures which aim at special artistic value, and are exhibited in important galleries, are of infinite variety of range in subject, and endeavour to realise within the conditions of artistic presentation almost any subject which has impressed an artist as worthy of permanent record. The instinct for beauty and the feeling for design may still have plenty of scope in accordance with the disposition of the artist, but they are by no means so prominent and necessary a part of art as they were; and many pictures have had immense fame which have been nothing but the baldest presentations of totally uninteresting everyday occurrences, without a trace of anything that shows a sense of either beauty or design.

It is much the same in literature. Nothing is more conspicuously characteristic of the present age than the immense increase of short illustrative stories which make vividly alive for all men the varieties of human circumstances and dispositions, from the remotest districts of India and the steppes of Russia, to the islands of Galway Bay and the backwoods of Australia. The few men that still have the instincts of great art cling to the great traditions and deal as much as they can with great subjects, but the preponderant tendency in all arts is towards variety and closeness of characterisation.

As has before been pointed out, the premonitions of this tendency are already discernible in Beethoven, and many other external facts in his time and soon after show in what direction the mind of man was moving. A characteristic feature which illustrates this is the much more frequent adoption by composers of names for their works; which evidently implies taking a definite idea and endeavouring to make the music express it. No one emphasises this fact more than Spohr. By natural musical organisation and habit of mind he was the last composer of whom one might expect unclassical procedure. Mozart was his model, and Beethoven was barely intelligible to him except in his least characteristic moods. But Spohr set himself in a very marked way to emphasise illustration. To many of his symphonies he gave definite names, and made it his endeavour to carry out his programme consistently. The well-known "Weihe der Töne" is a case in point. He meant originally to set a poem of that title by Pfeiffer as a cantata, but finding it unsuitable he wrote the symphony as an illustration of the poem and directed that the poem was to be read whenever the symphony was performed. Moreover, he endeavoured to widen the scope and design of this symphony to carry out his scheme, with eminently unsatisfactory results, as far as all the latter part of the work is concerned. His "Historical Symphony" has a similarly definite object, though not so close an application, as it was merely a very strange attempt to imitate the styles of Bach and Handel, Mozart and Beethoven in successive movements. More decisively to the point is his symphony called "The Worldly and Heavenly Influences in the Life of Man", in which the heavenly influences are represented by a solo orchestra, and the worldly by an ordinary full orchestra. The general idea is very carefully carried out, and the heavenly influences are made particularly prominent in the early part, and apparently succumb to the power of the worldly orchestra towards the end. Another symphony of Spohr's is called "The Seasons", which is a very favourite subject, and also a very suitable one, for true musical treatment.

Weber was naturally on the same side, both on account of his romantic disposition and the deficiencies of his artistic education. His one successful instrumental work, on a large scale, the Concertstuck for pianoforte and orchestra, deliberately represents a story of a knight and a lady in crusading times. The inference suggested is even stronger in the case of Mendelssohn, who was ultra-classical by nature, but gave names and indicated a purpose or a reason for the particular character of all his best symphonies—The Reformation, the Italian, and the Scotch. Even the symphony to the "Lobgesang" has a very definite and intelligible relation to the cantata which follows; while as far as musical characterisation is concerned, the overture and scherzo in the "Midsummer's Night's Dream" music are among the vivid things of modern times.

Berlioz

To all appearances the line which Berlioz took is even more decisive. But important as it is, the fact of his being a Frenchman reduces its significance a little. The French have never shown any talent for self-dependent instrumental music. From the first their musical utterance required to be put in motion by some definite idea external to music. The great Parisian lute-players wrote most of their neat little pieces to a definite subject; Couperin developed considerable skill in contriving little picture-tunes, and Rameau followed in the same line later. The kernel of the Gallic view of things is, moreover, persistently theatrical, and all the music in which they have been successful has had either direct or secondary connection with the stage.

Berlioz was so typical a Frenchman in this respect that he could hardly see even the events of his own life as they actually were; but generally in the light of a sort of fevered frenzy, which made everything—both ups and downs—look several times larger than the reality. Some of his most exciting experiences as related by himself are conceived in the spirit of melodrama, and could hardly have happened as he tells them except on the stage. This was not the type of human creature of whom self-dependent instrumental music could be expected; and it is no wonder that when he took to experimenting in that line of art he made it even more theatrical than ordinary theatrical music; because he had to supply the effect of the stage and the footlights and all the machinery, as well as the evolutions and gesticulations of the performers, by the music alone. His enormous skill and mastery of resource, brilliant intelligence, and fiery energy were all concentrated in the endeavour to make people see in their minds the histrionic presentation of such fit histrionic subjects as dances of sylphs, processions of pilgrims, and orgies of brigands.

Even the colossal dimensions of his orchestra, with its many square yards of drum surface, and its crowds of shining yellow brass instruments, is mainly the product of his insatiable theatrical thirst. It imposes upon the composer himself as much as it imposes upon his audience, by looking so very big and bristling to the eye of the imagination. But though it makes a great noise, and works on the raw impressionable side of human creatures, and excites them to an abnormal degree, the effect his music produces is not really so imposing as that of things which make much less show—for instance, the opening of Beethoven's B flat Symphony, which requires only seven different instruments to play it, and is all pianissimo. The means are in excess of the requirements; or rather what should be means becomes requirements, because the effect is made by the actual sound of the instruments, and often not at all by the music which they are the means of expressing. And this aspect of Berlioz's work is even more noteworthy in relation to modern musical development than the fact that he uniformly adopted a programme for his instrumental works.

He was a man of unusually excitable sensibility, and the tone of instruments appealed to him more than any other feature in music. He was also a man of literary tastes, and had no inconsiderable gifts in that line, and was more excited by the notion of what music might be brought to express than by the music itself. The result of such influences and predispositions was to impel him to endeavour to express literary or theatrical ideas in terms of colour and rhythm. He was the first composer who emphasised the element of instrumental tone quality or colour to such an extent; and so strong was his predisposition in this direction, that it can easily be seen that he often speculated in original effects of colour, and afterwards evolved or worked up musical ideas to fit into them, just as a painter might cover his canvas with the strangest tints he could devise, and work them up into a subject-picture or a landscape afterwards. But quite independent of these very marked peculiarities in his character, his genius and originality are incontestable. When the spirit of a situation like the opening scene of "Faust" or Margaret's meditation in the prison inspired him wholesomely, he was capable of rising to very high and genuinely musical conceptions.

The sum total of his work is one of the wonders of the art—unique in its weirdness and picturesqueness; and notable for the intense care with which every detail that ministers to effect is thought out. Not only are the scores very complicated in respect of the figures and rhythms of the actual music; but they are full of minute directions as to the manner of performance; extending to the putting of wind instruments in bags, and playing drums with sticks with sponge at the end, and many other original contrivances. The tendency to exaggeration is all of a piece with the high tension of his nervous organisation; but inasmuch as the whole object is to intensify characteristic expression in every conceivable manner, his work is very noteworthy as an illustration of the general tendencies of modern art since Beethoven. His methods have not found any very conspicuous imitators, though some very successful French composers have learnt a great deal from him in many ways. Indeed the modern French have more natural gift for colour, and a greater love for it, than for any other department of art. It appears to express most exactly their peculiarly lively sensibility; and their passion for it, and for what they call *chic*, has enabled them to develop in recent times a style of orchestration which is quite their own, and is generally very neat, graceful, finished and telling, especially for lighter kinds of music and opera.

. . .

Chopin

But by the side of the school of virtuosi, and in touch with it, the spirit of Chopin has laid a spell upon musical people all the world over, and has coloured a singularly wide range of musical activity in all countries His circumstances were specially suited to the necessities of the moment. The Poles are peculiarly different from the more happily regulated races of the western part of Europe; and the fact of having been unfortunate in their relations with their most powerful neighbours has intensified nationalist feeling. Such feeling, when repressed, generally bursts into song, and very often into very expressive song; and in Chopin's time everything combined to enhance the vividness and individuality of Polish music. Chopin, with Polish blood in his veins, and brought up in pure Polish surroundings, absorbed the national influences from his early years. Under such circumstances a national dance becomes a vital reality of more than ordinary calibre. A mazurka was a rhythmic expression of the national fervour. A polonaise symbolised the exaggerated glories of the Polish chivalric aristocracy.

Music which was so vivid and direct, and had such a touch of savage fervour, was not of the kind to go satisfactorily into sonatas. There needed to be very little intellectuality about it, but a great deal of the rhythmic element and of poetic feeling, and these things Chopin was eminently fitted to supply. On the other hand, his sensitiveness was acute even to morbidity; and being less gifted with force and energy than with excitability, he applied himself instinctively to the more delicate possibilities of his instrument. With him ornamental profusion was a necessity; but, more than with any other composer except Bach, it formed a part of his poetical thought. With most of the player-composers who cultivate virtuoso effects the brilliant passages are purely mechanical, and have little relation to the musical matter in hand. With Chopin the very idea is often stated in terms of most graceful and finished ornamentation, such as is most peculiarly suited to the genius of the instrument. Beethoven had grown more and more conscious of the suitableness of very rapid notes to the pianoforte as his experience and understanding of the instrument increased, and he had tried (in a different manner from Chopin) to achieve the same ends. But the reserve and grandeur of his style did not admit of the sort of ornaments that Chopin used; for these are made peculiarly vivid by profuse use of semitones and accessory notes of all kinds, which do not form part either of the harmony or the diatonic scale in which the passages occur. It gives a peculiarly dazzling, oriental flavour to the whole, which, joined with a certain luxurious indolence, a dreaminess of sentiment, and a subtlety of tone, makes Chopin's the ideal music for the drawing-rooms of fairly refined and prosperous people. But there is enough of genuine humanity and dramatic feeling to make his works appeal to a larger public than mere frequenters of drawing-rooms. There are even passages of savagery, such as those in the polonaises in A flat and F sharp minor, which sound like some echo from a distant country, and ring of the proud fervour of patriotic enthusiasm. The "Ballades" and so-called Sonatas and Scherzos convey a rich variety of moods and effects on a considerable scale, while the nocturnes, and some of the preludes and mazurkas, exactly hit the sensuous perceptions which are so highly developed in modern life.

Fortunately, with Chopin the general departure from sonata lines was no result of theory, but the spontaneous action of his nature. His music was the spontaneous utterance of a poetic and sensitive disposition, in the terms ideally suited to the instrument whose inner most capacities he understood more thoroughly than any one else in the world. Design of a classical kind was comparatively unimportant to him. He did not know much about it. But he most frequently cast his thoughts in simple forms, such as that of the nocturne—which Field had brought successfully into vogue just before his time—or the ordinary forms of the dance. When he struck out a form for himself, as in some of the best preludes and studies, it was like a poem on new lines. But the methods by which they were unified were much the same as those employed by J. S. Bach in his Preludes. Only in respect of their much more vivid colour, and intensity of feeling for modern expression, do they differ from the far more austere master. Of the degree in which expression is emphasised rather than form there can hardly be a question. But when the form is original it is extraordinarily well adapted to the style of the expression; as, for instance, in the preludes in E minor and D minor, where the form and expression are as closely wedded as in the most skilful and condensed poetical lyric. But such types of thought could not be expanded into great schemes of design. His largest works in original forms are the Ballades, and these are as unlike sonatas as any. The whole collection of his works is an illustration of the wide spread of possible variety which the new departure in the direction of expression, after the formal age, made inevitable.

Summary and Conclusion

If the art is worthy of the dignity of human devotion, it is worth considering a little seriously, without depreciating in the least the lighter pleasures to which it may minister. If it is to be a mere toy and trifle, it would be better to have no more to do with it. But what the spirit of man has laboured at for so many centuries cannot only be a mere plaything. The marvellous concentration of faculties towards the achievement of such ends as actually exist, must of itself be enough to give the product human interest. Moreover, though a man's life may not be prolonged, it may be widened and deepened by what he puts into it; and any possibility of getting into touch with those highest moments in art in which great ideals have been realised, in which noble aspirations and noble sentiments have been success-fully embodied, is a chance of enriching human experience in the noblest manner: and through such sympathies and interests the humanising influences which mankind will hereafter have at its disposal may be infinitely enlarged.

13 *The Music of the Seventeenth Century*

Introduction

Parry was commissioned to write *The Music of the Seventeenth Century* by Sir Henry Hadow and the Oxford University Press in late 1898. It was published in 1902 as volume III of the *Oxford History of Music*. Parry's ambitious undertaking was an attempt at a re-evaluation of the period; it was a painful process. By April 1900 the manuscript was more than double the allotted length. Fortunately Hadow's tactful encouragement ensured he cut more than a hundred pages out of his 'unlucky book' and Graves remarks that the following year 'he was engaged in a warfare with the Clarendon Press and the printers, each accusing the other of delays'.

E.J. Dent, writing in the *Athenaeum* in 1919, stressed that Parry was limited in his opportunities to study manuscripts in foreign libraries 'but would get manuscripts copied for him abroad' and 'whenever possible he went through the original scores'. Dent concluded: 'The value of his historical work depends on his critical analyses, and these are entirely his own. He differs from all other historians of music in that he approached musical history as a composer.'

Parry paid handsome tribute to Barclay Squire, the musicologist and librettist whom Parry appointed as Librarian of the R.C.M. Squire acted as Parry's assistant on the project, and his investigations took him as far as Venice in search of a Gabrieli Sonata. As early as 1889 he travelled to Italy with Barclay Squire and saw the codices in Trent, recording in his diary: 'We found things by Dunstable, Dufay, Binchois etc.'

This is Parry's most comprehensive book. The combination of telling a good historical story and a straightforward lucid musical analysis, replete with easy-to-read musical examples, makes even today for a rich, very enjoyable, but highly educational experience. This is the most difficult book to edit down and offer extracts. I hope the selection will induce the reader to investigate the whole book. Although Parry writes extensively, and with persuasion, about Henry Purcell, I feel that on balance his essays on Lulli and Schütz are more interesting since these composers relate more closely to his own work as a composer.

The Influence of French Taste

The influence of Monteverde is generally held to have passed into French Opera through his pupil Cavalli, who went to Paris in 1660 and 1662 in compliance with an invitation to produce operas to grace important Court functions. But French Opera was by no means the result of mere imitation of the Italian form. Its distinguishing traits were always very marked, and highly characteristic of the nation; and the features and qualities which it presents when it first comes decisively into view are the result of the fusion of several forms of French art and traits of French taste with important qualities and methods developed by the first two generations of Italian dramatic composers. The spirit of the dramatic material was to a certain extent Italian, and the attitude towards the emotional parts was Monteverdian; but the spectacular element and the dances were essentially French, and so also were some characteristics of the vocal music. The preponderant characteristics in the scheme of the typical French Court Opera were derived from the Mascarades, the actual record of which goes back as far as 1392, when a ballet was given in the hotel of the Queen Blanche in honour of the marriage of a knight of the house of Vermandois with a gentlewoman of the Queen's household; which ended grimly in the death by burning of several noble performers, as is related in the Chronicles of Froissart. Towards the end of the sixteenth century the records of such entertainments became numerous, and of one of them samples of music have survived, some of which are given in Burney's history. This was 'Le Balet comique de la Royne', given by command of Henry III, to grace the nuptials of the Duc de Joyeux in 1582. The music comprises some short rhythmic choruses, passages for solo voice, and a very sprightly and melodious piece of instrumental music.

Ex. 23

As specimens of theatrical music antecedent to the experiments of the Italian monodists, these small relics are of great interest, and indicate a line of development of art independent of the Italian movement. At the end of the sixteenth and the beginning of the seventeenth centuries France was exhausted by civil wars of the most merciless and murderous description, and was not in a condition to give opportunities for the development of any latent talent in her composers. But when there came a lull in the warfare, Louis XIII showed the usual taste of French kings for Mascarades. Of one great performance of the kind at Court, called 'La Délivrance de Renault', which took place in 1617, it is recorded that sixty-four singers, twenty-four viol players, and fourteen lute players were employed; and among other performers of high birth the king himself took a part as 'Démon du Feu'. The performances of the 'Ballet de Landy' in 1627, and the 'Ballet des Andouilles portées en guise de Momons' in 1628, and 'La prospérité des armes de France,' given at the Palais Cardinal in 1641, show that the form of art was in great favour. When Louis XIII died, and Louis XIV came to the throne, the taste for all sorts of theatrical entertainments manifestly increased. Mazarin, perceiving the liking of Anne of Austria for such things, encouraged and fostered them; and it appears that it was owing to him that Italian performers were first brought to Paris in 1645. The work performed on this occasion was 'La Festa teatrale della finta Pazza', by Giulio Strozzi, given partly in declamation and partly sung, and presented with great magnificence of stage accessories. The Court people received the Italians with mixed feelings. Mme. de Motteville gives an account of her impressions at one of these performances as follows: 'Le Mardi Gras la reine fit représenter une de ses comédies en musique dans la petite salle du Palais Royal. Nous n'étions que vingt ou trente personnes dans ce lieu, et nous pensâmes y mourir de froid et d'ennui'. In another place she seems to voice the impression produced on the French of the time: 'Ceux qui s'y connaissent estiment fort les Italians; pour moi je trouve que la longueur du spectacle diminue fort le plaisir, et que les vers naïvement répétés représentent plus aisément la conversation et touchent plus les esprits que le chant ne delécte les oreilles'. The French were much impressed by the vocal ability of Margareta Bertalozzi, but were unfavourably impressed by the Italian recitative, and thought their own ways of dealing with dialogue and songs much preferable; in which they foreshadowed the taste of more experienced audiences in later days; for the treatment of the dialogue in the Lullian form of opera, which was the outcome of French taste, was generally much more definitely musical than the conventional recitative of the Italians. Their preference for Mascarades to musical dramas, during the first half of the century, encouraged the poets who supplied the librettos to put much of the dialogue into neat little verses, which lent themselves readily to neat little vocal tunes, somewhat similar in general to those which were introduced into the English masques. Their acute feeling for dance-rhythm probably had some influence on the characteristic forms of their rhythmic songs, both in respect of the words and the music. A special type of dainty dexterously organized song has been characteristic of the French in all times from which musical examples have been handed down. They seem to take delight in simple ditties, which have no great warmth or force of expression about them, but in which the phrases and figures are very neatly manipulated. For, though a violently excitable people, they have a singular love of categorizing and systematizing in every branch of mental energy—as if they clung to the idea that a well-constructed organization would save them from the effects of uncontrollable savagery and violence. The Mascarades were obviously very favourable opportunities for such little ditties; and some dainty songs from such as were performed early in the seventeenth century have been preserved. One of the most successful composers of this kind was Pierre Guedron, who was Master of the Music and Composer of the Chamber of Louis XIII. Another composer of the same order was Guedron's son-in-law, Bosset, who was Intendant to Louis XIII; and yet another was Gabriel Bataille, Lutenist to the Queen. Their vocal music stands in marked contrast to the histrionic music of their Italian contemporaries, being essentially rhythmic and definite in form and melodic contour. The mere tunes of two of Guedron's songs from the 'Ballet de Madame' (which was produced on the occasion of Louis XIII's marriage with Anne of Austria) will be sufficient to show the difference between the French attitude towards vocal music and that of Monteverde and Cavalli.

Ex. 24

Ex. 25

The intention is obviously more structural than declamatory, and more intellectual than emotional. The French composers, if left to themselves, do not seem likely to have effected much in the direction of passionate expression. Their natural instinct, like that of their public, seems in the direction of gaiety and lightheartedness; impelling them to treat even pathetic situations with a sort of childish superficiality—as occasions for making something neat and pretty, rather than emotional or interesting. Their music seems to corroborate the inferences suggested by their history. The characteristic points of their early theatrical music are quite out of the range of the dramatic factors. The songs are dainty morsels in themselves, sometimes expressing very delicately the sentiment of undramatic words, but not in the high-coloured, emotional manner which was attempted by Monteverde and sometimes by his follower Cavalli. But, on the other hand, as the two schools progressed, the immediate and intrinsic relation of the music to the meaning of the words was closer in the French; and the difference became more marked when the Italian school drifted off into the formality of their arias and the absolute musical inanity of their recitatives; while the French school first found approximate expression of their ideals in the fine declamatory passages of Lulli; and, refusing to be permanently dominated by conventional ideas, attained a further point of vantage in the works of Rameau, and a more complete satisfaction of the difficult problems of musical drama in the works of Gluck. The process of the development of French stage music was therefore altogether in strong contrast to the Italian. The latter had begun with vague recitative, with hardly any salient features of any sort, and out of these somewhat chaotic conditions composers had by degrees modelled sundry concrete forms, such as the instrumental ritornelli and arias. The French approached the music drama with two kinds of ingredients already well defined, in the ballet-tunes and the chansons; and they aimed at the definite presentment of their first form of opera by amalgamating these with the scheme which had been worked out by the Italians.

The performances of Italian Opera in Paris, and the feeling of Parisians that the Italian methods in such music did not altogether satisfy their particular tastes, very naturally impelled the French to try to achieve something of their own on lines which were more congenial; and these aspirations found expression in the combined efforts of the Abbé Perrin as librettist and Cambert as composer about fourteen years after the first appearance of the Italian company. Perrin himself seems to have been the leading spirit, and, to judge by the letter which he wrote to the Cardinal de la Rovera soon after their first experiment, he had formed a clear idea of the points in which the Italian procedure could be improved upon from the standpoint of French taste. He shows that Italian composers had been content to set 'comedies' written to be recited and not to be sung; and he describes their music somewhat strangely for an Abbé, as 'plains chants et des airs de cloistre que nous appelons des chansons des vielles ou du ricochet'. The outcome of his speculations was performed with immense éclat at the house of M. de la Haye in the village of Issy in 1659. It is described in the collected works of Perrin as 'Première comédie française en musique représentée en France. Pastorale mise en musique par le Sieur Cambert.' It made such a favourable impression upon the courtly audience that it was repeated several times, and given by special command before 'their Majesties' at the château of Vincennes. Unfortunately, though there are fairly detailed reports about the nature of the music, and the poem is printed, the actual music seems lost beyond recovery. For works which throw any trustworthy light on Cambert's methods and abilities, we have to wait till fully twelve years later. Perrin was quite ready to follow up their success at once, and decided that the subject of the next opera should be 'Ariane, ou le mariage de Bacchus', and he even looked forward to following it up with a tragedy on the death of Adonis. But his immediate activity was put a stop to by the death of Gaston of Orleans in 1660, and of Mazarin in 1661.

[Lulli]

It was left for Lulli to infuse the dramatic element and complete the scheme, and for this he very soon had opportunity. The career of this remarkable man may be summarized in a few words. Born near Florence in 1633, he was brought to France by the Chevalier de Guise, who was attracted by his talent for playing the guitar. He got a footing at Court, and ingratiated himself with the King by his readiness in producing attractive songs and dance-tunes. The King made him director of the 'Bande des petits violons' in 1652, when he was barely twenty. He organised 'divertissements dansés' such as were dear to the King's heart, and found his first signal public opportunity in writing the music for 'Alcidiane', to words by Benserade, which was performed with much success at St. Germain in 1658, as has already been mentioned. In 1661 he received the brevet of 'Compositeur et Surintendant de la Musique de la Chambre du Roi'. In July, 1662, he was made 'Maître de la Musique de la Famille Royale', and in the same year he married the daughter of Lambert, who was 'Maître de Musique de la Cour'. Between 1664 and 1671 was the time of ballet writing, when among other works he wrote the music to 'La Princesse d'Elide' in 1664, to 'M. de Pourceaugnac' in 1669, to 'Le Bourgeois Gentilhomme' in 1670, and 'Psyché' in 1671. He had practically become the 'Intendant des menus plaisirs de la Cour', and quite indispensable to the King. And when the obscure differences between Perrin and his coadjutors brought their scheme of national opera into jeopardy, the King granted the exclusive privilege of the 'Académie Royale de Musique' to him by letters patent in 1672, and with him were joined Quinault for the poetry, and M. de St. Ouen for the 'machines'. The theatre in the Rue Vaugiraud was opened in 1672 with 'Les Fêtes de l'Amour et Bacchus', and from that date till his death Lulli produced at least one opera every year. In 1681 he was naturalized and ennobled; and in 1687 he died, about the age of fifty-four. He was one of the most remarkable examples of the successful 'entrepreneur' who ever lived; and as it has never been hinted that he was anything but a Gentile, his career serves as a striking exception to the theories generally held with regard to racial aptitudes for accumulating a fortune. He probably entered France without a louis d'or in his possession; but when he died, sacks full of them, with 'doublons d'Espagne', were found in his house to the extent of 20,000 livres; and his whole fortune was estimated at 800,000 livres, which he had accumulated mainly by shrewd investments in property in the growing fashionable quarters of Paris. For those who are in search of a strange psychological problem to unravel, Lulli seems ready to hand. The combination of composer and pelf-seeker [sic] is always repulsive, and the French of his time did not find it otherwise. But, notwithstanding the sordid, unscrupulous and worldly nature which his story suggests, it must be acknowledged that Lulli's work is characterized by a certain nobility, dignity, and breadth, and qualities of expression which command respect. The comparative absence of triviality and vulgarity may be discounted a little by the consideration that trivial and vulgar music is a matter of development like anything else, and till several generations of low composers had studied the likings of the vulgarest and most ignoble sections of society with the view of writing down to their level, composers really did not know how to be effectively trivial and vulgar. Now-a-days, when the poison has got thoroughly into the system of all arts, it is difficult for the most high-minded artist to avoid an occasional phrase which puts him in unfavourable contrast with Lulli. But, to give the man his due, Lulli did as little as any one to vulgarize the phraseology of music. Some of the credit may be due to his courtly audience. He certainly studied their tastes with considerable subtlety; and it may well be that, though the King and the Court took part in ballets and theatrical representations, they did such things in a sedate and courtly manner, without romping and buffoonery; and the music, which is such a delicate mirror of attitude of mind, paced with corresponding stateliness and show of courtly dignity. To modern audiences, accustomed to high colour, tinsel, and tricks of effect, the Lullian Opera would be quite unendurable, even supposing that it had not inherent defects begot of artistic inexperience and immaturity of method.

In one respect the Lullian Opera is mature, and that is in its purely theatrical features. It was an entertainment of an extremely artificial kind, developed on the basis of the time-honoured Mascarades, and, as a formal product of pure theatrical art, remarkably complete. It was as much through this fact as through the pre-eminent traits of Lulli's character, that French Opera came to a complete standstill for such a long time after his death. The puzzle had been worked out, and all the pieces so accurately fitted that a complete change of attitude was necessary before anything new could be brought into the scheme. Lulli himself made hardly any attempt to vary the general plan from the beginning to the end of his career. The typical French overture, the allegorical prologue with its alternate choruses and ballets, the dialogues of the drama in semi-recitatives, the laying out of the acts with but slight variations in the order of the divertissements and choruses, are all just as complete and articulate in the 'Thésée' of 1673 as in 'Armide' of 1685. As the type is so distinct, and as Lulli's works represent the final stage in one of the most important epochs in French theatrical art, the outline of 'Roland', which is one of the latest and best of the series, may with advantage be considered.

The overture is a dignified and massive piece of work, on precisely the same lines as the overtures of 'Pomone' and 'Les Plaisirs d'Amour', beginning with the slow movement—the main object of which is sonority and fullness—proceeding with a fugal movement, and ending up with another sonorous passage. After the overture comes the usual prologue, of the usual mythological allegorical description, with masses of people on the stage singing and dancing, and short passages of definite tune interspersed with suitable recitative, culminating in chorus and dance. After the prologue the overture is repeated, and then the play begins. Roland, the hero, is the impersonation of that abstraction so dear to the French mind, 'la gloire'. He is the ideal hero of effective and brilliant combats, who is returning from some warlike expedition in which he has played the conqueror, to seek the lady with whom he was in love before he started. Unfortunately, the lady has meanwhile found some one else, of the name of Medor, to supply his place during his absence, and very naturally keeps out of the way. Roland seeks her in country places, which afford excellent opportunities for the pastoral scenes and dances for which the courtly minds of Parisians seem to have had such a fancy on the stage. A rustic wedding is introduced, and, of course, rustic chorus and rustic ballet; and Roland sings, while the rustic music is going on, his assurance that he will find Angélique somewhere among the merry-makers. But, unluckily, the chorus begin to sing their blessings on the loves of Angélique and Medor, and the secret is thereby betrayed. Roland forthwith goes out of his mind, and sings a vehement solo about being 'betrayed, Heavens! who could believe it? by the ungrateful beauty for the love of whom he had forsaken his duty to "la gloire"'. Furious music is played while he tears up the trees and rocks and other practicable theatrical properties; and he concludes with a very fine piece of declamation, in which he expresses his having fallen into the darkness of the tomb, and the state of desperation induced by being crossed in love. The act in this case ends with solo music, and it is the only act in 'Roland' which concludes without mass of sound and crowded stage. The procedure shows Lulli's instinct very happily, as it obviates the monotony of an absolute similarity of effect in each act, and throws the situation, which is obviously meant to be the strongest point in the drama, into strong relief. A very good point is also made by beginning the last act with soothing music, to which the kindly spirit Logistille steps in to set matters right, exhorting Roland to give up his weakness, and resume the paths of glory, the music comprising one of the most famous tunes in the whole of Lulli's works. Roland, of course, feels the force of the appeal, and the chorus join in, and the whole concludes with excellent stage effect and great mass of sound.

The Beginning of German Music

[Schütz]

The first representative German composer whose gifts were sufficiently comprehensive to lead the way in the direction of modern forms of art was Heinrich Schütz. Born just a hundred years before Bach and Handel at Köstritz in Saxony, he began his musical career at the age of thirteen in the choir of the chapel of Maurice, Landgraf of Hesse-Cassel. After receiving a good general education, some of it at the University of Marburg, he was sent to Venice comparatively late in life by the Landgraf, who seems to have been smitten with the idea of introducing into Germany the methods of art for which Giovanni Gabrieli was so famous. To judge by the event, Heinrich Schütz was happily chosen for the experiment, and the Landgraf was singularly lucky or wise in his choice of the particular Italian composer to take as a guide.

As has been before pointed out, the Venetian tradition originally sprang from a northern source, and it had not yet lost its northern qualities. Of this tradition Gabrieli was the most powerful and characteristic representative. His music savours more of rugged force than of sensuous beauty. He seeks rather to interest than to please, and uses artistic resources to intensify the meaning of words rather than for purely artistic effects. Deeply speculative and enterprising, he passed beyond the limits of the old choral style fully as soon as the promoters of the 'Nuove Musiche,' but by a different road and with much greater musicianship and range of resource. His attitude was precisely of the nature to appeal to men of Teutonic race, and it was the appropriate outcome of inherent affinities that Germany alone of modern nations should initiate her own music under the influence of the great Venetian.

Heinrich Schütz was with Gabrieli from 1609 till 1612, when the master died, and the pupil went back to Germany. At first he remained in the service of the Landgraf who had afforded him the opportunity to go to Venice. But in 1616 a more favourable field was opened to him in the chapel of the Elector of Saxony in Dresden, of which he was made Cappellmeister. This Elector had aspirations also to be well to the fore in his chapel music, and Schütz had for a time the advantage of a band as well as an organ to accompany his choir. It was under these circumstances that he produced his most characteristic works, which have earned for him in some quarters the name of 'the father of German music.' The great majority of his compositions belong to the 'sacred' branch of art, the most important being numerous psalms and motets, a so-called oratorio of 'The Resurrection,' four 'Passions,' a musical rendering of the 'Seven Last Words on the Cross,' and several collections of 'Symphoniae sacrae,' which consist of settings of Latin and German texts of various kinds, some dramatic and some devotional, for voices and instruments. These works have many characteristics in common with Giovanni Gabrieli's, and it may be confessed that among them are a crudeness and speculativeness which frequently arrive at the point of being almost impracticable. But on the other hand Schütz, like Gabrieli, is personally interesting to a remarkable degree: a character of rare genuineness and fervour—a nature susceptible to beautiful and pathetic sentiments, and not the less attractive because his attempts to utter what he felt are so evidently bounded by the very limited development of artistic technique of his time. His attitude in relation to sacred words is happily illustrated by his setting of the 'Lord's Prayer' for nine voices and an accompaniment of two violins and bass. It begins with the following passage, in which the singular rising progressions evidently suggest the eagerness of pleading:—

Ex. 26

Each clause is preceded by the word 'Vater,' which is reiterated more frequently as the prayer proceeds. It is repeated three times before 'Forgive us our sins,' and four times before 'Lead us not into temptation.' The music to the words 'Erlöse uns von dem Übel' is developed at rather exceptional length, seeming to dwell especially on the word 'erlöse,' and thereby suggesting sentiment associated with the word 'Erlöser,' to which Germans attached a deeply mystical meaning. With the exordium, 'Father, thine is the kingdom,' in which the prayer ceases and an approach to doxology is made, there is a change of time and style, at first for some time with a single voice, and then for the first time the two choirs of five and four voices respectively come into action, answering and overlapping one another in the final phrase, 'Thine is the kingdom, the power, and the glory,' and so on, the two choirs being massed together in the last few bars to the words, 'Amen, Vater, Amen!' In the earlier part of the composition the whole of the voices hardly ever sing together, but only two and three at a time, with the evident intention of throwing the sonority of the last part into strong relief. This process lends itself at the same time to the individualization of each separate voice, as though each was personally concerned in his own utterance of the prayer, producing a kind of dramatic effect by a method which Schütz employed again for the choruses in the Passions.

Another interesting scheme, very apt to the words, is 'Nun danket Alle Gott.' It begins with a lively symphony, a few bars of which may be quoted as an example of Schütz's treatment of instruments:—

Ex. 27

The whole of the voices, divided into two choirs of six and four parts respectively, take up the words of the hymn in a massive succession of chords, and thereafter a kind of rondo form is attained by alternating passages for a few voices at a time in a semi-melodious recitative style (something in principle like the verses in the English anthems), with the reiteration of the massive 'Nun danket Alle Gott,' and the work is rounded off with a fine climacteric coda in which group responds to group with jubilant 'Allelujahs.'

The expressive intentions of the composer are shown in another aspect in the remarkable 'Symphonia sacra,' 'Saul, Saul, was verfolgst du mich?' Here the call rises from the lowest depths of available sound in broken ejaculations, the basses taking it first, followed by the two middle voices, and then by the two highest voices:—

Ex. 28

Then the same formula is given to the instruments still higher in the scale, and three choirs of six, four, and four voices alternate respectively the call *forte*, and then the words 'was verfolgst du mich' are given first *piano*, then *pianissimo*. Then single voices take up the words, 'Es wird dir schwer werden, wider den Stachel zu löcken':—

Ex. 29

and then the shout of all the choir comes again, the ejaculatory call alternating with passages of choral recitative, and the last outburst of 'Saul, was verfolgst du mich,' beginning *forte*, drops to *mezzo forte*, then to *pianissimo*, and then seems to die away altogether with the quasi-distant echo, 'was verfolgst du mich,' till only two voices are left out of the fourteen to end with.

It is worthy of note that the treatment is not in reality histrionic. The singular call rising from the depths and spreading over the whole of the vocal scale, beginning with the softness inevitable with such deep vocal sound, and increasing like a flood to the utmost force of the chorus, is more subjective than objective. It represents the throbbing of the inner man under intense excitement, growing more and more overwhelming as the emotion gathers force, until the whole being is vibrating with it, and then dying away like a fading image in the mind as exhaustion supervenes. This treatment does not suggest the scene, but the effect the situation produces on the human being. And it illustrates the just view of the Teutonic composer, that music deals with the inward man and not with what is external to him; with the mood induced by the external and not with the external itself. The external may be suggested secondarily by the exactness of the presentation of the inner feeling and mood; and when the mood is justly represented, a trait of external realism is justifiable as a help to define and locate the cause of the impression produced. The predisposition of men of Teutonic race to introspection and deep thought leads them in this respect in the right direction, and offers an additional reason why the German attitude led to such triumphant achievements in music.

The same characteristics of earnest simplicity and deep feeling are shown in Schütz's larger works. Of these the most important and the most comprehensive is the *Historia von der Auferstehung Jesu Christi*, which is frequently described as an oratorio, though in that category it stands, both for style and treatment, by itself. In this he employs chorus, a number of soloists, a small orchestra of strings, and an organ, for which only figured bass is given after the usual manner of the time. The treatment of the subject is similar to that employed in Bach's famous 'Passions.' The narrative portion, which is put into the mouth of the 'Evangelist,' is given to the tenor soloist, who is accompanied by four gambas, and it is sung in a curious kind of plaintive recitative, a great part of which is intoned on one note, diversified at the beginnings and ends of phrases and sentences by short passages of melodic rather than declamatory character, which have, in relation to the intonation, a very expressive effect. Most of the sentences throughout the work begin with the same melodic formula, consisting of a plaintive rise from the tonic to the fifth and the minor seventh and returning to the fifth again, which thenceforward becomes the reciting note. The reciting note is, however, not restricted to the fifth, but other notes are taken for various parts of the sentences, and the monotone is often diversified by isolated deviations of single notes for the purposes of accent on a syllable or the reverse. The following excerpt will serve to illustrate the process:—

Ex. 30

Ex. 30 concluded

The various characters are taken by various soloists as in Bach's 'Passions.' Thus, the two angels at the grave sing a kind of duet; the three Marys a trio; Cleophas a solo. The words of Maria Magdalena and the other Mary are given to two soloists, and so are the words of Jesus. All these individual utterances are in a kind of archaic recitative. There is not the slightest attempt at tune of any kind. The declamation is often on one note, as in the part of the Evangelist, but at prominent moments expression is obtained by rising or falling of the voice, and by the harmonies with which it is accompanied. As an example of the tender kind of expression obtained by the simplest means, the following from the scene between the angels and Maria Magdalena, comprising the pathetic utterance, 'They have taken away my Lord, and I know not where they have laid Him,' may be taken:—

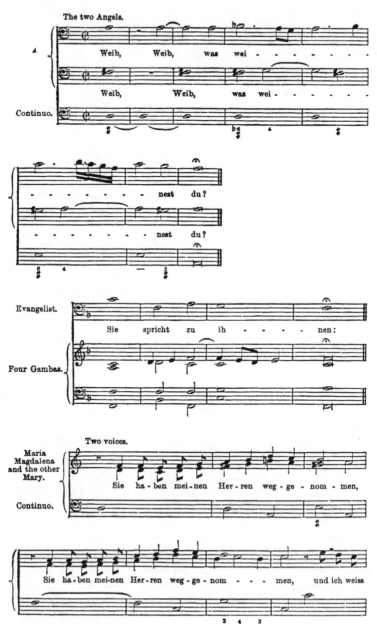

Ex. 31

The chorus is but little employed, in the body of the work only for the words of the disciples, 'The Lord is risen indeed, and has appeared to Simon', and there are two short choruses at the beginning and end—the first to give the formal words of preface, 'The resurrection of our Lord Jesus Christ as it is written for us by the four Evangelists,' and the final chorus, rounding off the whole, 'To God be thanks, who giveth us the victory through Jesus Christ'—followed by jubilant reiteration of the word 'Victoria.'

14   *Johann Sebastian Bach*: the St Matthew Passion

Introduction

Parry's relationship with Bach is so wide ranging and far reaching that it deserves a study of its own I hope a later Parry scholar will seriously consider doing this. A few salient points will have to suffice here. All of Parry's finest mature choral works show Bach's, and indeed Schütz's influence. Bachian counterpoint is often strikingly apparent in the development sections of his symphonic movements, and obviously throughout his organ music. As a performing musician and teacher, Parry preached Bach (the word is carefully chosen) throughout his life. While he was unsuccessful in passing on his love of Beethoven to his most illustrious pupil, Ralph Vaughan Williams, he was totally successful with Bach. Vaughan Williams worshipped the 'sublime bourgeois' almost to the exclusion of all other composers before Brahms.

That two spiritually troubled English agnostics should give the central position in Western music to the man now considered the principal musical spokesman for Christianity remains a paradox typical of the educated nineteenth-century Western mind. The usual explanation of this paradox, that music – even music with a text – is primarily abstract, and therefore not relatable to any doctrine, or philosophy, is a psychological sop to Cerebus and will not do. In our century Jung, his pupils and colleagues, have begun to remove this paradox by the re-discovery of the Gnostics, the Alchemical tradition, and a psychoanalytic interpretation of the pre-Christian religions and mythologies. Jung's discoveries made it possible once and for all to separate Jesus the Christ from Christianity. This was nearly impossible in the late nineteenth century: even the sharpest, most inquiring minds could not fully see the radiant prophet or understand the meaning of his words. Nearly two thousand years of political and theological dogma had distorted his image beyond recognition. It is now possible to make the distinction between the religions based on him and the essential nature of the man himself and what he taught.

That Bach, this glorious creative genius, with his enormous musical technique, combined with an authoritative but richly warm musical personality, should appeal so strongly to both men is not surprising. This book is Parry's central expression on the subject, but Bachian trajectories wind their way throughout all Parry's writings. Parry's essay on the St Matthew Passion is one of his most cogent pieces of writing while also typical of his approach. He writes intimately to his reader about music he knows well. He does not leave out basic factual information which the reader may not yet know, but he subordinates it to the basic discourse, so the writing never becomes pedantic.

Parry states, in the preface, his purpose is to present a 'condensed survey of Bach's life-work and his unique artistic character'. He goes on to argue that 'too copious a presentation of details is apt to obstruct that understanding of the works of any great composer or artist, and the manner in which human qualities are manifested in them, which is the object of all scrutiny of their lives'. He also delivers a salutary warning to all musicologists that 'musical analysis is, as a rule, quite unprofitable without the actual Music analysed', particularly of 'works which are hardly ever, if ever, performed.' This advice is particularly relevant to any assessment of Parry's own works for chorus and orchestra, of which nearly two dozen remain unrevived and unrecorded at the time of writing.

After many years of reflection, Parry began the writing of the book during the summer of 1901. It was finished during 1908, and published the next year by G.P. Putnam's Sons with the title *Johann Sebastian Bach: the Story of the Development of a Great Personality*. I have chosen his essay on the *Matthäus-Passion*, perhaps the finest and most moving words Parry has left to us.

The Matthäus-Passion

The records of the circumstances and conditions of composition which led to the achievement of the great "Passion according to St. Matthew", which is the richest and noblest example of devotional music in existence, are all as utterly blank as the other records of Bach's life. The work happily exists in all its lovable beauty, but how Bach lived and how he worked, how those in daily touch with him watched and possibly participated in the gradual unfolding of its inspiring pages, is unknown, and all the little incidents which would throw light upon his methods and habits of work are utterly vanished. Except for the manuscript score, which bears the tokens of the patient and steadfast labour of the composer, it might almost as well have been a supernatural accident.

Of the nature and quality of this unique form of art, for which unfortunately no other name has been discovered but "Passion music", sufficient has been said. Its source, growth and expansion have been outlined till the time of Bach's production of the "St. John Passion". It has further been indicated that after Bach came to Leipzig he not infrequently adopted a cosmopolitan style in his cantatas, temporarily allowing the romantic elements to be superseded by Italian modes of treatment. But the process of assimilation of the foreign methods did not in the least impair the fundamental qualities of his disposition, and from the outset of the "Matthäus-Passion" he shows that they were in no degree affected by the study and use of Italian forms. Indeed there is no work, even of the most fervent romantic styles of his youth, which breathes more consistently the romantic temperament of the race whose best qualities he represents so nobly.

The first chorus, which occupies the position of a prologue, is on the very grandest scale, requiring two orchestras of wind and strings, two choirs of four voices apiece, and a separate treble part which sings with steadfast gait against the multitudinous polyphony of the rest, the chorale, *O Lamm Gottes, unschuldig*. The first words of the chorus, *Kommt ihr Töchter, helft mir klagen*, suggest indirectly to the mind of the worshippers the attitude worthy of the subject. The alternation of the utterances of the two choruses, rising at times to almost dramatic intensity, and the rich flow of sad phrases and harmonies punctuated by monosyllabic interjections, lay a groundwork of the utmost dignity and solemnity. Then the voice which takes the part of the Evangelist (the counterpart of Historicus in Carissimi's little oratorios) takes up the story, plunging at once into the midst of it with the words, "When Jesus had finished all these sayings, he spake to His disciples," and then follow the words of Christ, "Ye know that in two days will be the Passover, when the Son of Man will be betrayed." The passage is given to a bass solo accompanied by strings in harmony, as is invariably the case where Christ is made to speak in His own person. The story is made to pause for a moment while the pathetic chorale, *Herzliebster Jesu, was hast du verbrochen*, is sung.

Then the Evangelist tells of the meeting of the high priests and scribes in the palace of Caiaphas, and their plan to take and kill Jesus. There follows the first chorus of what was technically called the "Turba", being the words of the assembled priests, "Not on the feast-day," in a vigorous and decisive vein, such as characterises nearly all the choruses which belong to the action of the story, and makes them stand out in clear and unmistakable contrast to the reflective choruses and the chorales. The episode of the woman with the vase of precious ointment is fully dealt with, and is followed by the commentary recitative *Du lieber Heiland du*, which presents a characteristic procedure frequently adopted by Bach in the Passions; as the movement is accompanied throughout by a sad and tender figure played on two flutes, almost always either in thirds or sixths, below which the chords, filled in by pizzicato strings and "continuo", recur in absolutely strict and regular slow beats. The movement is really out of the category of recitative, for, though the melodious voice part is free and elocutionary, the unbroken persistence of the figure of the flutes and the recurrent chords on the strings establish a principle of expression and coherence of an invaluable kind which differentiates the type both from the purely informal recitative and the aria. It is the more serviceable in this Passion, as it distinguishes the quasi-recitative of commentaries from the unaccompanied recitative of the Evangelist who relates the story.

The relation of the treacherous compact of Judas with the high priest is followed by a very pathetic aria, *Blute nur, du liebes Herz* in full *da capo* form, but with no other trace of Italian influence. The warning of Christ to his disciples, that one of them should betray Him, is followed by a graphic little chorus of the disciples asking, "Lord, is it I?" the voices rapidly alternating one with the other, a scheme which had been anticipated with the object of suggesting actuality by Schütz in his Passion. Closely following upon this is the solemn episode of the symbolical offering of the bread and wine, which has that singularly tender and solemn feeling before described as characterising the music put into the mouth of Jesus by Bach. This in its turn is followed by the recitative *Wiewohl mein Herz* which is a counterpart of the quasi-recitative *Du lieber Heiland*, the accompaniment this time being given to a duet of plaintive oboi d'amore. The confidence in his own courageous loyalty expressed by Peter invites a pause for reflection, which is afforded by an appropriate chorale; and thereafter follow the poignant episode of the Garden of Gethsemane, and the words of Jesus, "My soul is exceeding sorrowful even unto death," which naturally suggest further reflections. And these Bach most amply presents in two movements of extraordinarily tender beauty, in both of which his favourite device of alternating the solo voice with chorus in intercommunion of sentiment is most aptly used. The tenor voice in the first of these movements expresses the anguish of the thought, *O Schmerz, hier zittert das gequälte Herz*, with accompaniment of two flutes and two oboi da caccia and organ. The choir answers with the first phrase of a soft unaccompanied chorale; then the solo voice takes up the plaint again and is answered by the second line of the chorale, and so on throughout. The movement does not come to a definite end, but merely turns to the dominant of the coming key, C minor, and so makes way for a movement in which the scheme of alternation of solo voice and chorus is similar, but the voice part is of more definite character, as befits its designation as an aria. The words make an innocent attempt at comfort, as the solo voice utters "I will watch my Jesus," and the chorus answers referring to His sleep, "So may our sins be put to sleep," with a singularly characteristic and innocent tune. The wide expansion of this group of movements was probably deliberately made with the view of keeping the mind occupied with this mournful episode of the tragedy proportionately to its significance.

The whole story of the betrayal follows in detail with many remarkable instances of emphasis on the situations; for instance, the choir bursts in upon the tender flowing lament which is given to the soprano and alto, "So ist mein Jesusa nun gefangen," with the sharp, angry interjections "Lasst ihn, haltet, bindet nicht," which, as it were, punctuate the whole movement with reiterated protests, thereby in some measure preparing the ground and the mind for the tremendous rush of the chorus, *Sind Blitze, sind Donner in Wolken verschwunden*, an example of graphic and raging energy such as had never been heard before. The strides of the sequences, the explosion of the sudden chord of F sharp major after the central close in D, the alternation of the choruses seeming to contend with one another in their shouts: "Eröffne den feurigen Abgrund, O Hölle," (first Choir) "Zertrümmre," (second Choir) "Verderbe," (first Choir) "Verschlinge," (second Choir) "Zerschelle," seem to typify a perfect cataclysm of nature at the horror of the betrayal of the sinless Son of God. Thereafter follows in Bach's version the relation of the episode which ends with the words "And all the disciples forsook him and fled."

This is as far as Bach takes the story in the first half of the work, and the commentatory chorus which follows and completes it (in the existing version) is the marvellously rich and expressive movement which originally stood at the beginning of the Johannes-Passion, *O Mensch bewein' dein' Sünde gross'*. It is practically a noble adaptation of the form of organ music known as the "Chorale-fantasia," but almost incredibly enriched by every known resource of art to intensify the expression and bring men's relation to the tragedy home to their minds. The beauty and aptness of the Passion form could hardly be more exquisitely displayed, but in order to realise it, it is necessary to consider the innermost meaning of the situation. The regular rotation of routine which is inevitable in ecclesiastical functions has the tendency to deaden the impression of what is related in sacred narrative or offered in the abasement of devotion; and so it comes about that such a poignant moment in the story might pass almost unnoticed. The disciples, the friends, the intimates, the choicest of flower of those to whom He had daily revealed the treasures of His mind, those whose belief in Him had been so absolute and heart-whole and should be the means through whom His message was to be conveyed to mankind, are close at hand; but the moment which tests their loyalty comes, their courage fails, and He, sinless and betrayed, has not so much as one friend left to comfort Him. The contemplation of a situation so utterly forlorn, in which the cruelty of public injustice is accentuated by the refined torment of the disloyalty of beloved friends, suggests the condition of stupefaction in the minds of those who hear the story with complete perception. The music, which in this chorus summons the mind to concentrate itself on the poignant episode, seems to express the kind of pain that comes on the mind when something happens which transcends man's power to estimate and express. It floats like the subtle suggestion of a mood of sorrow filled with remembrance. The instruments—flutes, oboi d'amore, strings—discourse their tender phrases for a while, till, as though human contemplation had arrived just at the point of utterance, the trebles of the chorus quietly begin the chorale, *O Mensch bewein' dein' Sünde gross'*, to which the other voices respond by taking up the same words and amplifying the expression of the sentiments with those intimate touches of realistic suggestion of which Bach always availed himself. The implication is, of course, a figurative one, as the men who are exhorted to bewail their sins are not the disciples who had fled. Their transgression is here but a type—the reminder of the universal inadequacy of mankind,—and the devout address their admonition to themselves; as much as to say: "It was for us that this was endured, and yet we are as little steadfast in our loyalty as the disciples in the time of need."

The form of the "Chorale-fantasia" is especially apt for the contemplative state of deep sorrow. Each phrase of the chorale is followed by a short interval in the vocal utterances, during which the instruments maintain their plaintive discourse. And the effect is essentially true of the human state in such conditions. It is as much a fact of experience as of theory that short sentences interspersed with pauses have a very powerful effect in impressive situations. As examples of Bach's insight in the matter, reference may be made to the strangely fragmentary chorale at the end of the motet, *Der Geist hilft uns*, and the chorale at the end of the dialogue cantata, *O Ewigkeit*. The profound effect of the sentences "Man that is born of a woman," etc., in the English burial service, may be also recalled in this connection. The effect in this case was obviously not Bach's invention, but a

Ex. 32

property of the form. But the manner in which he manipulated the details shows how deeply he was moved by the words. They seem to govern and direct every progression and every melodic phrase. Type-figures there are no doubt—as an example may be quoted the type [Ex. 32] which Bach very often used to express a kind of sympathetic wail, as for instance in the *Farewell Capriccio* to his brother, and the sonata in B minor for violin and clavier, and the fugue in F sharp minor in the first twenty-four preludes and fugues. But the figure is only one out of many and is not subjected to many variations, but is, indeed, itself a variation, which seems to reveal itself as an afterthought.

As an example of the extent to which Bach's mind is alive to the emotional undercurrent of the words, the treatment of the chorale phrases in this movement may be pointed out. In almost every case the treble voices anticipate all the other voices in leading off each phrase, till near the end. They fall behind a little in the penultimate phrase, and in the last of all the subordinate voices have several bars to sing before the chorale phrase is uttered. It is as though the soul found it difficult, through sheer distress, to utter the final words "Wohl an dem Kreuze lange".

But in truth the extent to which Bach was moved in this case and the thoughts that crowded in upon him as he wrote make the chorus almost impracticable. It is so full of expressive details that even conductors who have not surrendered to the entirely gratuitous theory that Bach's deep meditations are to be set going like a lot of noisy machinery in a factory, are driven to abandon in despair the attainment of a performance which will adequately represent what any sympathetic person can see that Bach intended. So far the amplest experience conveys the impression that the ideal expression of the chorus must remain unattainable till conditions of rehearsal and the attitude of those who lay stress on barren tradition are entirely changed. Meanwhile those who are capable of understanding derive some consolation from the contemplation of the exquisite devotional poetry of Bach's personality which is here so amply revealed.

This chorus completes the first half of the work, and undoubtedly sundry religious exercises were gone through before the second part was entered upon. This begins with the tender plaint of an alto solo, evidently prefiguring the Church, in the words "Ach, nun ist mein Jesus hin," to which the chorus answers with the question of the Song of Solomon "Wo ist dein Freund gegangen, O du Schönste unter den Weibern?" The movement obviously supplies an additional prologue for this act to make each part of the work complete. Then the story is resumed: Jesus brought before the high priest, the false witnesses, the high priest's verdict "He has spoken blasphemy," the chorus of Jews "He is worthy of death," the insults, the mockery, each episode with attendant reflections tenderly expressed in chorale or recitative and aria. Then follows the episode of Peter's denial of his Master, and the affecting episode of the cock-crow, which recalled to Peter the words of his Master, "Before the cock crow shalt thou three times deny me," and Peter's instant remorse, expressed in a melismatic passage of recitative, which is one of the most touching passages in the whole work, and one of the most remarkable examples in existence of the use of such a device for the purpose of expression. This is followed by one of the most beautiful movements in the work, the soprano aria with violin solo in Bach's most expressive vein, *Erbarme dich, mein Gott*, which symbolically transfers the remorse of Peter to the worshipper. It is a notable proof of the completeness of Bach's assimilation of the Italian form of the aria, as the whole is most deeply Teutonic both in its sentiment and in the richness of the artistic treatment of instrumental and vocal melody for the ends of expression.

The tragedy proceeds with the binding of Jesus and His being sent by the high priest to Pilate as a malefactor, and the dialogue between Pilate and Jesus, the appeal of Pilate's wife, Pilate's question to the Jews: which should be liberated and handed over to them, Jesus or Barabas the murderer? and the immediate and spontaneous shout of the Jews: "Barabbas!" the absolute realistic terseness of which is so overwhelmingly effective; Pilate's question: "What then shall I do with Jesus?" and the fierce answer of the crowd: "Let Him be crucified!" and Pilate's answer, "Why, what evil hath He done?" which is followed by the tender recitative, accompanied by two oboi da caccia, *Er hat uns Allen wohlgethan*, and an aria with an accompaniment, which seems to hover in the air, for two flutes and two oboi da caccia, *Aus Liebe will mein Heiland sterben*. A repetition of the fierce chorus "Let Him be crucified!" follows. And so the tragic story proceeds step by step, each individual taking his part and the "Turba" vociferating dramatically till the final scene is reached.

This gives rise to a singularly touching alto recitative, *Ach, Golgatha, unsel'ges Golgatha*, with an accompaniment of two oboi da caccia and violoncello, which is one of the most perfectly apt pieces of colour in the whole work, and is followed by the aria *Sehet Jesus hat die Hand* for alto, which is interspersed with the questioning cry of "Wohin" by the chorus, the scene of the Crucifixion, and the bitter cry of the Crucified: "My God! My God! Why hast Thou forsaken Me?" the rending of the veil of the temple, and the earthquake, graphically suggested in the realistic manner which Bach's sincerity generally made convincing, the application of Joseph of Arimathea for the body of Jesus, and a solo for bass, *Am Abend, da es kühle war* (which Bach headed as a recitative, but which is in reality an exquisitely expressive and melodious arioso), and the story ends with the burial and the watch set over the grave. The work itself is completed by the reflections of the worshippers in the recitative, *Nun ist der Herr zur Ruh' gebracht*, with the pianissimo answer of the chorus, *Mein Jesu, gute Nacht*, breathing that touching intimacy which was characteristic of Teutonic feeling towards Jesus; and the marvellously noble and tender double chorus, *Wir setzen uns mit Thränen nieder und rufen dir im Grabe zu*, which again bespeaks the loving sorrow of those who have listened to the unfolding of the world-moving story and taken it to heart in all its deeply impressive and suggestive meaning.

The genius of Bach has so enriched it with every device of expression, dramatic force, variety and aptness of musical material, and interest of artistic resource that notwithstanding the pauses at every episode for reflection and contemplation, the whole story seems to proceed with constant speed, even for those who can only partially realise in imagination the circumstances for which the work was written and the peculiar fascination of the conditions in which it was originally performed. There are frequent cases where the glamour of surroundings suffused with ancient associations and deeply rooted sentiments lends special enchantment to works of comparatively little intrinsic value, whose aptness to the surroundings is fortuitous, and which, when removed from them, manifest no traits which recall them. Bach's "Matthäus-Passion" is at the extreme opposite pole from such works. Though it is absolutely impossible to revive the conditions for which it was intended—chiefly because the particular type of worshipper's mind to which it was addressed, as well as the material surroundings, are gone forever from the world— it suggests the sublimation of all the finest traits of those conditions and surroundings in every page. It is probably the most beautiful expression of a beautiful phase of religion.

It need not be supposed that a devotional attitude so supremely ideal could have ever had a general practical existence. Even in Bach's time the majority of the congregation would have been quite unworthy of the work as a scheme of religious art. It can at least be said of them that they put themselves in a position to afford Bach the opportunity of knocking at the door of their hearts and offering his view of the manner in which the story of the Passion might be profitably taken. And there can be no manner of doubt that most people who have ever heard the work with any attention, were they ever so little in touch with the devotional attitude at the outset, would be touched with some glimmer of the divine light of love before the work is over. For truly the keynote of the whole, as has been said in connection with the "Johannes-Passion", is the divine manifested in man. The beautiful conception of the supreme sacrifice of self willingly undertaken by the Supreme Being in taking the form of man and voluntarily submitting to suffer every indignity and cruelty, and even death at the hands of man in order to redeem him, puts the ideal of absolute self-sacrifice at the very highest point the human mind is capable of conceiving.

Bach's "Matthäus-Passion" presents the recognition of this conception by Teutonic religion in very marked guise, inasmuch as the Godhead of Christ is scarcely anywhere apparent. The tragedy is unfolded in its purely human aspects, as the sacrifice of the man who was ideally adorable as man rather than on account of his divine descent. The situation recognises, as it were, the absolute abnegation and the full acceptance of the brotherhood of man; it sets aside the glamour of the divine origin and appeals to men's hearts direct, to look upon the story of unsurpassable human goodness, patience, endurance, loving-kindness and suffering, to dwell upon every moment of it and set it before mankind as the highest state to which manhood can attain, redeeming humanity itself by the proof of its supreme possibilities of selflessness, and winning the title to divinity by a life and a death which surpassed all the experiences of mankind.

It was probably not intentional, but in the very first short passage of recitative this situation is suggested, for when Jesus predicts the coming betrayal and crucifixion he speaks of himself as the "Son of Man" not as the "Son of God," and the answering chorale echoes the same feeling, "Deeply loved Jesus, what law hast Thou broken that man should such judgment pass on Thee?" The same attitude persists throughout, with the rare exceptions of such movements as the "Thunder and Lightning" chorus, the portents at the time of the Crucifixion, and the quotation of "Surely this was the Son of God" near the end, which are just sufficient to keep the superhuman element in sight without disturbing the concentration upon the human aspects of the tragedy. It is indeed in such regions that Bach was so pre-eminent. His music is almost invariably intensely human in its expression, and, notwithstanding the enormous amount of church-music which he wrote, unecclesiastical. It is intensely spiritual, deeply devout, nobly and consistently serious, but with the largeness of temperamental nature that reaches out beyond the limitations of any four walls whatever into communion with the infinite. The story of the Passion as told by him would appeal not only to the Christian but also to a pagan who had but the slenderest knowledge of the traditions of Christianity. It was the outcome of Teutonic Christianity of the time, and yet it transcended it in the far-reaching power of the music and makes an appeal which can be answered by humanity at large.

Of the power and variety of art which it displays it is hardly necessary to speak. After passing through the various phases which have been described, his mastery of all the methods of art then cultivated was supreme. He had, indeed, extended their range far beyond the standard of any composer of his time, and brought all that he had mastered into exercise for the first time in this work. For however great many of his previous works had been, they none of them range so widely and so richly as this; and at the same time the unity of the whole work in style, spirit, and texture is almost incredible. The strength and consistency of the man's nature, completely matured, make every page glow with his personality, and with a humanity so noble and far-reaching that it stands alone and unique without any works which share a place with it, or anything which in its peculiar qualities and scheme could follow it.

It appears that when the "Matthäus-Passion" in its first form was first performed on Good Friday in the year 1729 it was not fully appreciated. It could hardly be expected that it would be. Whether he had it performed in succeeding years cannot be verified. It is only ascertainable that the original version was considerably altered by him, and that the final version as it is now known to the world was performed under his directions in the year 1740 or soon afterwards. It continued to be performed in Leipzig even after Bach died, but did not become known to the world outside till, just a hundred years after its first appearance, it was performed at Berlin on Mendelssohn's initiative and under his direction on March 12, 1829.

The complete survival of the "Johannes-Passion" and the "Matthäus-Passion" is probably owing to the fact that at Bach's death they came into the hands of his son Philip Emanuel. He is known to have written three other Passions, but they are all lost, apparently beyond rediscovery; and it is supposed that it is owing to their having been in the hands of Wilhelm Friedemann, the eldest son, and the irregular and ill-balanced member of the family, through whose carelessness they were lost. Parts of the music of a "Passion according to St. Mark" are said to be preserved in the "Trauer Ode" written for the funeral ceremony of Queen Christina Eberhardine in 1727.

There is also, strangely enough, a complete "Passion according to St. Luke" in Bach's handwriting; but it is evidently not by him, as it does not bear any resemblance to his musical personality at any period of his life. A vivacious letter of Mendelssohn's to a man who had been so unlucky as to give a large sum for the manuscript, under the impression that it was Bach's work is worth quoting. He says:

I am very sorry you have given so much money for the "St. Lucas Passion." True it is that, as an undoubted manuscript, it is not too dear at the price, but, all the same, the music is not by him. You ask "On what grounds is the 'Lucas' not by Sebastian Bach?" On intrinsic grounds. It is hateful that I must maintain this when it belongs to you; but just look at the chorale, "Weide mich und mach' mich Satt"! If that is by Sebastian, may I be hanged!—and yet it is unmistakably in his handwriting. But it is too clean. He has copied it. "Whose is it?" say you. By Telemann, or M. Bach, or by Alt Nichol, Jung Nicol, or plain Nichol? What do I know? It's not by Bach!

This verdict must be emphatically endorsed.

15 *Style in Musical Art*

Introduction

Parry based his sixth book on the series of lectures he gave at Oxford from 1900 to 1908 while holding the Heather Professorship of Music. The lectures were, in part, based on material to be found in earlier talks and writings. The Inaugural Lecture, from which the book derives its title, was given at Oxford University on 7 March 1900. Serious health problems however forced him to resign his professorship in February 1908 and the lectures were not completed.

The book's tone is influenced by the same preoccupations that animate the series of *Ethical Cantatas* which he composed in tandem with the lecture series. Parry attempts to place his concepts of music history and compositional techniques within an overall view of Western civilization In many ways this is a transitional work – from the composer and musicologist, in the widest sense, to the would-be philosopher of his last book, *Instinct and Character*.

As might be expected the musical and psychological aspects of the discourse are the more rewarding: Parry's attempt at an all embracing view of Western culture, using music as both the centre and departure point, is only occasionally successful. The reader is well aware that the book's moral historicity is that of an Edwardian gentleman from the upper classes – however enlightened and exceptional he may have been. Parry placed himself in a false position. He would have been on stronger ground had he argued that great art only flourishes in a society which has an enlightened aristocracy to offer financial and emotional support to the creative artist.

Parry, whose distrust of the aristocracy grew considerably with age, was probably looking for alternative answers to the problem, but had not formulated any idea definite enough to write about. 'The members of the leisured classes at both ends of the social scale drift into loafing' but 'Commercialism becomes the most powerful means of degrading art'. History has not solved the dilemma for him – after twenty years in the field, I am painfully aware how hopelessly inadequate modern Arts Councils, Arts Associations and Music Charities are to solve a problem which society itself does not want to face. Thus, many of Parry's social comments on the arts continue to be apt. In contrast it is noticeable that the sections on music *per se* tend to be drier and less enthusiastic than in his earlier books.

Nonetheless, *Style in Musical Art* contains much interesting writing, with a more than usual number of quotable quotes, and it exudes a great deal of that famous charm which caused George Bernard Shaw to keep his distance. Parry explains in his preface to the book that 'the originals have been for the most part rewritten, several lectures have been omitted as unnecessary in the changed conditions and chapters which cover the ground originally planned have been added.' This adaptation was carried out in 1909/1910, the book was published by Macmillan in 1911 and reprinted in 1924.

Form and Style

It may be as well to recognize in good time that style and form are nearly akin, and that they are not only liable to be confused, but that from some points of view their provinces seem to overlap. As has been said before, the test of style is the consistent adaptation of the materials of art or literature to the conditions of presentment; which is as much as to say that it is influenced by the nature of the material in which it is executed, the disposition and standard of intelligence of the audience or spectators to whom it is meant to appeal, and the circumstances or situations in which it is to be presented. But it must at once strike any one who gives thought to the matter that "form" is based on the same influences. The forms of works of art also vary with the qualities of the materials in which they are executed as much as their styles. If they are executed in iron or wood or stone, they must necessarily differ in form in accordance with the inherent properties of the materials. The form of a literary work is influenced by the purpose it is meant to serve. The form of a work which is meant to be presented on the stage is bound to differ from the form of a work which is meant to be read and lingered over in privacy and quiet seclusion; and the form of addresses made to an excited mob in a political agitation would be different from the form of the address of a scientist to fellow-men of learning Moreover, it is common to speak of the form of details, such as the form of a sentence or the form of a musical phrase; and such form is easily confused with the style of such details. Hence it is obvious that form and style both take their characteristics from the same sources and influences, and are evidently so closely interwoven that it is often hard to keep them apart and to discuss one without getting into the domain which it has been customary to consider as belonging to the other. It therefore becomes unsafe to discuss style in detail without anticipating the status and nature of form, and trying to find an adequate basis of distinction and to show that if the lines of demarcation are not absolutely decisive, any more than the lines of demarcation between the animal and vegetable kingdom, still there is a central idea which attaches to the respective conceptions.

It will be easier to judge of the relation of form to style if precautions are taken against haziness of definition; and as the word "form" has been unfortunately very much in evidence in the discourses of theorists and analysts of music it is well to give it some little attention. It would indeed be preferable to speak of organization, because the word form is so liable to be misunderstood. By form in music men really mean the particular scheme or system upon which a work of art is organized. They mean the principles by which the thoughts which the artist wishes to express are brought within the real range of art. Chaos is as preposterous in art as it is impossible in nature; the essence of art is to be perfectly organized. Mere wild exuberance in the outpouring of excited feeling or sensuous intoxication in colour and tone is not art at all. Till the feelings which a man wants to express are systematized upon some principle which will stand the test of intellectual analysis they do not come within the range of art; to lack organization is to be merely idiotic and incoherent.

True it is that ingenuity and subtlety of form have often been overvalued. Form is not an end, though it is an essential. It is the means by which thought or feeling or aspiration is brought within the domain of art, but if there is no impulse in the man beyond it, the product is mere vanity and emptiness. From the excess with which it is emphasized by writers on music people might be misled into supposing that some of the highest achievements in the art attained their pre-eminence on account of the intricacy and ingenuity of their construction. But in truth a great work of art is great because of the thought or the feeling which it expresses and only secondarily for the scheme or plan in which the thought or feeling is presented. The method of organization or form may be especially admirable on account of its aptness to the thoughts or feelings which the artist has to convey, and it may merit consideration on account of the manner in which it brings them home to the mind.

But no amount of ingenuity in the manipulation of the scheme of presentment can raise commonplace or trivial thoughts to a high place among the great manifestations of art. And it seems very probable that great thoughts imperfectly organized are more valuable than indifferent thoughts presented with extraordinary skill of organization. The highest justification of organization is to be exactly apt and proportionate to the thought which has to be expressed. To elaborate the form of presentment of a commonplace thought which could be adequately expressed without any elaboration is not only superfluous; it makes the commonplace more exasperating.

The reason for difference of degree in elaboration is easily made intelligible. The higher kinds of art, like the higher kinds of human beings, are more highly organized; for being so enables them to effect more than such as are lowlily organized. The snippets and trivialities of the variety entertainment, the songs of the ballad opera, and such types of art have their lowly organization, parallel to that of the lowest organisms in nature, such as the confervæ, the infusoria, the amœbæ, the jelly-fishes; and such lowly organization is adequate for lowly and insignificant purposes. Man attained his pre-eminent position in the sphere of living things because he was capable of being developed to the highest pitch of complex and subtly efficient organization; for the art of the highest quality similarly copious methods of organization are required. And the methods of organization of art, like the multifarious organization of all the components of the body of man, are the fruit of long processes of development. They may be said to be, as in the case of man, the result of the reactions of the environment upon the sensitive material. Art in its slow growth continually found new means by which organization could be effected, new processes by which the thought of the artist could be clearly and attractively presented to other human beings. And as each branch of art evolved its more perfect identity it developed principles of form which were more and more perfectly adapted to the conditions of its presentment.

It is of great importance to realize at the outset that the possible varieties of principles of organization are practically illimitable. It is not so long ago that the musical world passed through a strange phase in which the almost miraculous perfection of the manipulation of "sonata forms" by such great masters of instrumental music as Mozart and Beethoven so monopolized men's attention that even philosophical and learned writers on the art failed to observe that the conditions to which these orders of form were adapted, and for which they had been laboriously evolved by men of the highest genius, were of a special kind, and were only admirable in the highest degree when employed for special types of art. In the highest sense sonata forms are only suitable for instrumental music, and indeed only for instrumental music of a certain well-defined type. For those whose dispositions were specially appealed to by perfection of organization, the sonata type seemed the highest manifestation in music. It may even be admitted that the type of mind to which such qualities appealed was a high one, and that it was often combined with the faculty of understanding and of being in touch with the great or beautiful thoughts for whose exposition the highest types of artistic form were employed. But it clearly was a misconception to infer that, because this type of art presented the finest examples of analysable form so far realized, there could be no other branch of art which could approach it in importance or prestige, and that all other branches of art must follow the same methods of organization in order to merit the full approbation of men of taste and understanding.

It is indeed becoming apparent that one of the drawbacks of sonata forms is that they are too limited. The strict and very definite schemes on which they are based do not admit of much expansion without ceasing to represent faithfully the sonata type. Moreover, the type tended to emphasize the formal at the expense of the spiritual. It was specially adapted to a particular period and a particular class of people who combined a high standard of cultivated artistic intelligence with an elaborately constituted code of conventional habits and criterions. They were people who believed with a completeness of conviction which had become second nature in the efficacy and importance of formalities. It was essential to them that human beings should be in their right places; the elegant courtiers and hereditary gentlefolk at the top and the common men at the bottom. And when the position of the aristocratic classes ceased to be based on higher efficiency and ability to lead and rule and administrate, it had to be maintained by artificial means, such as subtle conventions of manner, speech, and livelihood; and these conditions induced a formal and even conventional habit of mind, which applied to their arts as well as to their manner of living. And in art as well as life these formalities of everyday existence had a tendency to dull and discredit human feeling and to make people regard a display of it as a token of base origin and inferiority.

The sonata type of form was just adapted to this type of society. The scheme of organization which had been elaborated by the concentrated efforts of several generations of composers covered a very large field of artistic requirements, aesthetic as well as intellectual, but it had become so subtly balanced that if one of the factors were missed out or a departure made at any point from the essential principles of the scheme, the whole would be thrown out of gear. The typical scheme was devised instinctively, from the very first infantile attempts till the most marvellous perfection was attained by the greatest masters of the form, for absolute, self-contained music. It provided for the presentation of certain musical ideas or subjects in certain relations of contrast and affinity to one another, for their dissection and development, and for their definite recapitulation in such a manner as to re-establish the feeling in the mind of the auditor of the particular position in the scale from which the movement had started; one of the essential features in the scheme being that the mind should be kept away from that point from the moment that it had been adequately established as the point of initiation till the concluding paragraphs made it return to its home again. Within the limits of this scheme there is a wide range of possible variation; but the fact that it became too familiar through the profusion of examples produced and that expectancy of systematic procedure always weakens the emotional capacity, made it unfit to be applied to any purposes but those which were in force in the days of its highest perfection. The sonata was essentially an aristocratic form of art, and it was inevitable that as soon as the aristocratic phase of modern history reached its apogee and approached declination the art which was so highly and so worthily characteristic of it should also begin to disintegrate. One of the most interesting features in the situation was that the composer of all others whose disposition was most fervently democratic should have brought the aristocratic form to perfection and proceeded, before he had done with it, to introduce features which were bound to effect its dissolution.

It was the spiritual fervour of Beethoven which exalted the sonata to its highest phase, and there it hung poised for a short while at the extreme limit of possible adjustment of spiritual exaltation and perfection of design; and the composer evidently began to find the accepted scheme of organization which he himself had brought to perfection too constraining and restrictive to the impulse of his thought, and therefore endeavoured to find new types of form and to revive sundry earlier types of organization and combine them in various ways which departed from the essential principles upon which composers had been working for generations. From which arises the obvious implication that to the greatest of composers of sonatas the scheme, as established in his earliest complete examples, no longer appeared adequate for the expression of the new type of musical impulses and ideas which a changing order of society engendered. The suggestion may be hazarded that there is very deep-set parallel between the choral music of its great period— the latter part of the sixteenth century—and the sonata type of its greatest period. For as in the one case the only possible type of pure uncontaminated style in music associated with words is presented by the choral music, in the other the only pure examples of intrinsically perfect style and musical design in absolute wordless music is presented by the sonata forms of what may be called the sonata period. The sonata, therefore, is of all things the most perfect representative type of abstract principles of organization. It can only exist under conditions in which nothing hinders or distracts the attention of the composer from manipulation of design. Directly words are used, the sonata type becomes not only an anomaly but an irrelevancy. The value of the sonata as a type lies in its being absolutely and unqualifiedly an exposition of certain ideal principles of design or organization. To adapt it to words would imply the necessity that the writer of the words should also write them in sonata form. The absurdity is at once apparent. The sonata form is essentially a form devised for music; it is no more adapted to literature (except as an occasional sport) than it is to crockery ware. Parenthetically also it may be said that the style of sonatas is equally unappropriate for other depart-ments of music. For it must be obvious that the more perfectly anything is carried out to suit special conditions the more impossible is it that it should serve equally well for totally different conditions. And this is indeed what practical experience has proved to be the case where predetermined forms of the sonata order and the reserved style of the sonata kind have been employed for operas. It is true such works may have great beauties and a special charm of their own, but they cannot be regarded as adequate or final solutions of the problems of either opera or song or any music wedded to words, either in form or style.

This leads to the recognition of the fact that the problems involved in all the various forms of art can only be solved finally in the respective spheres to which those kinds of art belong. Mere transference of methods, or of form, or of style from one branch to another must remain inadequate, unless the conditions are in some wise so much alike that a transformation can be effected within the range of the essential qualities in which the branches agree.

The Influence of Audiences

Those who keep their ears open and observe, notice how explosive the music is which rapidly gets a vogue. How full it is of big words and the semblance of violent feeling, which is fed by the desire to get a response from all the least trustworthy promptings of ill-regulated temperament in the audience, often by the mere love of feeling excitement of some sort. But as a matter of fact the apprecia-tion which is the result of mere excitement is not truly artistic appreciation at all. It is appreciation of something which is incidental to art without representing art in itself. A great mind may be excited by some supreme and wonderful stroke of art, but lesser minds are excited by the very things which are antagonistic to art in the higher sense. The big words and violent gesticulations impose upon the ignorant and those whose minds are undeveloped. The artistic qualities appeal to the minds which are capable of discerning fineness of thought and skill in presentment—to those who understand. The multitude who do not understand carry all things before them for a time by weight of numbers. But in the end quality tells against quantity. The few who are intelligent and spacious minded are in a sense organ-ized, and the masses who are not intelligent are not organized; and the effect of organization is to stand firm, and of that which is not organized to dissipate and fall to pieces.

There are some underlying principles of adjustment in such things. Men of the finer type are not so desperately eager for notoriety or applause as men of a lower type. Those whose temperament is likely to produce work of a high order prefer the endorsement of the few whose good opinion is worth having to the acclamations of the millions who have no understanding. They can go on their way independently doing what they know to be good without feeling cast down or disappointed that their names are not bruited abroad and their recreations reported in periodicals to impress those who would not understand their works.

It is not in the competence of the very big public to encourage really first-rate men in any branch of art or literature. Average minds may be brought to appreciate their work by slow degrees, but the appreciation comes too late to be of service to the producer. Where the wide contemporary audience exerts a powerful influence on art the effect is to induce a type in which lack of power of continuous attention is no drawback. It induces a kind of music which becomes intelligible by referring to something concrete outside music, whether of the programme or the rhapsodical order. The undeveloped mind, which has no real musical intelligence, likes to be helped by being told the music represents something it can understand, even by realistic suggestion of an obvious kind. It likes music which is constantly pretty or exciting or sentimental, with the sentiment laid on heavily. It likes a sort of mosaic of nice attractive phrases of the type which happens to be fashionable and to which it is therefore accustomed; and does not care in the least if the phrases are not coherent, or even whether one is completed before another drops in to occupy its easily distracted attention. The art which is highly organized, closely knit, and finely developed is of no use to it. It requires intrinsic effects rather than the fineness of relations which are appreciated by the higher type of mind. The results are perceptible in all directions; and one of the worst of them is that the undeveloped and unstable mind is especially subject to be imposed upon, and to fall a prey to the devices of commercialism.

Commercialism inevitably ministers to that irresponsible and incoherent pursuit of superficial pleasure which is the mark of undeveloped minds. Such pursuit is ominously in evidence at the present day, especially in quarters where the influence of a leisured class is predominant. The members of the leisured classes at both ends of the social scale drift into loafing. Grown-up people lose the power of application and attention because they have nothing definite whereto to apply their minds, and they ruin their children because they think they are, monetarily, sufficiently provided for, and that therefore it is unnecessary to bore them with any serviceable kind of education; and the children grow up with the sole idea of filling their lives with amusements. Here and there individuals find out that the results are disappointing; that unless there is something to occupy the mind the pursuit of pleasure entails intervals of intolerable boredom, or ceaseless change which ends in sheer dissipation. Their minds do not mature and they go through life with the notion that the innocent aspirations of the golden age of childhood are sufficient for the full-grown man. The classes which are very much the reverse of leisured think that those who can live without work are fortunate in being able to amuse themselves all day long, and that whenever they have time to amuse themselves they are likeliest to succeed by following their example. The habit of pleasure-hunting becomes contagious, and the attitude of mind of the well-to-do filters down into the ranks of the ill-to-do. Music wherever it happens to come into the scheme of things becomes merely a form of superficial pleasure. The music which requires any exercise of higher faculties and could arouse genuine interest is considered tiresome. But the object of trade is to get as many buyers as possible and quick returns. Therefore commercialism must be always trying to find out what people can take pleasure in most widely and most quickly; and to boom such things as will appeal to the largest number of superficial minds. The effect is to make minds more and more superficial, and more and more susceptible to what is cheap and specious, and more capable of being speedily hoaxed by advertisement.

So it comes about that commercialism becomes the most powerful means of degrading art. It looks for the weaknesses of careless humanity and exploits them; and careless humanity in its millions is even enthusiastic about what it pays the commercials to hoax them with. Were it not that even some of the commercials themselves have souls above the commercial standards it would seem as if genuine art must be throttled. Though commercialism has had such disastrous effects, even in such quarters humanity reveals the persistence of higher ideals. The purely futile minds are fed full of futilities by those whose object is only to make money; but there is a residue still that understand better how life may be made worth living, and the higher type of publishers find their choice pay in the end, because what they like will go on selling while the stuff that produces quick returns presently becomes unsaleable.

The spirit of every age has many phases. At all times there are some elements of noble aspiration, of earnestness and deep feeling and honesty and mental energy, flourishing below the kaleidoscopic and bewildering phenomena of the purely surface life; and the varieties of composers have varieties of opportunity to represent different phases of the life forces of their time. The composer or artist who appeals to the highest kind of mind and temperament has a harder and harder task as time goes on. To be fully adequate he must be in touch with the loftiest and most advanced thought of his time, he must be on the crest of the wave which in his own sphere represents true progress. And this entails his steeling his heart to lack of general appreciation, and being content with the appreciation of the few. It has often been observed that the finest works of art are only produced by those who have to experience hardship, pain, and difficulty. Men even distrust the productions of those whose lives seem too easy. There is a dim recognition of the fact that the steel of true nobility must be tempered in the fire. So the paradox seems to be suggested that where the public are too ready to be kind their too easily gained favour reacts unfavourably on the composer, and there are plenty of actual instances which confirm the idea. It seems as though it were a necessary preliminary to the higher kind of achievement for its maker to find it difficult to win appreciation.

The trivial and unintelligent crowd and the composers who supply them with what they want mutually react upon one another. But so do the choicer spirits at the other end of the scale. If there is a part of the great general audience which is always making for deterioration there is also another and a more steadfast part that is always making for betterment. It is the sympathy of the higher type of mind and temperament which feeds the higher artistic natures, and sustains them in the independent exercise of their imagination and their artistic intelligence by the higher standard of their enlightenment and vitality.

Yet people so endowed very rarely put such sympathy into words. It is only in the strata of low-class art and low-class minds and productions of every sort that men are constantly flattering and congratulating one another on their perform- ances and their successes. Among men of higher mettle compliments which must inevitably be suspect are tabooed. The principles of the highest courtesy are under- stood; which are to treat the baser cravings, which are always so eagerly suscept- ible, as absent. The unintelligent mind does not realize that the appeal to a low desire for flattery is the reverse of a compliment, and it is always looking for means to excite and feed such lower cravings in its acquaintances. It is one of the most familiar tokens of what is called vulgarity, and is very much in evidence in the wealthiest ranks of society. The more strenuous mind goes so much to the other extreme that friends of the higher mettle sometimes pass through life together without arriving at certainty whether the opinion of each of the other's work is favourable or the reverse.

In reality all men who think frankly admit that a man is strengthened by the necessity of being self-dependent. The man who wins popular success often forgoes his independence to keep it. The man who estimates rightly the inability of the widest contemporary public to recognize the highest in art forgoes immediate suc- cess, but maintains his independence; and the few whose minds are large enough endorse his attitude—even when they do not fully understand it themselves.

Theory and Academicism

The tendency of academies to breed academicism is well known, and it requires no great perspicacity to see that the causes of it are, on the one hand, the necessity of assimilating the principles upon which instruction is given in order to make it systematic, and, on the other hand, the difficulty of identifying and making the most of those individualities and idiosyncrasies and aptitudes which are the neces- sary foundations of every kind of pre-eminence. These facts are not by any means confined to music. The difficulties are felt in every quarter where education is conducted on any scale. It cannot be administered to groups of human beings without being systematized. But a thing which is systematized is stiffened into formality—often premature formality—and it generally happens that if a system becomes inadequate in the onrush of human motion (one need not pin oneself to its being progress) it may be impossible to reconstruct and adapt the system adopted without causing a complete breakdown of the whole educational organi- zation. One reason would be sufficient to show the practical bearing of this—that all the experienced teachers would be sure to be saturated with the only partially adequate system which had been in vogue, and that a radical and sweeping change would reduce them to impotence long before there was any one ready to teach on the remodelled system, and therefore for a time education must come to a stand- still, and the enterprising educational establishment where the new system is adopted would have to put up the shutters.

But it all points to the same uncomfortable fact that theory—in whatever department of human affairs it is met with—must rightly and always be regarded with distrust and suspicion. The fruits of human experience must be systematized in order to be communicated, but theory which precedes practice is always liable to stultify practice because it is founded upon too limited a range of experience to apply to the particular kind of practice for which it may be required. And as we have seen, a theory once formed cannot be adapted to new contingencies quickly enough to prevent breakdown while it is being reconstructed. The only safe theories will be the ones which may be proposed when the world comes to an end and practice will be no longer necessary. However, theory cannot be dispensed with, and those who have not strength and independence enough to realize the absolute pre-eminence of individual personal responsibility will go on clinging to fetishes and formulas and dogmas of all kinds to relieve themselves of the effort of thinking independently. Such being the circumstances, and theory being so firmly rooted, the utmost one can do is to point out its invariable untrustworthiness, and to note the piles of obstructive and useless lumber to which it gives rise and the misdirection and waste of human energy of which it is the too fruitful cause, of which academicism in all kinds is one of the most piteous manifestations.

But educational institutions do not necessarily produce academicism; nor is all academicism the fruit of academic training. There is a spurious academicism which is the result of lack of training and knowledge of standards. This is the fruit of the superficial impulse towards correctitude, and is like the purely artificial respectability of certain classes which is kept for special occasions, and is familiarly represented by rooms which on ordinary days are only inhabited by d'oyleys and antimacassars, ormolu clocks, sham flowers and sham china, and gilded chairs which are not warranted to carry more than ten stone. This kind of academicism, though much in favour in special strata of society, requires no more than a regretful glance. It is all so piteous, because, on the whole, though it is only describable as the paltriest veneer, it is so well meant; and it is rather a misunderstanding than a lack of appreciation and respect for refinement and the higher developments of the human mind. Academicism is, after all, in one sense, the tribute of the man who does not understand to the man who does, the acknowledgement of the actuality of a high ideal, even though it may not be intelligible to the man who makes the acknowledgement; and in days when purely theoretic enlightenment teaches the distrust of everything which cannot be reduced to a formula, and tabulated and put into a pigeon-hole, even academicism may have its useful function.

There is a phase of music which is just as little worthy of being called music as academic music, which ultimately takes its rise in misconceptions as to the meaning of art, and ministers to the glorification of abstract theory, and to total obliviousness of the requirements of style. The respect which is paid to certain music on the ground that it is scientific or learned is due to the fact that the number of people who can appreciate the really highest achievements of art is very small; that is to say, the number of people who can really get to the heart of it as art, not as clever manipulation. People who have not the capacity to come into touch with the thoughts themselves, but have an estimable disposition to respect things which instinct tells them are great and true even when they do not understand them, are led, quite amiably, to expatiate on the purely mechanical aspects which are always of a high order in connection with great works of art, and to praise the works for being wonderful examples of musical science. A composer may find that what he has to say requires and invites a vast amount of elaboration, which involves the employment of a great range and variety of artistic methods and devices. He may have to write a work for special conditions of performance to which a class of really musical effects are appropriate which may make great demands upon his knowledge of artistic devices. These for a time may bewilder the auditor by the very complexity of the experience; and if he is unfriendly he will abuse what he did not understand as being dry, and if he is friendly he will praise on the ground that the composer is scientific. But as a matter of fact if the work were only scientific it would not be music; and it is very unfortunate that the advocates of musical culture should so often lay so much stress upon what is called scientific music. True it is that great mastery of technique and procedure is indispensable for the adequate exposition of great thoughts, and great artistic achievements require a delicate adjustment to the requirements of style so subtle and so highly organized that only one single human being in millions is capable of attaining to it. But it is not attained by science nor by scientific methods, but by the development of a favourable artistic instinct. All the scientific methods which ever were devised could not develop such a subtlety of sense for style as is shown, for example, in Beethoven's Quartet in C sharp minor, and the 2nd movement of the Quartet in B flat, Opus 130. The composer who has been rightly developed by the means appropriate to an art may produce works on which the scientist may well expend his powers. But the synthesis which must follow analysis in order to produce a work of art is not the scientist's business and never can be; and scientific music is simply a misnomer. No such thing is possible. Art and science are different in their inception, their practice, their objects, and their procedure. When science is so amply mastered as to pass into philosophy, the philosopher may take the hand of the artist; but there is no bridge before the most advanced stage of the journey is reached.

Notes

Sh. P. indicates a document from Shulbrede Priory; BL and CUL refer to documents in the British Library or Cambridge University Library.

Preface

1. Many points in this Preface first appeared in Bernard Benoliel, 'Parry before *Jerusalem*' in *Music and Musicians* (June 1985).
2. Graves, Charles L., *Hubert Parry: his Life and Works*, London: Macmillan (1926).
3. Dibble, Dr J.C., *Hubert H. Parry: His Life and Music*, Oxford: Clarendon Press (1992).
4. Parry maintained a diary from 1864 until a month before his death. These all survive with the exception of 1887 from which only Dorothea's transcripts for C.L. Graves are available. In addition there are a number of notebooks by Parry. Lady Maude Parry's diary is complete for the years 1887–1893 when it apparently breaks off. No others are extant. There is a large collection of letters from Parry and Lady Maude to each other and to other members of the family. Various diaries and letters from other members of the family survive, including Thomas Gambier Parry, Charles Clinton Parry, Dorothea Ponsonby and her husband Arthur, later Lord Ponsonby of Shulbrede. Shulbrede Priory is the source for all of their diary entries and letters quoted, unless otherwise cited in the footnotes. This material awaits a systematic study by future Parry scholars.

1: Formation of a Creative Personality

1. White, Edmund (1993), *Genet*, London: Chatto & Windus. Translated by White from *L'Atelier d'Alberto Giacometti* by Jean Genet, published in *Oeuvres complètes V*, Editions Gallimard (1979).
2. Dorothea Ponsonby, from an unpublished notebook (written for C.L. Graves's biography), Sh. P.
3. Graves, Charles L. (1926), *Hubert Parry*, London: Macmillan, I, 7, quoting the diary of Henry Fynes Clinton.
4. Drew, M. (1930), *Mary Gladstone (Mrs Drew), her Diaries and Letters*, ed. Lucy Masterman.
5. Parry was in many ways a typical Pisces. Allen Oken in his inimitable book on astrology, *As above, so below*, entitles his chapter on Pisceans: 'I seek myself and I don't seek myself'. The sign's glyph depicts the inherent dualism of the fish: 'one of the arcs represents the infinite consciousness of man: the other, the infinite consciousness of the Universe'. He goes on to point out, of the Piscean, 'his need to completely sacrifice his own wishes for the sake of others while at the same time exercising complete control over those around him in order to complete his personal goals.' Because the individual born under this sign can sympathize with almost any individual or situation it may become impossible for him to choose a specific path in life. See Oken, A. (1973), *As above, so below*, New York: Bantam Books Inc.
6. Parry, diary, 3 January 1904.
7. Parry, diary, 6 December 1866.
8. Parry, letter to Ernest Gambier Parry for 'Annals of an Eton House', in Graves, *Parry*, I, 24.
9. Graves I, 21
10. Lewis Majendie, letter to Parry, March 1865, Sh.P.
11. Graves II, 105.

12. Parry, diary, July/August 1867.
13. Graves, I, 88.
14. H.H. Pierson, letter, Sh.P.
15. Charles Willeby, who knew Parry well, wrote in *Masters of English Music* (1894), New York: Charles Scribner's Sons, 262: 'Pierson, he says, did him an enormous amount of good. On leaving the University he desired nothing better than to be allowed to devote himself exclusively to his music. But his father would not hear of it.'
16. Modern psychological thinking on this subject originates with Freud, but long after I had written this study, I discovered a useful book on the subject *In search of the Lost Mother of Infancy*, Lawrence E. Hedges, Ph.D., Jason Aronson Inc, New York, 1994. Hedges states: 'Those who lose their mothers at birth have a major shift to make that leaves its history in their personalities.' (page 4) and continues: 'Green (1986) speaks of the "dead mother" who is known through sensual pleasure and then, when she fails to appear when needed, becomes internalized as lost or dead. Green holds that the dead mother interject remains as a blank or empty place in our psyche where love and desire once held forth. He shows how we then search the world for the rest of our lives for the lost mother of infancy. But, as Green so aptly points out, although we may search for her ' "out there" in the world, where love once was, she is not there. She for whom we search is inside ourselves, and she is dead. Her love and her loss have left its mark as an emptiness, a lack, a desire that we search to fill.' (page 5). (See Green, A. (1986), 'The dead mother', in *On Private Madness*, London: Hogarth Press.)

2: Lady Maude

1. Arthur Ponsonby (*c.* 1938), *Brief Glimpses: Hubert Parry*, unpublished, Sh.P
2. Graves I, 101, Parry, diary, 24 August 1868.
3. Lady Herbert, letter to Parry, 20 June 1870, Sh.P.
4. Letters, 1871, Sh.P.
5. On the basis of Parry, Burne-Jones, Genet and other notable individuals who have not known their own mothers, the author has formulated a theory on how this affects both their creative processes and their relationship with the unconscious feminine side of their personality, i.e. 'anima' in C.G. Jung's definition. The author calls this the 'Snow White syndrome'.
6. Lady Maude Parry, diaries (1887–1893), Sh.P.
7. Lady Maude commented in her diary for 10 October 1887 that, while Parry was getting ready to leave for the College: 'I looked over an article of his on musical analysis before he started and tried hard not to understand it but found it quite simple.'
8. Sir Philip Burne-Jones, painter and cartoonist, was the only son of Sir Edward Burne-Jones; he was a constant frequenter of the Parry household throughout the 1880s and 1890s, and harboured a romantic attachment to both Lady Maude and Dorothea.
9. Thomas Gambier Parry, letter, 3 November 1872, Sh.P.
10. Parry's overture *Vivien* is now lost and was apparently never given a public performance.
11. The Ionides were a wealthy Greek shipping family who settled in London and became important patrons of the Pre-Raphaelites. Constantine Ionides' daughter, Mary Zambaco, became a model for Rossetti and Burne-Jones.
12. Parry, diary, 23 December 1877.
13. Ibid, 5 December 1874. However, it is clear that Maude's condition did not inhibit her capacity for enjoyment: 'I danced every dance and didn't stop until 5 o'clock in the morning so that at last I fell like a worn out old cart horse.' (Letter to Eddie Hamilton, January 1874.)

14. Mahler, A. (1968), *Gustav Mahler: Memories and Letters*, ed. Donald Mitchell, London: John Murray.
15. Gambier Parry, letter to Parry, 1 April 1875.
16. Parry was friendly with Tora Gordon's family during this time. Tora married Victor Marshall and fades out of Parry's diaries.
17. Parry, diary, early 1876.
18. Parry, letter to Eddie Hamilton 7 May 1876, BL Add. MS 48621. Dibble, J. (1992), *C. Hubert H. Parry*, Oxford: Clarendon Press, 138. At this point Parry abruptly switches subject without supplying the salient noun. In fairness, he writes this letter after being cooped up in quarantine for several weeks and he opens by explaining how Maudie 'has been getting along splendidly', nor does he blame Maude for her aristocratic attitudes. However, he does admit that 'This is a bellyful by way of a letter – I think I'd better pull up – '.
19. Parry, letter to Eddie Hamilton, 18 May 1881, BL. Add. MS 48621. Dibble, 196.
20. Lady Maude Parry, letter to Eddie Hamilton, 1883. BL Add. MS 48621.
21. A series of eight London concerts in May 1877 which included excerpts from *Die fliegende Hollander, Die Walkure, Götterdammerung*, and *Tristan*. On the evening of 4 June Parry went to see the Wagners off at Victoria. The event was an artistic triumph but financially disappointing for Wagner.
22. Dorothea Ponsonby, diary, 19 May 1917. E.D. Morel was a writer and journalist, and founded the Oxford Dramatic Club.
23. Lady Maude Parry, diary, 1890.
24. Lambert, A. (1984), *Unquiet Souls*, London: Harper and Row.
25. Lady Maude Parry, diary, 24 June 1892.
26. Ibid.
27. Graves, I. 230.
28. Drew, M. (1930), *Mary Gladstone (Mrs Drew), her Diary and Letters*, ed. Lucy Masterman, London: Methuen.
29. Parry, diary, 27 June 1889.
30. 'Lady Maude utterly wild but very well, wearing down all who come into contact with her, almost an Edgar Allen Poe Story', Arthur Ponsonby, diary, 29 January 1930, in Jones, R.A. (1989) *Arthur Ponsonby: The Politics of Life*, London: Christopher Helm.
31. Johnston, A. (1929), *The Life and Letters of Sir Harry Johnston*, London: Jonathan Cape. In his last long illness, Lady Maude was the only visitor he liked to see.
32. These highly gifted women living on the brink of the modern age, but powerless fully to enter it, learned to serve their famous husbands, by acting out their spouses' negative anima characteristics before their very eyes – assuring these great men of at least some outward equilibrium and inner peace.

3: The Ambivalent Road to Dr Parry and Sir Hubert

1. Schopenhauer, A. (1969), *The World as Will and Representation*, trans. E.F.J. Payne, London: Dover Press, 267.
2. Graves, I, 129. Parry, diary, spring 1871.
3. Parry, C.H.H. (1887): *Studies of Great Composers*, London: Routledge & Kegan Paul, 'Conclusion', 361.
4. Parry, diary, 24 September 1896.
5. Delius, letter to Granville Bantock, 21 December 1907, *Delius: A Life in Letters*, ed. Lionel Carley (1988), London: Scolar Press, Vol. I, 323. Delius, about to be exposed to Parry's *Job* for the first time in September 1909, speculated on the prospect to Granville Bantock: 'How a man rolling in wealth, the lord of many acres & living off the fat of the land can write anything about Job beats me entirely, unless it is a cantata

expressing H.P.'s satire and derision at Mr. Job's mode of life – I'm really curious.'
Delius: A Life in Letters, Vol. II, 24, 24 April 1909.

The author, who shares Parry's own grave doubts about the aristocracy, feels that this line of thinking is a half truth. It is not so much that the wealthy classes cannot produce great artists, but sadly that they do not have the desire to. The composers Don Carlo Gesualdo, Prince of Venosa, and Ernest Chausson are two notable exceptions.

6.   Drew, M. (1917), *Some Hawarden Letters*, London: Nisbet & Co., 117, Parry entry at Sh. P.
7.   Parry, diary, 13 July 1898.
8.   Graves I, 223, Parry, diary, 1881.
9.   Graves I, 227, Parry diary, December 1881.
10. Ibid, 216, Parry diary, November 1880.
11. Shaw, G.B. (1981), *Shaw's Music*, ed. Dan H. Lawrence, London: The Bodley Head, vol. I, 493: '[it] may be inferred that he is a gentleman of independent means.' 21 May 1887, in *The Star*.
12. Drew, M. (1930), *Mary Gladstone (Mrs Drew), her Diary and Letters*, London: Methuen.
13. That artistic freedom so valiantly fought for by Beethoven, Berlioz and Wagner, and indirectly by Handel, Gluck and Mozart before them.
14. See C.G. Jung's definition of 'the anima'.
15. Parry, diary, 16 January, 1886.
16. Graves I, 253, Parry, diary, 16 June 1885.
17. Ibid, 257.
18. Ibid, 217.
19. Ibid, 256. Letter to C.H. Lloyd, 23 January 1892.
20. Parry, diary, 24 February 1892.
21. Graves II, 261. Letter to C.H. Lloyd, 4 March 1892.
22. Ibid. 257.
23. Graves I, 261, Parry diary, 18 September 1885.

4: 'Beethoven's Business' – Parry the Symphonic Composer

1.   This whole chapter is based closely on my CD notes for the Parry/Chandos CD series, Nos. 8896, 8955, 8961, and 9062 (1990, 1991, 1992).
2.   Quellette Fernand (1973), *Edgard Varese*, trans. Derek Coltman, London: Calder & Boyars, 125. First published in 1966 in Paris: Editions Seghers.
3.   It was mistakenly revived in April 1995. This concerto is the instrumental equivalent of *Job*. Its style is uncertain – vacillating uncomfortably between Liszt and Schumann. The melodic material is feeble, almost nonexistent, and the orchestration blatant. Its emotional world is so ambivalent and insincere that it is downright unpleasant to listen to, a travesty of its models and forebears.
4.   Graves I, 235.
5.   Ibid. 243, Parry, diary, April 1883.
6.   Fortunately Parry's heirs were able to preserve nearly all the original performing material which was later used for the 1991 Chandos recording. It was conducted from a reproduction of the Bodleian Library manuscript full score used by August Manns at the 1883 Crystal Palace performance.
7.   Willeby, C. (1894), *Masters of English Music*, New York: Charles Scribner's Sons, 226. Willeby, who was friendly with Parry, wrote: 'But four years later – after the third in C had made its appearance – it was reproduced by Richter with its first and last movements entirely rewritten and the other two revised.'
8.   Parry, diary, May 1882; Graves, I, 230.

9. Parry, letter to Philharmonic Society, 14 December 1888. BL loan 48: 13/26.
10. Dibble, Dr J. (1992), *C. Hubert H. Parry: His Life and Music*, Oxford: Clarendon Press, 278.
11. Shaw, G.B. (1981), *Shaw's Music*, ed. Dan H. Lawrence, London: The Bodley Head, vol. I, 638, 21 May 1889, *The Star*: 'And here I must protest at the cruelty of these professional exercises in four mortal movements'.
12. Graves II, 235, *The World*, 24 December 1890.
13. A pupil for several years and admirer, especially of Parry's orchestral music, he was one of the people to encourage Parry's reawakened interest in symphonic writing after 1900.
14. Graves II, 52.
15. Graves II, 182, Parry, letter to Herbert Thompson, 10 September 1911.
16. Parry's championship of Schoenberg to Dr Strong (see pp. 114–15) and his attendance at performances of the *Five Pieces for Orchestra* and *Verklärte Nacht* in 1913, suggest his knowledge of Schoenberg's music went back earlier than diary references can prove. The Quartet No. 1 was published in 1907 and the *Kammersymphonie* in 1912, whilst copies of *Pelléas und Mélisande* were available to musicians. There are several similarities in structure and orchestration between Parry's Fifth Symphony and these early Schoenberg scores. It is not logical that Parry only investigated them after he composed the symphony when the famous first performance (September 1912) of the *Five Pieces for Orchestra* occurred only three weeks before Parry commenced serious creative work.
17. 'Masters of the English Musical Renaissance', Forelane UCD 16724/25, 1981.
18. On the basis that Parry was then about to embark on his Wagnerian fiasco *Guinevere* and the work has no parallel in his other orchestral music.
19. This work has been recorded several times, including twice by Boult. The second time, for EMI, was an accident. The orchestral library mixed up the *Symphonic Variations* with the *Symphonic Fantasia* Fifth Symphony. Sir Adrian only realized when he brought down the baton in rehearsal. Rather than waste the session it was decided to include the piece on Sir Adrian's final recording with Parry's Fifth Symphony.
20. Parry, C.H.H. (1920), *College Addresses*, ed. H.C. Colles, London: Macmillan.
21. The performing materials produced by the Ralph Vaughan Williams Trust for *From Death to Life*, *Symphony No. 4*, *Elegy for Brahms* (edited by Alasdair Mitchell) and *The Soul's Ransom* are available on hire from Faber Music.
22. Only the *Fifth Symphony* was published in full and miniature score by Goodwin and Tabb (1922). Novello published the *Second Symphony* (1906) and the Third (1907), *Symphonic Variations* (1897) and *Overture to an Unwritten Tragedy* (1906).
23. G.B. Shaw had similar reservations about Haydn as he did about Parry: 'Haydn would have been among the greatest had he been driven to that terrible eminence.'

5: What Shaw Understood

1. *Shaw's Music* II, 869.
2. The four commissions were *Eton*, *De Profundis*, incidental music to *The Frogs*, and *The Lotos Eaters*.
3. Jung, C.G. (1913), 'The Theory of Psychoanalysis' in *The Collected Works*, vol. iv: London: Routledge and Kegan Paul.
4. Parry, letter to Sedley Taylor, 20 July 1894. CUL Add. MS 6259.
5. If Job is the archetypal myth of the individual confronting the collective historical concepts of good and evil, the Pied Piper stems from the biblical and Hellenic tales of the prophet being rejected by the living collective, i.e. a corrupt society; Parry's artistic intuition fails here as miserably as it did in *Job*, though in a musically less obvious way.
6. Parry, letter to Gambier Parry, 15 December 1873, Sh. P.

7. *Interviews and encounters with Verdi* (1984), ed. Marcello Conati, narrated by Richard Stokes, London: Victor Gollancz.
8. *Shaw's Music* III, 174.

6: 'As befits an Englishman and a democrat' – the Creation of a Modern Choral–Orchestral Tradition

1. Performing material is available from Novello for all these pieces except the *Magnifica* and *A Song of Darkness and Light*. The performing material for both the 1902 and 1911 versions of *I was Glad* is available from Westminster Abbey Library.
2. Graves I, 200: *Pall Mall Gazette*, 2 April 1879.
3. Prosper Sainton, letter to C.H. Lloyd, published in the *Musical Times*, 1 June 1899, 373.
4. Based on programme notes for the Bach Choir Parry Concert, Royal Albert Hall, June 1985.
5. Vaughan Williams, R. (1987), *National Music and Other Essays*, London: Oxford University Press.
6. Vaughan Williams, R. (1955), *A Musical Autobiography*; published in *National Music and Other Essays*, (1963), London: Oxford University Press.
7. Vaughan Williams, R. (1955), *A Musical Autobiography* in ibid., 182.
8. Based on programme notes for the Bach Choir Parry Concert, Royal Albert Hall, June 1985 and notes for Chandos CD 8990, 1991.
9. Parry, diary, 3 January 1892.
10. On permanent exhibition in the Mauritshuis, Den Haag, The Netherlands, and undoubtedly known by Parry.
11. Based on programme notes for a City of Bath Bach Choir performance, Bath Abbey 23 April 1988 and Chandos CD 9025, 1992.
12. Parry, diary, 30 April 1896.
13. Based on programme notes for the Bach Choir performance, June 1985.
14. Parry, diary, 24 June 1902.

7: The Soul's Ransom – Parry and the Ethical Cantata Concept

1. The author is an ardent devotee of 'the great Mr. Handel'; indeed Handel created the basic concept of English Oratorio. In most respects his influence was enormous but his idiom was an unique, all embracing European one and at the end of the nineteenth century he did not seem nearly so English as Purcell.
2. *Bergman on Bergman*, interviews with Ingmar Bergman by Stig Björkman, Torsten Manns and Jonas Sima, trans. P.B. Austin (1973), London: Secker & Warburg.
3. Vaughan Williams, R., *A Musical Autobiography*. The complete paragraph reads: 'Parry once said to me, "Write choral music as befits an Englishman and a democrat." We pupils of Parry have, if we have been wise, inherited from Parry the great English choral tradition which Tallis passed on to Byrd, Byrd to Gibbons, Gibbons to Purcell, Purcell to Battishill and Greene, and they in their turn through the Wesleys to Parry. He has passed on the torch to us and it is our duty to keep it alight.'
4. This analysis is in part based on various programme notes for *The Soul's Ransom* written since 1981 and the Chandos CD 8990, 1991.
5. Graves II, 32, quoting W.S. Hannam, Secretary of the Leeds Festival and an ardent supporter of Parry's music.
6. Parry, diary, 24 September 1907.
7. Elgar, letter, 18 May 1909, Grave II, 49.

8. In the 1950s Gerald Finzi, on behalf of Parry's heirs, presented several major manuscripts and working papers to the Bodleian Library including the full score of *The Soul's Ransom*. This was indeed fortunate since Novello's destroyed the original performing material when they moved from Wardour Street. In 1980 the Ralph Vaughan Williams Trust commissioned a new full score and orchestral parts from the Bodleian manuscript. I sent the score to June Gordon, Lady Aberdeen, who conducted the first modern performance at Haddo House on 10 May 1981. Felix Aprahamian, reviewing that performance in the *Sunday Times* called it 'A Ransom worth playing . . . the whole a resounding and noble vindication of a generally neglected composer'.

8: The People who Knew Parry – and the People Parry Knew

1. Stirling M.W. (1926), *The Richmond Papers*, London: Heinemann, 254.
2. Parry, C.H.H. (1920), *College Addresses*, ed. H.C. Colles, London: Macmillan, 4.
3. Gurney, I. (1984), *War Letters*, ed. R.K.R. Thornton, London: The Hogarth Press, 209; letter to Marion Scott, 29 September 1917.
4. Graves I, 27.
5. Ibid., 41 and 59.
6. Lambert, A. (1984), *Unquiet Souls*, New York: Harper & Row, 26, Lavinia Lyttelton's diary, 9 November 1866.
7. Graves II, 63, letter to Dorothea Ponsonby, December 1913.
8. Drew, M. (1930), *Mary Gladstone (Mrs Drew), her Diaries and Letters*, ed. Lucy Masterman, London: Methuen, diary, 21 June 1870.
9. Drew, 9 February 1871.
10. Graves I, 143; Parry, diary, November/December 1873.
11. Graves II, 143, Parry Notebooks.
12. Graves I, 322.
13. Ibid., 152.
14. Lambert, *Unquiet Souls*, Laura Tennant's diary, 12 January 1885, 28.
15. Graves I, 253.
16. Ibid., 271.
17. Drew, M. (1917), *Some Hawarden Letters*, London: Nisbet & Co. 184, letter from E. Burne-Jones, 1 May 1886.
18. Lambert, *Unquiet Souls*, 65, Wilfred Scawen Blunt, *Secret Memories*, 14 January 1895.
19. Graves I, 317.
20. Balfour, A. (1992), *Letters of Arthur Balfour to Lady Elcho 1885–1917*, London: Hamish Hamilton.
21. Lady Maude, diary, 3 January 1892, Sh.P.
22. Letter from Parry to Willie Leigh, 4 August 1904; in the possession of the author.
23. Brendon, P. (1979), *Eminent Edwardians*, London: Secker & Warburg.
24. Graves II, 43, Parry, diary, November 1907.
25. Dibble, *Parry*, 274. Abdy, J. and Gere, C. (1984), *The Souls*, London: Sidgwick and Jackson, 63. This incident occurred in 1884.
26. Dibble, 275. Parry, diary, 24 November 1888.
27. Graves II, 31.
28. Graves I, 403.
29. Lady Maude, diary, 11 June 1892.
30. *The Richmond Papers*, 229.
31. Graves I, 284 and 343; Parry, diaries, 1887 and December 1891.
32. Ibid., 324.
33. Ibid., 271.
34. Graves II, 126.

35. Ibid., 11.
36. Ibid., 3.
37. Ibid., 41, letter from Alfred Lyttelton, 10 February 1907.
38. Graves II, 289.
39. Weintraub, S. (1973), *Bernard Shaw 1914–1918: Journey to Heartbreak*, London: Routledge & Kegan Paul, 242 and 243.
40. Mackenzie, C. (1963), *My Life and Times*, vol. 3, London: Chatto & Windus, 223.
41. Graves II, 358.
42. Ibid., 39, 22 October 1906.
43. Graves I, 184.
44. Ibid., 330
45. Lambert, *Unquiet Souls*, 187 and 188.
46. Graves II, 128.
47. See Parry's diaries and letters to W.S. Hannam; also see Plunkett Greene's biography of Charles Villiers Stanford (1935).
48. Dibble, 263, Parry's letter to Hamish MacCunn, 13 July 1887.
49. Graves I, 363, in Vaughan Williams, R., *The Music Student*, 1918.
50. Graves I, 383.
51. Ibid., 398.
52. Boult, Sir A. (1973), *My Own Trumpet*, London: Hamish Hamilton, 20.
53. Graves II, 192, Eugene Goossens writing to C.L. Graves in *c.* 1925.
54. Graves I, 385–6.
55. Graves II, 60.
56. Gurney, I. (1984), *War Letters*, ed. R.K.R. Thornton, London: The Hogarth Press.
57. Walton, Lady S. (1988), *William Walton: Behind the Façade*, London: Oxford University Press.
58. Kennedy, M. (1989), *Portrait of William Walton*, London: Oxford University Press.
59. Moore, J. Northrop (1987), *Elgar and His Publishers*, vol. 2, London: Clarendon Press, letter from Elgar to Jaeger, 8 October 1907.
60. Delius, F. (1988), *Delius: A Life in Letters*, vol. 1, ed. Lionel Carley, London: Scolar Press.
61. Bax, Sir A. (1943), *Farewell My Youth*, London: Longmans, 27.
62. Dibble, *Parry*, 317, P.M. Young (1980), *George Grove*, London: Macmillan.

9: *The Last Journey to* Jerusalem

1. Graves II, 47.
2. Ibid., 51. There is a touching letter from Coleridge's father to Parry, following the publication of the lyrics in 1909: 'Your music married to Mary's poetry is a wedding for ever memorable and dear'.
3. Parry, diary, 27 February 1908.
4. Ibid., October 1909.
5. Ibid., 7 December 1908.
6. Parry, letter to Edward Elgar, 21 November 1910. HWRO 705: 445 5247/8; Dibble, 434.
7. Graves II, 46; Parry, diary, March 1908.
8. Ibid., 51.
9. Parry, diary, May 1909.
10. Parry, diary, 1910.
11. Parry, letter to Edward Elgar, 7 May 1909 in Dibble, 421. HWRO 705: 445 5247/8.
12. Graves II, 49, letter from Elgar, 18 May 1909.
13. Graves II, 72, Parry, diary, 17 December 1914. Given Parry's punctuation, it is open

to question whether he is referring only to *A Sea Symphony* or to all the works in the concert, which is a more interesting thesis at that stage in the war.

14. Parry, diary, 18 November 1908.
15. Ibid., September 1910.
16. Parry, *College Addresses*, 57, Address, September 1910.
17. Dibble, 446, Parry, diary, 30 October 1911.
18. It is possible that by 1912 Parry somewhat identified with David in Browning's poem. Elgar had written most of his masterpieces and was known internationally, Vaughan Williams was well on his way to becoming Elgar's successor in public estimation. Both composers are impossible without Parry as their precursor.
19. Parry, *Instinct and Character*, 149. An atypically fine paragraph, it suggests that by the time Parry came to grapple with *Instinct and Character*, he had already moved beyond its combination of Darwinism and late nineteenth-century humanist philosophy. A book on the spiritual aspects of creativity would have been an appropriate sequel to his first six books and could have proved the literary counterpart to the music of the Indian Summer.
20. Graves, II, 157. This idea is closer to primary Buddhism than early Christianity.
21. The *Ode on the Nativity* was recorded in 1983 on Lyrita under the auspices of the Ralph Vaughan Williams Trust, with Sir David Willcocks, the Bach Choir and the London Philharmonic. This recording is currently not available on CD.
22. *The Times*, 8 October 1918.
23. Graves II, 149.
24. This idea is a paraphrase from Schopenhauer, *The World as Will and Representation*.
25. The legend concerns the medieval Feast of the Virgin. It was traditional to lay gifts at the feet of the statue of the Virgin. All social strata, including royalty and nobility, hoped that in recognition of their gifts the Virgin would give a sign of assent. After the poor had made their offerings a juggler came before the statue; as he had nothing material to offer at all because of his poverty, to the astonishment of everyone he began to practise his art at the foot of the statue. When he had finished and was bathed in sweat, the Virgin moved down off her pedestal and wiped his brow with the sleeve of her dress.
26. Bruckner's Seventh Symphony was heard in London during 1887, but Parry's diary is missing for that year. The same day that *Blest Pair of Sirens* was performed at the 1903 Duisberg May Festival, Bruckner's Ninth Symphony received its German première (in the atrocious disfigured version by Ferdinand Löwe), programmed with his *Te Deum*. Bruckner's *Te Deum* has some strong formal similarities to the *Ode on the Nativity*. In his diary, Parry does not refer to the specific works programmed apart from Strauss's *Tod und Verklärung*.
27. Parry, diary, 22 February 1912.
28. Jung, C.G. (1961), *Memories, Dreams, Reflections*, New York: Random House Inc., chapter vi, 'Confrontation with the Unconscious'.
29. Parry, diary, 17 January 1914.
30. Ibid., 21 January 1914.
31. Ibid., 20 July 1914; Dibble, 466.
32. Ibid., 10 June 1914.
33. Ibid., 9 March 1914.
34. Ibid., 27 March 1914.
35. Property of Mrs Ursula Vaughan Williams and printed with her kind permission.
36. Dibble, *Parry*, 493, letter to Macmillan, 30 May 1918, BL Add. MS 55239. Compare Graves II, 362 where Graves prints the original draft.
37. Parry, diary, 22 May 1916.
38. Ibid., 26 November 1915.
39. Graves II, 92.
40. Graves II, 92, letter from Mrs Fawcett, 5 March 1918.

41. Graves II, 172, from an 'Appreciation' of Parry's songs, written by Harry Plunkett Greene for Graves's biography.
42. Parry, diary, 4 October 1916; Dibble, 487.
43. Graves II, 91.
44. Parry, diary, 26 July 1918; Graves II, 96.
45. Graves II, 98, Parry, diary, 6 August 1918.
46. Parry, diary, 6 September 1918. It is evident from Parry's diary entries for the last two months that Emily Daymond became increasingly difficult for Parry to deal with. In contrast, Maude seems to have spent a serene summer and at the time of Parry's accident was busy organizing a croquet party.
47. Dibble, 496, diary of Arthur Ponsonby, 12 October 1918. It should be noted that Ponsonby did not write this entry until five days after Parry died, suggesting that there is an element of literary artifice to the description here. The story of the bird is more significant.
48. Howells, Dr H. (1968), text of the Crees Lecture, delivered at the Royal College of Music, 7 October 1968, published in the RCM Magazine.

Part II

10: *Contributions to Grove's* A Dictionary of Music and Musicians

1. Dibble, 127.
2. *The Strand Magazine*, May 1904; see Moore, J. Northrop, *Edward Elgar: A Creative Life*, Oxford: Clarendon Press.

Index

Index of Parry's works